Robert William Elliston
Manager

Robert William Elliston
Manager

Christopher Murray

LONDON
The Society for Theatre Research
1975

FOR KATHLEEN

Because of that great nobleness of hers
The fire that stirs about her, when she stirs,
Burns but more clearly.

Yeats

First published 1975
by The Society for Theatre Research
14 Woronzow Road, London, N.W.8

© The Society for Theatre Research 1975

ISBN 0 85430 005 8

Designed and printed at
The Compton Press Ltd., Compton Chamberlayne
Salisbury, Wiltshire

Foreword

IT IS NOT a good time to make a puff for Elliston. His kind, like the theatre of his time, appears remote from our increasingly subsidized theatrical scene. In order for performers and directors to live, it is no longer imperative that they beguile the public into thinking that it is pleased.

For Elliston, the box office was the dictator and the guide. Elliston's public was bludgeoned by crude publicity and wooed by immense personal charm. He wrote the copy and he exuded the charm. As performer, manager, parent, rake, author, litigant (to name a few facets), Elliston put on a show and starred in it. Insufferable and irresistible, he was always a popular favourite.

There is something perverse in attempting to give a permanence to so essentially ephemeral a phenomenon as a great theatrical character. The well-delivered anecdote can convey a hint of the man better than a printed chronicle. Yet it is our trick, in the Society for Theatre Research, to get as near to a just assessment of theatrical ghosts as we can. We welcome a book on Elliston. Mr. Murray's book is the more to be welcomed in that it directs attention to Elliston's real long-term significance as a pioneer as well as a performer. Contemporary accounts of Elliston generally endorse Charles Lamb's famous summary of the man (cited by Mr. Murray), and we can have no doubt of Elliston's success as a performer with the public of his time. Until now, however, we have not had a considered presentation of Elliston's managerial aims and methods.

Elliston was involved in management at the most confused period of English theatrical history. Mr. Murray has done a good job of untangling the various threads so that we may apprehend something of the complexities and absurdities of early nineteenth-century theatrical life. It is for readers to be aware, as they enjoy the form that Mr. Murray has set upon events, that Elliston himself was confronted with the indigest: the day-to-day business of running a theatre; paying employees; coping with a pretty rum collection of playwrights; and generally manipulating the whole enterprise so that a capricious and uncertain public might be cajoled into thinking that it knew what it wanted and was getting it.

The following pages help to give solidity and integrity to a man whose eccentricities and faults have received far more attention than his achievements. The chief lesson of those achievements is that, in the theatre, it is the executive artist who really pioneers and rarely gets the credit for it. Such players and managers prepare the way for dramatists, and theatrical theorists, whose written evidence is easier for writers, teachers, and students to deal with, and can seem to demand no practical knowledge of theatrical practice.

Take him for all in all, it is probably as well that we shall not see Elliston's like again. But it is right for us to salute him and to be reminded that, whatever the age, theatrical concerns demand theatrical imaginations. His rakish and extremely charming ghost also reminds us that, in spite of Honours Lists, learned societies, and scholarly expositions, the theatre has no business to be respectable.

CLIFFORD JOHN WILLIAMS
Editor for The Society for
Theatre Research

Acknowledgments

WRITTEN LAST, to be read first, this is the most pleasant part of my task. I wish to thank, personally and sincerely, a large number of people who helped me to write this book. To rehearse the names of all would be to tell sad stories of the death of some, such as my mentor, the late Professor Jeremiah Murphy of University College, Galway; while a full roll-call would hardly be appropriate, since help in the writing of one's first book connotes the history of one's life. But I should like to say that I am grateful to all those whose help might be considered indirect, although it was very great in its effects; I mean my parents, my teachers in Galway, my friends. In particular, I should mention Professor Alois M. Nagler, of Yale University, under whose supervision the thesis was written on which this book is based; and those members of the Society for Theatre Research who answered all my queries with as much promptitude as thoroughness, Miss Sybil Rosenfeld and Miss Kathleen Barker. I am grateful also to Mr. George Speaight and the members of the Publications Committee of the Society for Theatre Research for undertaking the book.

For twelve months I could refer casually but impressively to "my editor." I am not sure of the manner in which he referred to me, but I am sure that Mr. Clifford John Williams must be an ingenious director. With tact and understanding, he brought the best out of me during the months of rewriting. For the faults that remain in my work, he is as little to blame as Professor Nagler. I have to thank Mr. Williams also for writing the Foreword. If he will allow me to say so, it was most generously done.

In addition, I must express my appreciation to the library person-nel who assisted my research and provided many of the illustra-

tions. Miss Helen D. Willard, late of the Harvard Theatre
Collection, Miss Dorothy Mason, of the Folger Shakespeare
Library, Mr. W. H. Crain, of the Hoblitzelle Theatre Arts Library,
and Mr. A. S. Latham, of the Department of Prints and Drawings,
Victoria & Albert Museum, are among those to whom I am most
indebted.

To the editors of *Theatre Survey, Theatre Research/Recherches
Théâtrales,* and *Theatre Notebook,* I express my gratitude for permission to use material already published in the form of articles;
to Mr. M. B. Yeats and the Macmillan Company of London and
Basingstoke for permission to quote the lines from "The Folly of
Being Comforted," from *The Collected Poems* of W. B. Yeats,
which appear in the Dedication; and to Mrs. O'Casey and Messrs.
Macmillan for permission to quote from Sean O'Casey's *Juno and
the Paycock,* in the epigraph to the final chapter.

Finally, to my wife, for her encouragement and tactful criticism, I pay sincere tribute.

University College, Dublin
December 1973

Contents

List of Illustrations

10. The coronation procession as presented at Drury Lane, 1821. A sheet of characters for the toy theatre, published by West 1821, reprinted 1825. Courtesy the Victoria and Albert Museum, Enthoven Collection. Photo Crown copyright.

11. Elliston as George IV, Drury Lane, 1821. A theatrical portrait published by West, 1821. Courtesy the Victoria and Albert Museum, Enthoven Collection. Photo Crown copyright.

12. Elliston as Falstaff. Engraving by T. Wageman, 1826. Courtesy the Folger Shakespeare Library.

13. Elliston in a triple role as the three Singles in a musical farce, *Three and the Deuce* by Prince Hoare. Engraving published by Walker and Knights, 1812. Courtesy the Harvard Theatre Collection.

14. Madame Vestris as Don Giovanni being expelled from Hell as a nuisance, Act I scene 2 of *Giovanni in London* by William Thomas Moncrieff as produced by Elliston, Drury Lane 1820. Engraving from a drawing by Gaetano Marinari, the scene designer at Drury Lane. Courtesy the Harvard Theatre Collection.

15. T. P. Cooke and Miss Scott in *Black-Eyed Susan* by Douglas Jerrold. Engraving from a drawing by Robert Cruikshank, 1829. Courtesy the Harvard Theatre Collection.

16. Master Joseph Burke, child star at the Surrey, 1827–30, as himself and in character. Courtesy the Victoria and Albert Museum, Enthoven Collection.

17. Robert William Elliston, a portrait by G. H. Harlow, *c.* 1808. Courtesy the National Portrait Gallery, London.

Illustrations not otherwise acknowledged are from
originals in the author's collection.

ONE

Enter Mr. Elliston

'The king for my money: he speaks all his words
distinctly, half as loud again as the other. Anybody
may see he is an actor.'

Fielding, *Tom Jones*

IT IS IMPOSSIBLE to read Charles Lamb's two essays on Robert
William Elliston without being impressed with a sense of intense
vitality. Elliston, one feels, comes alive from the Elian page like
a character in Dickens. This fictive exuberance makes its own
ironic comment on the personality of Elliston, who indeed once
stoutly claimed that he was "the same person *off* the stage that I am
on."[1] Wherever one looks in his career one finds a story-book
quality. He was one of those people who had no reason under the
sun to take to the stage. Nobody in his family history had any
connection with the theatre. Born in Bloomsbury on April 7, 1774,
Robert William was the only child of a watchmaker, an alcoholic.
He had no less than two fairy godfathers, or uncles to be precise,
who, as they were both Professors at Cambridge, took it upon
themselves to supervise the education of young Robert. From the
age of nine he was a pupil at St. Paul's, and he spent his holidays
at Cambridge. A respectable, not to say clerical, career seemed to
be mapped out for him. Avuncular dismay may be surmised when
at the age of seventeen, like Roderick Random or Peregrine Pickle,
Robert ran away from his home in London to go on the stage in
Bath.

This was in 1791, and his first appearance on the public stage
(he acted in private theatricals as a schoolboy) was on April 14, as
Tressel. Thereafter, as the saying goes, he never looked back. He

became one of the best actors ever to tread the Bath stage. When he moved on, inevitably, to the London arena he was equally success- ful. By 1807 he had no rival in high comedy, and was ranked just behind John Philip Kemble and George Frederick Cooke in tragedy. Leigh Hunt, at this time, had no hesitation in calling Elliston, "the greatest actor of the present day."[2] Physically, he was best equipped for comedy. As Hazlitt wrote of him in 1820: "There is a joyousness in his look, his voice, and manner; he . . . writes himself comedian in any book, warrant, or acquittance; hits the town between wind and water, between farce and tragedy; touches the string of a mock heroic sentiment with due pathos and vivacity; and makes the best strolling gentleman, or needy poet, on the stage."[3] He sustained his reputation in comedy until his death in 1831. In general, few would quarrel with the assessment which appeared in his obituary: "Elliston was undoubtedly the most versatile actor of his day."[4]

But there was another side to Elliston. There was Elliston the actor-manager. The qualities that made him an interesting manager are implicit in his career, once one penetrates its apparently fictional façade. Elliston's motive in taking to the stage was at first a mystery to himself, but within three years he had found it out. For his benefit night at Bath, on March 6, 1794, he composed an address considered important enough for publication. Entitled *The Love of Fame,* this attempts to define the impetus governing the lives of such various figures as the poet, the soldier, the buck, the actor, etc. "Chimeras" the ambitions of such figures may be, but they spur activity. The actor "To publick candour gladly trusts his cause,/And pants for FAME in popular applause."[5] Fame was the spur in Elliston's life, impelling him into management of so many theatres that he was widely known as the Napoleon of the drama. To follow him on this course is to take a tour of the English theatre in Regency times.

The conditions of Georgian theatre are well known, especially through the work of Professor Allardyce Nicoll. But there are two aspects of it which require special emphasis in relation to the present study. One is the monopoly question, and the struggle for a free stage; the other is the audience, and its emergence as the final arbiter of public taste. In both of these areas Elliston's career takes on a certain significance.[6] He began as manager of a London minor theatre: in all, he had three terms of management of minor theatres. It is fair to say that by his work in this area he paved the way for the repeal of the Licensing Act. Elliston's relationship with the audience is closely linked with his whole acting style. Leigh Hunt used an expressive image for this style: "His feelings follow each other like the buckets on a water-wheel, full one instant and empty the next."[7] We should call such a style romantic. Hunt's term is "duplicity,"[8] connoting not only rapid transitions of feeling but, as it were, hypocrisy, or sharing a confidence with an audience while deceiving characters on stage. Elliston shone in roles which were a compound of benevolence and rakishness, such as Charles Surface; his particular quality was seen to best advantage in double and even triple roles, such as Duke Aranza in Tobin's *The Honey Moon* or the three Singles in Prince Hoare's farce. A good example is also provided by *The Venetian Outlaw,* a melodrama which Elliston adapted from the French, and in which he himself played the lead at Drury Lane in 1805. The Venetian Outlaw, Vivaldi, acts as a double agent between the Doge and some conspirators, revealing his third and "real" face only to his wife, the Doge's daughter, in a key scene. The play is so contrived as to exploit situations demanding sudden alternations in Vivaldi's demeanour. As John Genest remarked in *Some Account of the English Stage* (VII, 650), *The Venetian Outlaw* acted far better than it reads: it was obviously only a vehicle for Elliston's talents. Unhappily, Monk Lewis brought out a rival version of the same play at Covent Garden, and this cut short any ambitions Elliston may have had of having a life-long role as the Man with the Three Faces: Lewis's version became a hit, while Elliston's played only five times.

Underlying his acting style was a specific attitude towards an audience. Elliston kept no secrets from his audience; he confided in them familiarly; he appealed often to their generosity. This treatment was really a projection of his style as a stage lover: he wanted communion with his audience. As manager this attitude had several effects. Most importantly, it implied a unified audience, a refusal to see any difference between an audience at the Royal Circus and that at Drury Lane. Elliston did not tailor his performances to suit a class. This approach underlay his whole managerial career, blurring the traditional distinctions between specific centres of entertainment. A second effect was Elliston's

habit of addressing an audience. It had its elements of the ludicrous, to be sure, but behind it lay his conception of his calling.
Fortune had blessed him with a certain physical resemblance to
the Prince Regent: Elliston lived to impersonate George IV in a
coronation spectacle on the stage of Drury Lane. It was considered
the height of absurdity when one night during this spectacle
Elliston raised his hand and said to the audience, "Bless you, my
people!"[9] But this was not hallucination; it was projection. In an
age which saw the decline of royal patronage to the theatre, Elliston
stepped in and played the king. There is about all his managerial
undertakings the air of one conferring an inestimable favour upon
the public. This air was fused with that of appeal through the
technique of "duplicity." Elliston was king *and* comedian,
unceasingly.

As an actor and a personality, Elliston has been well enough
served by his biographer, George Raymond. As a manager, however, he has been neglected. The reason for this is implicit in the
Elliston myth. One does not theorize about the managerial abilities
of Bully Bottom or of Mr. Crummles. In reality (to which the
present study hopes to adhere), Elliston had a keen mind and was a
born administrator. Neither in the two-volume *Memoirs of Robert
William Elliston Comedian* (1844–45), nor in the more widely
known condensed *Life and Enterprises* (1857), does Raymond do
justice to Elliston as manager. Succeeding historians of the theatre,
such as William Archer,[10] have accepted Raymond's study as
definitive. Only E. B. Watson, in a perceptive eight pages,[11] to
which the present writer is indebted, has shown any appreciation of
Elliston's managerial competence. There is need, therefore, for a
detailed study of Elliston's managerial career.

Succeeding chapters will deal with Elliston's management of the
two London minor theatres, the Royal Circus and the Olympic
Pavilion; the management of Birmingham Theatre Royal; the
management of Drury Lane; and finally of the Surrey. Such a survey
spans the history of the English stage from 1809 to 1831, coinciding
with the period of the Regency, of which Elliston could be said to
be the abstract and brief chronicle. To quote Charles Lamb again,
"Wherever Elliston walked, sate, or stood still, there was the
theatre."[12] A final chapter will attempt an analysis of Elliston's
abilities as manager, showing his interest in rehearsal, his emphasis
on discipline, and concluding with an estimation of the place of

Elliston in the history of the nineteenth-century English theatre.

In the eighteenth century before one achieved the status of manager one had as a general rule to establish oneself as an actor. Consequently, Elliston's earliest attempts to break into management were hinged upon his success as an actor. One must distinguish, perhaps, between management and production, but from the first time he took to the stage, as a schoolboy, Elliston showed an interest in controlling a theatre. In taking part in private theatricals at the Lyceum, while still at St. Paul's, he would not only play the leading role but also take charge of production.[13] It was during his years at Bath, however, that he made his first strong bid for managerial control.

When he stepped onto the stage of Bath Theatre Royal, Orchard Street, on September 26, 1793, it was as an actor schooled in one of the best circuits in England. During his two years with Tate Wilkinson on the York circuit he had acted on 149 nights, appearing in a total of 44 different roles.[14] Wilkinson himself paid tribute to Elliston as an "actor of rising merit."[15] During his first year at Bath he played more than forty parts,[16] starting with the role recommended for him by John Philip Kemble, namely Romeo.[17] He was immediately well received. He had all the Georgian requisites, "propriety," "passion," a voice full of "force" and "melody," an "understanding" sound and "well cultivated,"[18] and of course he *"made love like an angel."*[19] His reception on his benefit night, March 6, 1794, is some indication of his instant popularity. In a theatre where capacity receipts were in the region £140–£145,[20] Elliston brought in £102, which topped the receipts of the manager, William Wyatt Dimond, by £25.[21] Though he was as frequently on stage the next year, acting forty roles across the range of eighteenth-century drama, he was in the position of all apprentice actors. "In such characters as Mr. Dimond may think proper to relinquish," as the *Bristol Journal* put it,[22] "he has found in Mr. Elliston, a respectable successor." Unless he could produce some sensational stroke, Elliston would have to wait in line until older actors retired. He was gaining a reputation, indeed, as Tate Wilkinson somewhat to his "astonishment" noted,[23] and soon attracted the attention of George Colman the Younger, who invited him to play a few nights at the Haymarket in the summer of 1796.

How Elliston triumphed before a London audience in roles

associated with the great Kemble is probably too well known to detail here. His Octavian, in *The Mountaineers,* was immediately acclaimed, though it made less of a stir than his success in the role in which Kemble had earlier failed—Sir Edward Mortimer in Colman's *The Iron Chest.* Back in Bath, Elliston's London achievement meant increased popularity. For his benefit on July 11 he repeated at Bristol the role of Octavian, "to one of the most brilliant and crowded audiences ever seen at Bristol Theatre since the time of the celebrated Powell."[24] It was noted with approval that Elliston "displayed all that discrimination and force of expression for which he was so justly praised in London." Together with *The Mountaineers,* Elliston presented a spectacle entitled *The Siege of Quebec.* Since the production of this afterpiece was left in his own hands, it is of some interest as an indication of Elliston's theatrical style.

The Siege of Quebec was a "pantomimic ballet" in five scenes, narrating in mime and song part of the story of General Wolfe, a part played by Elliston. The playbill contained an "epitome" as follows:

SCENE I
*Day break. A View of the River St. Lawrence, and the
Heights of Abraham*

The Boats with the British Forces are seen moving slowly up the River; after which, General Wolfe with a small party of his Troops effect their landing, surprize the Enemy's out-posts, and dismiss some Pioneers who choose a place for their Encampment.

SCENE II
A Plain in Quebec

General Wolfe receives the congratulations of his Friends upon their providential debarkation, and obtains an account of the number and situation of the Enemy from the French Centinels.—In the meantime, the rest of the British Army accomplish their ascent and proceed to the Camp.

SCENE III
The Tent of the General

General Wolfe and his Council arrange their plans of future operations, and afterwards indulge themselves with wine, joining several loyal and patriotic Toasts and Songs; among which is introduced the celebrated Song by General Wolfe composed the night before the Battle, of 'How *stands the glass around?'* The Aid-du-Camp then announces the arrival of a Deserter, who is brought in and betrays the Enemy's design of making a vigorous attack early the next morning. The General dispatches his Officers in haste to prepare their regiments for advance, and appears affected by a sentiment of his death—but, humbly submitting himself to the merciful Disposer of all events, resolves to suffer no such terrors to abate his duty, and retires to encourage the spirits of his Soldiers.

SCENE IV
The British Camp and Review of the Troops

By Permission of the Right Hon. Earl NORTHAMPTON, a selected body of the *Northamptonshire Militia* will in this scene perform various Military Evolutions; after which General Wolfe exhorts his Soldiers to conquer or to die, and they march off in full Chorus to Purcell's popular Air of *'Britons, Strike Home!'*

SCENE THE LAST
The Field of Battle

This Scene will display the Engagement of the Troops, the Defeat of the French, and the Death of General Wolfe; which will be faithfully presented after the celebrated Print engraved by WOLLET from the Picture of WEST.[25]

The form of this piece derives from the London minor theatres, where dialogue on stage was not permitted. Elliston saw theatrical potential in this form which he later exploited not only at the minor theatres but indeed at Drury Lane itself. It is clearly related to melodrama, a form first seen on the English stage several years later, in 1802.[26] And melodrama, as Eric Bentley reminds us, is "drama in its elemental form; it is the quintessence of drama."[27] With its use of dumbshow, spectacle, a battle scene and a pathetic tableau of death, *The Siege of Quebec* had all the ingredients of a productive theatrical formula. In its anticipation of audience responses, political and moral, the playbill offers also an introduction to the Elliston style. Bland assumptions are made of unquestioning emotional accord, awe, and admiration. To reinforce the awe, Elliston laid special emphasis in his advertisements on his engagement of the militia, while on the playbill he further informed his "Friends" that "no expence has been spared to render this Ballet worthy the public approbation." In its melodramatic form, then, its appeal to middle-class feelings, and in the tone of puffing that

surrounded it, *The Siege of Quebec* offers a paradigm of the
Elliston style.

Producing a piece like this was all very well in its way, but what
Elliston really wanted was to get directly into management. When
Keasberry, who was joint acting manager with Dimond, retired in
1796 Elliston hoped to get a foot in. His uncle, Dr. William Elliston,
Master of Sidney College, had somehow been won over as a backer.[28]
Elliston was disappointed, however, and Dimond became sole
manager, choosing Charlton as his assistant.[29] Elliston persevered in
his ambition, and in 1800 his hopes rose again. In the intervening
years he had consolidated his reputation as an actor, acquiring
gradually more and more major roles, the best, in fact, of
Shakespeare, modern comedy, and even opera. Nothing was denied
him. He was the spoiled child of the West country. His articles
were due for renewal in 1801, and at this time also Dimond was due
to retire. The question of Elliston's future in the management
then became positively topical. One night when he was playing
Macbeth, after the scene where Ross saluted him with his new title,
Elliston went downstage and repeated with conspiratorial significance, "Glamis and Thane of Cawdor! *The greatest is behind,*"
which was taken as an allusion to his own ambition.[30] He tried to
make a share in the theatre the condition on which he would stay
on after 1801; he would accept a raise from three to five pounds a
week if a promise of proprietorship were given.[31] The real decision
lay with John Palmer, virtually the father of the Bath-Bristol
theatre, who was still administrator. Palmer was unwilling to sell
a part-share to Elliston.[32] He did not even get the position of acting
manager; this went to Charlton.[33] Up to the building of the new
Bath Theatre Royal in Beaufort Square, in 1805, Elliston kept
up an interest in proprietorship, abandoning his efforts in the end
only when a place in the new theatre proved too difficult to establish.[34] Much later, in 1817, when he was well entrenched in the
field of management, he made one final bid to become lessee of
Bath, but once again without success.[35]

The tale of these thwarted attempts is not without significance
in Elliston's career. It is fair to say that the Bath theatre formed
him as a theatrical force, and that he never forgot it. During the
years he lived there, 1793–1804, Bath was at the height of its reputation as a fashionable watering place.[36] The theatre formed an

integral part of this fashionable life, as Jane Austen so happily testifies in *Northanger Abbey*. The theatre was, in fact, a "converging point," as the actor John Bernard expressed it, "where strangers could obtain a view of the 'beauty and fashion,' without the trouble of introduction. Our boxes, indeed, did not much exceed in dimensions a large drawing-room,—with this difference, that a splendid party could always be entertained there without a *crush*."[37] Moreover, the Bath theatre was one of considerable standing. It was, after all, the first provincial theatre in England to receive a royal patent (in 1768); from 1779 to 1817 it was run in circuit with the theatre in Bristol,[38] and during this time it was regarded among the best theatres in the British Isles. During his years at Bath, Elliston not only shared in the success of the theatre, but he also found Bath a most hospitable environment. After his marriage in 1796 to a local dancing mistress he brought his parents to live there. Bath became for him a home. Thus it was that Elliston's idea of a theatre was founded on his experience of Bath. Every managerial concern he afterwards became involved in somehow took on the shape of Bath. The theatre as fashionable rendezvous, the theatre as cottage industry, the theatre of versatility and ingenuous charm: such aspects of his own techniques can be traced to Elliston's years at Bath.

When he left Bath in 1804 it was to take up the position of leading actor at Drury Lane, lately vacated by John Philip Kemble. In the meantime, he had dabbled a little more in management, in episodes that throw further light upon his style. After 1797, when he was again at the Haymarket, Elliston spent the summers in the provinces, where he found himself a favourite of that good-hearted theatregoer, George III. In August 1799 he was invited to Frogmore to participate in festivities celebrating the birthday of Princess Amelia. Details of this affair are not available, but apparently the royal family was pleased with the manner in which Elliston entered into the spirit of the occasion. The following year he was invited to act in a similar fête, and in 1801 he was given complete charge of the festivities held at Radipole, under the supervision of Princess Elizabeth. The fête took place on August 1. A large tent was erected to accommodate the royal family, and a stage area was created in front of it, with six other tents deployed around for the use of the two hundred guests. The festivities opened with actresses dressed as Dryads strewing flowers before the king and queen; then came a masquerade and a little gypsy scene, both interspersed with songs. Then while dinner was in progress Elliston entered in the guise of a monk, announced victory over the *"Invincible* army"[39] and lay at the king's feet ensigns captured by Nelson and Abercrombie. This action was suited by words penned by Princess Amelia, alerting George to the monk's scarcely controllable ecstasy.[40] Thereafter Elliston was likely to pop up again in the guise of a naval officer, and, to the accompaniment of a hearty chorus of jolly sailors, pay homage to his beloved monarch. Numerous bands were loud in their imprecations for royal salvation, and songs were not wanting in support of panegyrics on native vigour. Many of these *divertissements* were threaded in and out of a Bartholomew Fair setting, with stalls, and shops, and even a lottery. In the evening, regular theatre replaced mere spectacle, when a comedy, *The Wheel of Fortune,* and a farce, *The Deaf Lover,* were presented. These pieces, of course, were old favourites, and were not, it seems, given any novel interpretation. George III, it need hardly be said, was no Louis XIV, and the entertainments at Radipole have little in common with those at Versailles in the days of Molière and Vigarani. Yet they did, no doubt, call for a certain amount of organization, if not theatrical imagination.

There were many restless attempts to break into management before Elliston's competence found a real outlet. In 1801 he speculated upon opening a new theatre in London, perhaps relying on his favour with the king to obtain him a patent. He consulted with friends, however, as he always did before taking a decision, and he got sound advice from one, Lord Harcourt, whose opinion was "that the king would not be inclined to grant another patent; and were his Majesty so disposed, the opposition of the existing patentees would induce the king to yield to their prayer in petition against it."[41] Elliston abandoned the idea for the moment, but it was to remain an ambition which was to exercise his attention later, from 1809 until his "capture" of Drury Lane in 1819. Meantime he turned his eyes northward where the Liverpool Theatre Royal was advertised to be let in 1802. Here he was outbidden by the joint application of Lewis and Knight, and the summer of 1802 saw him managing instead two tiny theatres at Wells and Shepton Mallet. He drew upon actors in the Bath theatre for this season.[42]

Presaging the puffs of his later career, the *Bristol Journal* announced that Elliston's company was "superior to any summer one in this kingdom," and went on to observe that "the elegance with which he has fitted up the theatre, the correctness of the performances, and the conduct of the performers, has deservedly merited the countenance and support of the polite and fashionable city of Wells." The truth was less flattering. So meagre was his company that Elliston was forced to act most of the roles himself, whether Harlequin, clown, or Shakespearean. On one occasion, indeed, he played both Richard and Richmond in *Richard III,* dashing off and on stage from alternate sides, until the last scene, when Richmond was played by the scene-shifter.[43] In contrast to the triviality of this venture was the attempt to open a theatre in Oxford, which would operate during the summer, using personnel from not only Bath and Bristol, but also from the Haymarket. Though he tried to exert special pressure in a characteristically aggressive way, i.e., through enlisting the influences of some friend in the University and refusing to take no for an answer, he had finally to accept the decision of the Chancellor himself against the opening of such a theatre.[44] As it happened, Elliston had other fish to fry, a concern which made all of these tentative, though furiously pursued, objectives ultimately irrelevant.

In September 1802 he suddenly heard once again from George Colman, offering a four-month engagement during the following summer. It had been five years since Elliston had appeared before a London audience. Now he was not only to be leading actor in Colman's experiment of a newly extended season,[45] but was offered the position of acting manager as well. After some haggling, Elliston accepted Colman's terms of fourteen pounds a week with a benefit for each of his official capacities.

For opening night, May 16, Colman wrote a little impromptu entitled *No Prelude!* which preceded the bill of *The Jew* and *The Agreeable Surprise. No Prelude!* is of interest for the comment it supplies on the part Elliston was to play in the Haymarket scheme. In a skilful piece of fourth-wall theatre, Colman introduces the Prompter and Mr. Elliston as characters who discuss the problems facing the theatre. After an opening scene in which the Prompter anxiously reads a witty but unhelpful letter from Colman, Elliston enters and is seized upon:

Promp:—But I may gain some intelligence, now;—for You (as report says) are our Manager.

Ellis:—Pshaw!—Reports are as false in the petty States of Theatres, as in the important States of the world.—I am to assist in the mechanical drudgery of Stage arrangements but our Proprietor will always manage, (or mis-manage, as he laughingly says) for himself—On matters of emergency I shall be forthcoming before the curtain:—and whenever I step forward and present the audience in my own person with an *Apology for an Actor*, I trust I shall find the 'usual candour and indulgence.'—

Promp:—That's modestly said, sir.

Ellis:—No, faith;—tremblingly said;—for I tremble at what I have undertaken—knowing the exigencies of the scheme, I have rashly promised to put on the Sock as well as the buskin.

Promp:—Be cautious!

Ellis:—Oh! I am aware of the prejudice. I am scarcely known in London, but as an actor with an Onion in his handkerchief;—Yet I must throw it away, now and then, and try if the Town will not be as kind to me in my efforts to make them laugh, as to make them cry.— 'Tis from no vanity, believe me, of my own:—All for the good of the cause, Waldron!—[46]

Among the company of virtually unknown actors (Charles Mathews made his London debut on this same night), Elliston more than held his own. By the end of the season, four months later, he had acted no less than twenty-two roles, across the range he had developed at Bath. Reviews were favourable, and on May 25 the royal couple commanded *The Heir at Law* with Elliston as Pangloss. Royal attendance was something of a tribute, since it had been lacking at the Haymarket following a fatal accident some ten years previously.[47] Now the king and queen attended four times during the first two weeks of the season,[48] thus lending the project an air of solid respectability.

The impact he made on the Haymarket audience brought renewed offers from Drury Lane too good to be refused. Although he had one year's articles still to serve,[49] the Bath management allowed him to accept the Drury Lane contract for September 1804. Since he was scheduled to join Colman again for the summer he was further obliged by the Bath management in taking his benefit prematurely, on February 28. With lines of provincial praise ringing in his ears, Elliston then bade farewell to the West country early in May, and faced the challenge of the Drury Lane stage.

With Elliston's career as actor this survey is concerned only insofar as it can be associated with his formation as a manager. In the present context, this association was indirect, being linked with a wide experience of the contemporary stage. Elliston's debut, as Rolla in *Pizarro*, on September 20, was less than spectacular. The reviews were decidedly unenthusiastic. They scarcely improved as Elliston went through Doricourt, Archer, Charles Surface, Don Felix, Orlando, Octavian, Benedick, Falkland (*The Rivals*), Delaval (*Matrimony*), Hamlet, and Richard III, all before the end of 1804. Elliston may have been right in complaining to his uncle that he was having to "encounter a host of formidable foes, and all the intrigue of envy and malice."[50] It was really not until he appeared in *The Honey Moon*, on January 31, that the critics conceded him anything above mediocrity. The part of Duke Aranza in this play, which was very loosely based on *The Taming of the Shrew*, gave full scope to Elliston's combination of romantic sensibility and air of solemnity. He was found "admirable; whether as the submissive lover, or the cool, determined husband."[51] Leigh Hunt considered it a "perfect performance," because "all is natural."[52] It seems to have laid whatever opposition there may have been against Elliston within Drury Lane. Following as it did upon a performance in *Matrimony* with Mrs. Jordan, it opened up a vein of romantic comedy which Elliston made his own. Of the twenty-seven parts he played at Drury Lane this year, sixteen were in comedy or farce.[53] In spite of the constant remarks by critics which imply a tendency on his part to over-emphasize versatility, it remains true that over the $4\frac{1}{2}$ years he was at Drury, 51 of the 83 roles Elliston acted were in comedy or farce. This vein admirably suited the Haymarket, of course, and a similar pattern is to be observed in his performances there: in 1805, for instance, he played twenty-seven roles, the majority of which were in comedy, such as Rover in *Wild Oats*, Vapid in *The Dramatist*, etc. He was exceedingly popular at the Haymarket, as his notorious benefit nights testify.[54] But though he was an asset in this respect, he created certain problems also. His success at Drury Lane meant in effect the end of Colman's independent policy: in 1805 Colman opened his doors to other established actors, which meant the end of his experiment. A second effect of Elliston's success concerned his personality, and rendered his managerial demeanour less than popular among his fellow actors.

Elliston was a Regency man to his fingertips, an ebullient personality, fond of his wench and his wine, a frequenter of gaming-houses and masquerades, a veritable scandal to wife and family. All this can be admitted with complacency: Raymond documents it extensively in his anecdotal fashion, James Winston with less amusement in his Diary. In truth, there was no reforming the man. Ultimately, this Dionysian dimension, to give it a lofty reference, was to exact its toll; a pattern which allows the historian to maintain his moral superiority and regard the antics of Elliston as he would those of a fictional Lord of Misrule. But one tends to forget that the extrovert nature of an Elliston has as its complement an inner turmoil, a cantankerousness even, which can make life very difficult for those around him. Put another way, no great comedian is charming to the prompter. At the Haymarket Elliston's duties were not limited to "the mechanical drudgery of stage arrangements," to quote the terms of *No Prelude!* He also had a say in the engagement of actors,[55] and in the acceptance of new plays.[56] From the first he displayed an energy which was not easily distinguishable from aggressiveness. After the end of his first season he was taken to task for his unwillingness to take orders from Colman. "Have you," enquired Colman with that acid he could so effectively employ, "installed yourself Theatrical Pontiff, and assumed Infallibility?"[57] What Colman had in mind may be illustrated by Elliston's handling of a situation involving the failure of a new play.

A piece called *Village; or, The World's Epitome,* opened at the Haymarket on July 18, 1805, with Elliston and Charles Mathews in leading roles. At this time, a new production meant a good deal at the Haymarket, which as a rule contented itself with a repetitious repertory of light entertainment, with no more than two or three new productions per season. *Village* got a bad reception on opening night, but was saved for a second performance through an appeal made by Elliston. Upon repetition it was so badly received that it was allowed to finish only after Elliston begged the audience's indulgence on his bended knee.[58] It may indeed have been a bad play: it was never printed, and Genest dismisses it without his usual summary of a new piece.[59] Elliston took the damnation personally. Backstage, before the afterpiece began, and while the audience continued to register its disgust, Elliston tackled Mathews and accused him of not doing his best, a charge which led to blows. The audience continued to howl for somebody's blood. True to form, Elliston appeared before the curtain, and after winning an expectant silence pronounced himself "so much *agitated* on account of the TREATMENT I have received *behind* the scenes that I cannot NOW speak; but I will shortly address you."[60] This startling overture, betokening unimaginable scandal, was succeeded by the assurance that "*no consideration whatever* should deter him from *speaking* the TRUTH," an article which "produced the loudest applause from an almost bursting *curiosity*." He expatiated on the "triple duty" he owed to audience, proprietors, and author, but kept to himself the promised account of his ill-treatment. As a sequel he published a letter next day in the *Morning Post* flatly denying the rumour that he had been floored by Charles Mathews; on further reflection, in a letter to *The Times* on July 22, he stoutly defended his practice of making speeches to the audience. This, he claimed, was one of his management duties. And in the age of Nelson and Wordsworth, duty was hardly a laughing matter.

All this seems harmless enough. Colman may have thought differently. When he was forced through financial difficulties to sell half a share in the Haymarket patent, in the course of this year, Colman chose David Morris, his brother-in-law, and Thomas Dibdin, the playwright, as shareholders. Dibdin dallied for a time and finally declined Colman's offer. Elliston, eagerly waiting in the wings, fully expected to be called upon next. But for some reason Elliston was passed over, and the quarter share was divided between two others, Tahourdine, an attorney, and James Winston. The latter, author of *The Theatric Tourist*, had made his acting debut at the Haymarket in June 1805.[61] He was now appointed stage manager, Elliston being "deprived" of the position,[62] although he retained the post of acting manager. Bagster-Collins, the biographer of Colman, says Elliston resented Winston's presence at the Haymarket.[63] It is true that he was "greatly disconcerted" over his failure, as Raymond indicates,[64] but it was Colman he blamed and not Winston. In fact, as succeeding chapters will indicate, Winston became not only Elliston's right-hand man in management but also a loyal friend, and ultimately sole executor of his will; he also collected the papers and letters which provided the material for the first biography of Elliston. On the other hand, Elliston left the Haymarket in 1805 without making the last-night speech—awesome omen!—and the following year, on applying to the proprietors for the use of a farce by Colman for his benefit at Drury Lane, he had a letter from Colman himself politely but coldly refusing him.[65] He did not appear at the Haymarket again for many years after 1805.

With his secession from the Haymarket Elliston's abortive attempts at management came to a close. In 1806, indeed, he attempted, without success, to gain an opera licence for the Lyceum in London.[66] But for the most part he was content to reap the benefits of his acting career. In March 1807 he signed articles with Drury Lane for a further five years, at an agreed salary of twenty-eight pounds a week, a handsome figure for those days.[67] He set up house at 9 Stratford Place, Oxford Street, a fashionable address which made his friends fear for his temerity. "Garrick," he was warned, "did not so presume, and Kemble does not venture beyond the bourne of Bloomsbury."[68] But Elliston cared little for such tact. He had achieved the fame of schoolday dreams, and for many years to come 9 Stratford Place was to be something of a royal seat for him.

While he waited for Fate to take the next step, Elliston was not without a keen sense of the mutability of his present popularity. From the start he had not been blind to the risks involved in the profession he had so romantically adopted. During those first years with Tate Wilkinson he had to come to terms with feelings of guilt and family disapproval, especially that of his uncle, Dr. Elliston of Cambridge. In letters to his uncle, who at first refused to know him more, he agonized over the conflicts his choice was providing, and at length was able to decide that an actor "may possess the most amiable virtues & be worthy the patronage of the publick & his relations."[69] One may smile at the naïveté of this, but it is true, as a fellow actor remarked that "there was a capital parson spoiled the day Elliston turned player."[70] As time went on the moral risks were forgotten: Elliston had none of the love-hate attitude of William Charles Macready. He became fully of the stage and for the stage. And he had the charm to convert his uncle to patronage, a performance worthy of Charles Surface himself. But the professional risks remained, and though he was at the pinnacle of his fame at the time of his uncle's death, in February 1807, he knew that pinnacles are commonly precarious. He spent the summers after 1806 in the provinces, pillaging, as he himself put it.[71] His letters to his wife on such occasions are not usually noteworthy, but now and again there is a phrase or two that cuts through the rhetoric and shows the man within, self-seeking, indeed, but honest. "If God preserve my life," he wrote to his wife from Edinburgh in July 1808, "and give me fortitude to pursue my hopes, our happiest days are yet to come, though I myself may pass into comparative obscurity."[72] Elliston, while aware of the insecurity of his popularity, could never conceive "obscurity" as being any degree lower than "comparative."

On February 18, 1809 an advertisement appeared in *The Courier* announcing that the Trustees of the Royal Circus were ready to treat with any person of "indubitable responsibility" regarding the lease of the theatre. Five days later Elliston sent his "ultimatum" to the Trustees. He offered to lease the Royal Circus for six or nine years, at their option, at an annual rent of £2000, plus ground rent and taxes.[73] If the lease was to be for six years, Elliston added, "I should desire to have a clause inserted allowing extension of the term to nine years at my option on the payment of a fine not exceeding £300."[74] He clearly had plans for a lengthy stay. The details of the proposal indicate his shrewd instinct for business. He insisted that his liability was to be limited, and he made payment of rent contingent on this clause. He wished, he stated, to avoid "even a possibility of litigation." This from the man who was to prove, in Hazlitt's phrase, the Widow Blackacre of theatrical disputations![75] The agreement reached was for seven years lease at an annual rent of £2100.

This was opportunity, and challenge. Yet had not Fate stepped in the following night, February 24, the idea of leasing a Circus in London might have been no more than whimsical. For on that night Drury Lane theatre burned to the ground. Just five months after the destruction of Covent Garden the second major theatre was now gone. For poor Sheridan this was tragic; for the crowd of one hundred thousand that gathered to see the fire it was the finest spectacle since the Great Fire of London.[76] For the leading actor at Drury Lane it was an omen most favourable. He arrived at the scene from a party: since it was a Friday in Lent there was no performance. He got into his dressingroom and salvaged his possessions.[77] While Sheridan lost everything Elliston lost no more than his watch to one of the ever-busy pickpockets. The gods, perhaps, were smiling now. Elliston was lessee of a summer theatre at which horses and pantomimists were the stars. Were one given to flights of metaphor one might imagine the hush that fell over London as the roaring flames died out like preliminary applause. The stage was set for a manager's career.

TWO

Shakespeare Versus *Harlequin*

'He's a good pony at bottom,' said Mr. Crummles,
turning to Nicholas.

Dickens, *Nicholas Nickleby*

APOLOGY seems the appropriate tone for the discussion of theatres
such as the Royal Circus. But as that well-known manager of the
Dickensian circus, Mr. Sleary, was in the habit of remarking, people
must be amused. Elliston, upon appearing for the first time before
the audience at the Royal Circus, was as conscious of that theatre's
low standing as he shared, albeit unwittingly, the philosophy of
Mr. Sleary. Elliston spoke as follows:

> At home, then, view me—where, unaw'd by rule,
> The gravest sometimes dare to play the fool;
> To cheer the heart, make every plan their choice,
> And e'en turn singers, *unpossess'd of voice*:[1]

The Royal Circus was an unfortunate theatre. It was situated in
the undeveloped south side of London, in soggy St. George's
Fields, between Blackfriars Bridge and the Obelisk. From its
opening in November 1782 it had known little but interior dissen-
sion and exterior harassment.[2] In particular, it was victimized by
the patent theatres, determined to uphold their monopoly on
legitimate drama. In 1789, for example, John Palmer (the original
Joseph Surface), being then within the Rules of the King's Bench,
was employed at the Royal Circus: because he dared to use
dialogue on the stage of a minor theatre, in a piece called *The Fall
of the Bastille,* he was charged under the Licensing Act and im-
prisoned as a vagrant. The following year Palmer and another actor
were similarly convicted, and the theatre was forced to close its

doors. Upon reopening in 1795, the managers, John Cross and
James Jones, took good care to present little better than inexplic-
able dumbshow and noise, or, more accurately, pantomimes, ballets
of action, and burletta scenes involving songs and doggerel chanted
to a piano accompaniment. Horses, rope-walkers, popular singers,
and liquor, however, were what really drew the crowds. In August
1805 the Royal Circus burned to the ground, and although a fine
new building was erected on the site within a year, it was unable
to compete with Astley's Amphitheatre, rapidly establishing itself
as the only circus in town.

In spite of this lugubrious history, the Royal Circus had a reputation for lively material. Its pantomimes and ballets of action
were staged with great attention to detail. John Cross was author
of many of these, published in two volumes in 1809 as *Circusiana*.
Looking through them, one is struck by the vividness and theatri-
cality of the setting and playing called for. For example, *Black-
beard; or, the Captive Princess* (1798) is a stirring melodrama in all
but dialogue. Through dumbshow, it contrives to give expression
to such primary feelings as terror, melancholy, desire, anger at
injustice and joy at its violent removal. It would, one feels, make
first-rate television. Cross's pantomimes, e.g., *Niobe; or, Harlequin's
Ordeal* (1797), and *Rival Statues; or, Harlequin Humourist* (1803),
are similarly impressive to read. One cannot help thinking that
Cross somehow anticipated the taste of the early nineteenth century. Certainly, soon after Elliston arrived on the Drury Lane stage
a new theatrical ambiance was rapidly forming. Thomas Holcroft's *A Tale of Mystery* (1802) established the vogue for melodrama on the legitimate stage; Thomas Dibdin's *Mother Goose*
(1806) gave pantomime a new place in "respectable" entertainment.
Old hierarchies began to crumble, though many years were to pass
before Shakespeare would make peace with Harlequin, in the age-
old struggle between literary and non-literary values, the poet
and the *metteur en scène*.

Talk of ambiance is always vague, but if it can be accepted that
the interest in pantomime, ballet of action, drama of terror and
pathos, etc., serves to characterize the English drama around 1800,
then Elliston can be said to be a product of his time. As an actor,
he was adept at mime. Leigh Hunt has a lengthy account of a
lover's quarrel enacted between Elliston and Dora Jordan in

Kenney's *Matrimony* (1804); relying heavily on dumbshow, the actors conveyed the classical *integratio amoris*. "Altogether the most complete scene of amorous quarrel that I have ever witnessed," was Hunt's verdict.[3] In 1805 Elliston starred in a melodrama he wrote himself, *The Venetian Outlaw*, the stage directions of which called for dumbshow of the minor-theatre variety. It is significant that in later years, when *The Times's* critic sought for a comparison to illuminate the skill of Grimaldi, the best mime of the age, he should say (December 27, 1824): "There was so much intelligence about every thing he did. It was as good as the performance (and not unlike it) of Elliston, or Liston."

When Elliston described himself as "at home," then, at the Royal Circus, he was perhaps speaking truer than he knew. This was on the night of his debut, June 15, 1809. The theatre had been open since April 3, with John Cross retained as manager, presenting its usual bill of fare. During this time, Elliston finished out the season with the Drury Lane company at the Lyceum. Aware of the momentousness of his move to the Royal Circus, he issued a lengthy statement on June 13, aimed at setting to rest public anxiety over the wisdom of his intentions. Not surprisingly, the document is a blend of openhearted confession and barefaced advertisement. It concludes:

MR. ELLISTON would certainly not have lent himself in this way to the scheme of any other individual; but, in his own house, and uncontrolled by the authority of any judgment but his own, he may surely take liberties with himself, with an impunity he could not reckon upon elsewhere. He proposes, by a previous address, which his friends will probably see in the papers, to prepare the public mind for his appearance in so new a shape. In short, he has no doubt . . . that he may for a short time amuse himself by riding on the outside of the coach, (for so this stage may perhaps be deemed as to his profession), without in the slightest degree relinquishing his claim to his place within.[4]

To entertain his guests on June 15, Elliston presented the pantomime, ballet, and tight-rope acrobatics usual to the Royal Circus, but he included also a production which indicated a new departure. This was an adaptation of *The Beggar's Opera*, in which he himself played Macheath. This was the thin edge of the wedge that was to enable Elliston to present legitimate drama on a minor-theatre stage. The technique was simple enough. John Cross cast Gay's prose into rhymed recitative (i.e., with musical accompaniment), totalling some eight hundred lines, retained thirty-four of the original sixty-nine songs, and added a new one. He also interjected a contemporary flavour by setting the scene of Macheath's capture in a *"Splendid Pavilion, Appropriately Decorated for a Grand Masquerade."*[5] The music of Pepusch and Linley was retained throughout, and a lot of mime gave the thing the quality of melodrama. It was billed as a burletta, and apart from Elliston it drew upon the talents of the stock Royal Circus company, e.g., Johannot as Peachum, Mrs. Hatton as Lucy Lockit, and divers singers, Harlequins, and low comedians in the beggarly roles. The ballet-master, Giroux, with his two daughters and Mrs. Taylor, gave the traditional hornpipe of four in fetters in the second act. The following day, readers of the *Morning Chronicle* were informed that the production, "having been received by a numerous and brilliant Audience, with the most flattering and unequivocal marks of approbation," would be repeated nightly.

Probably from curiosity, crowds flocked to see Elliston, and he made good use of the appearance (perhaps by invitation) of social notables: lists of such visitors were published in *The Times*. Such lists were combined with "puffs" for the performance (of Elliston) —almost the only form of criticism to appear, if one disregards the quatrain in the *Monthly Mirror*:

> Quantum mutatus!
> *'Terrible show,'* you well may say—
> Indeed it is too bad,
> With gain, so mean, to make Cross *Gay*,
> And Gay so very *sad*!

The show was popular, in any event, and ran for fifty nights.

The Beggar's Opera was but a feeler for what followed, i.e., a production of *Macbeth* as a burletta. The advertisement which appeared in the press on August 30 described the show as a "Ballet of Music and Action, founded on MACBETH." Since the aim was to "illustrate" the play, special attention was paid to scenery and machinery, by Greenwood, Marchbanks, and Branscomb. The banquet scene was under the direction of Alexander Johnston. Locke's music was augmented by an overture and other pieces by Dr. Busby, the organist and composer. Elliston was to play Macbeth, Mrs. Hatton his "ruthless consort," Makeen, the equestrian at the Royal Circus, was Banquo, and Ellar, the Harlequin, was the Physician. The choral witches, according to the playbill,[6] numbered sixteen, and the singer Slader as Hecate led the three witches. The whole production was mounted under the direction of Elliston.

Elliston introduced the play that evening with a prologue written by Dr. Busby, his "laureat," as he liked to call him. This prepared the audience for the style of the production—"The emphatic gesture, eloquence of eye . . . And what we must not *say,* resolve to *do.*"[7] The play itself was, in Professor Sprague's phrase, a "*Macbeth* of few words," with a total of only 326 lines in the three acts, the bulk of which occur in the witches' scenes.[8] The rest is silence. There was one textual restoration, however: Lady Macduff, usually omitted at this time, appears in Elliston's version. So too does Edward the Confessor, who has four lines, in which he pledges to Malcolm's cause an average of two thousand five hundred men per line.

This adaptation was once again the work of John Cross, who virtually translated *Macbeth* into the medium of serious pantomime. The stage directions, as for *The Beggar's Opera* adaptation, are very full, and suggest the style in which the piece was acted. The words "appears" and "seems"—so detested by Hamlet—are the key words, indicating the broad visual impact the actors had to make. Conventional attitudes and gestures, exaggerating the expression of emotion by conventions such as kneeling, pressing hand to heart, striking the forehead, pointing to the ceiling, and reacting violently, were the techniques used.[9]

Apart from mime and rhymed recitative, there were songs and the use of banners or scrolls to advance the plot or evoke atmosphere. One of the most effective uses of song was in the scene where Macbeth murders Duncan. Just as he approaches the bed a spirit sings, "Sleep no more! /Macbeth doth murder sleep."[10] Linen banners or scrolls were essential at a minor theatre, containing information painted in large letters. Thus, after the witches departed in I, iii, a messenger entered with a banner announcing, "*By Sinel's death, Macbeth is Thane of Glamis,*" while shortly afterwards Macduff entered with the news, "*Duncan doth create Macbeth Thane of Cawdor.*" Other banners included the message to Macduff, "*Your Castle is surprised, and wife and babes murdered,*" to Macbeth, "*The Queen is dead,*" and "*The wood of*

Birnam moves towards Dunsinane." Such moments would turn the whole theatre into a vast classroom, as the eager auditors painstakingly spelled out the latest bulletin.[11]

Macbeth is replete with opportunities for spectacle, few of which Elliston missed. At the Royal Circus the murders of Duncan and Banquo were presented on stage, with much gore, though an exception was made in the Lady Macduff scene. The witches were given full rein, providing "a mystical dance . . . and an introductory *Pas de troix*," before the descent of Hecate from the clouds. The banquet scene was one of the biggest spectacles, with the ghost of Banquo, "surrounded by clouds," coming and going through a trap with unsettling regularity. But the big scene was the fight at the end, described in great detail in the printed promptbook. Macbeth, as in all melodrama, wins hands down for most of the general battle, even wounding Macduff "slightly." He leers at Macduff: "Swords I smile at, weapons laugh to scorn/Brandish'd by man that's of a woman born."[12] Macduff, however, has an obstetrical couplet to throw back, as a result of which "Macbeth seems inclined not to fight; but being shewed the banner, he summons new courage," casts four dauntless lines in Macduff's teeth, fights again, falls and dies. "The crown is presented to Malcolm by a nobleman on his knee; and the curtain drops amidst a flourish of trumpets."

It also dropped, by all accounts, to tumultuous applause. The reviews (and the fact that there were reviews at all concerning a minor theatre, is, it is clear, unusual) were all favourable. Elliston had captured the imagination of the town. The *Morning Chronicle* (August 31) testified that "with the exception of the dialogue, the performance was almost exactly the play of SHAKESPEARE," and that Elliston had "certainly rendered it a splendid and interesting spectacle." The scenery was declared to be "magnificent, and in some instances, especially in the descent of *Hecate* from the clouds, an improvement on the scenery of the play as represented at the Winter Theatres." *The Times* (September 1) admitted that "much as we might have been inclined to condemn the experiment, we were really most agreeably surprised at the event," finding that the performance,

so far as action went, was uncommonly expressive and clear; and the incantations of the witches, from being given in scenery the most appropriate (we must say) we ever saw, boasted a more grand and imposing effect than we ever before witnessed. In fact, the whole was produced with that attention to costume, scenic splendour, decoration and embellishment, that the greatest admirer of our immortal bard could but regret his divine language was precluded.

And the *Morning Post* of the same date asserted that the audience was pleased with the production, adding: "never did a performance more progressively rise in fascinating an audience, and proving to conviction, that the attention to scenic display, embellishment, and decoration, is one of the necessary supports of the Drama. We never witnessed a piece upon the whole so well got up."

Even the galleries appreciated *Macbeth*. After one performance they called loudly for Elliston who appeared and took his bow. Then the audience called for Banquo whom they also had appreciated; but Banquo had gone home. The audience was rather firm in its insistence on having the privilege of congratulating Banquo in person; so he was sent for to his home, and arrived, in due time, flushed and harried, on the stage. The audience, which had become rather vocal, fell silent, staring in surprise at the actor, whom they did not recognize. At length a voice cried out from the gallery, "Who is that chap?" while the much-called-for actor stood awkwardly awaiting his doom. "Don't you know," another voice answered from the depths, "why you fool, that's the Author."[13]

After a two week run, *Macbeth* was rejoined by *The Beggar's Opera,* in both of which Elliston played nightly. No "orders," or free passes, were admitted, an indication of full houses. The audience for his benefit night, September 27, reflected the general interest Elliston had aroused, for it was "altogether as respectable and brilliant as we have ever beheld in the best days of our Winter Theatres."[14] Though the theatre stayed open until November 4,[15] Elliston behaved as if this were the last night. He formally addressed the audience, expressing his gratitude at the support shown him during his first season. He also outlined the principles that had guided him throughout the season: attention to the audience's comfort and convenience; a determined effort, within the limits of his licence, to bring about "such a change in the Entertainments of the place as might hold out amusement in an elegant and rational form," and with a firm determination "not to degrade my stage" to aim at "a succession of novelty equal to that of any well regulated

Theatre."[16] Should these objects have been achieved, "I shall never consider that my own personal exertions have been misplaced," for where the audience approves, "I must have reason to be proud."

Elliston was far from being satisfied with the silly restrictions circumscribing his productions at the Royal Circus. Now that Drury Lane was out of commission he intended to take full advantage of the critical state of London theatre and make a bold bid for a substitute. His attempt to found such a theatre falls into two stages.

His initial machinations were really incidental to the Royal Circus. That is to say, he merely used his status as a *soi-disant* respectable manager of a thriving concern as a self-recommendation for his claim to be given permission to operate a more legitimate theatre. He had, in fact, another theatre up his sleeve ready to fill the lacuna caused by the Drury Lane fire if only he could get a suitable licence. This was the Pantheon Opera House in Oxford Street, which he intended to operate in association with one Colonel Greville, noted impresario of the Argyle Rooms.[17]

On July 25, 1809, Elliston, through the Lord Chamberlain, memorialized the King for an extension of Greville's licence to include regular drama. His opinion of the current licence, which precluded dialogue, indicates what must have been his view also of the Royal Circus restrictions. He considered it impossible that performances, "cramped & perplexed by the Disadvantages of Recitative, should prove lastingly attractive; or produce any of the solid Ends of dramatic Representation."[18] He begged, in view of his managerial responsibility, not to say success, amply illustrated by his recent prowess at the Royal Circus, to be allowed to better serve a deprived public by "the promotion of rational amusement."

When answer finally came from the Lord Chamberlain, who did not send on the memorial to the King, it was to reveal that Greville had already got permission to use dialogue. A neat double-cross had been perpetrated. Sheridan had stepped into the picture persuading Greville to forget about Elliston and the Pantheon, and instead to allow Sheridan to make use of this licence for the Drury Lane company at the Lyceum.[19] The only revenge Elliston could take was to refuse to act in such a company.

Thus it developed that as 1809 drew to a close Elliston was in the rather precarious position of having nothing but the Royal Circus theatre with which to earn a living. The obvious move was to try to raise the status of this theatre, be it ever so humble, as a contender for legitimate honours. The immediate impetus for this next step came from an unexpected source.

On October 9, 1809, the committee for a subscription theatre in London published their prospectus. Ever since Drury Lane burned down, a group of theatre-lovers, dissatisfied with the monopoly system and its evil effects on drama, had combined to form a movement for a new legitimate theatre, which would be organised along the lines of a limited company. The Lord Mayor of London, a brace of aldermen, five members of Parliament and seven prominent citizens, hereafter referred to as the Third Theatre Committee, formed the nucleus of the movement. It savoured of amateurism, if not a coterie, and as such could not at first be taken seriously. But now, with the publication of a prospectus and at the end of October an announcement of a petition to Parliament for leave to build a new theatre,[20] the committee aroused great interest. By November 2, startlingly, the subscription for the petition was declared full, i.e., £200,000 had been raised. No longer could the amateurs be thought innocuous. On behalf of Drury Lane, Peake, the Treasurer, voiced alarm, condemning the committee as opportunistic; he also scoffed with Macbeth-like confidence at the idea of a third theatre. Drury Lane, he assured all the world, was sure to be rebuilt, using its "dormant" patent for authority.[21] The Third Theatre committee's reply was as alarming as Macduff's, casting into doubt the validity of the Drury Lane patent and making the reasonable point that if there were three patents in existence there should be three theatres. Since there were, of course, only two patents in existence, from Davenant and Killigrew's time, and Drury Lane was actually operating under a licence while its original patent, discovered in 1792 to be in the possession of Covent Garden, was not in fact being used, it looked as if the Third Theatre committee had a point. The question could do with an airing.

A stir came over the metropolis. Arnold of the Lyceum theatre, sitting pretty with Greville's licence, looked on himself as the true representative of the third theatre, if such could possibly exist. Greville had Sheridan's assurance that he could have the Drury

Lane "dormant" patent when Drury Lane was rebuilt; so he too looked on himself as the true Messiah. Elliston lost no time in putting in his twopence worth. He penned another Memorial to the King forthwith (November 16), and this time enlisted a friend, Colonel Taylor, to present it to the King in person.[22] Taking over the general arguments of the Third Theatre committee, Elliston cites the increased population of London and the beneficial role played by the theatre in society as reasons for a new theatre. Innocently, he mentions the talk of a possible application to Parliament for an additional theatre; he humbly submits that his own theatre (the Royal Circus) is fully competent to fill this role.

A copy of this went to the Lord Chamberlain, a day later, significantly enough. To the Lord Chamberlain Elliston insisted he had no intention of proposing a new theatre "without previous sanction."[23] Nothing to get alarmed about, is the point he wishes to make; he merely does not want, as a theatre owner, to be the victim of this committee. He also dissociates himself from Greville at this point, wishing now to go it alone.

On November 18 Elliston took off for a brief engagement at Bath and Bristol, followed by a trip to Manchester Theatre Royal, which he had leased for a twelve week season beginning December 4. He was not on the spot, therefore, to know how his Memorial to the King fared. His solicitor, Allen, wrote to him, however, that "no assent" was the verdict. "At all events," consoled Allen, "it secures you this, that no one, *by application to the King,* can have a preference to you."[24]

While Elliston settled down to managing the Manchester theatre, using the Royal Circus company for the most part, Allen kept him well informed from London on the latest developments in the Third Theatre movement. On February 8, 1810, the committee petitioned the King, the first step that led to the appeal to Privy Council in March. On February 9 Allen acknowledged receipt of another petition from Elliston; this was presented on February 14. Allen advised Elliston to follow up, like the Third Theatre committee, with a Bill to Parliament. Although he anticipates heavy opposition Allen thinks Elliston has a just cause, and he encourages him to press forward in the fight against the subjection of Drama "to the Police."[25]

Following Allen's advice, Elliston enlisted Sir Thomas Turton to undertake the presentation of a Bill to Parliament; several interested citizens wrote Turton on Elliston's behalf. On March 1 Elliston wrote to the Prime Minister, Perceval, in person, formally asking for his petition to be heard; this letter he published as a broadsheet.[26] He also canvassed the magistrates and residents of the Borough of Southwark for support, and elicited from them a petition in his favour. This latter paid tribute to Elliston's first season at the Royal Circus: "Instead of this Theatre as heretofore the Resort, for the most part, of the lo[wer] orders of Society the same was nightly filled by persons of Rank & Fortune thereby rendering the said [Theatre] a place of Entertainment very desirable & agreeable."[27] These loyal supporters considered that the necessity of constant musical accompaniment during performances at the Royal Circus was a "restriction which cannot in any manner benefit the public . . . whilst it operates as a great drawback upon the Merits of the Operatic & other Musical Pieces . . . by depriving them of their proper musical Variations in the diff[t] parts." The privileges Elliston is asking for would obviate these artistic shortcomings, and keep the theatre on "its present respectable footg."

Elliston felt sure Sheridan would oppose his Bill in Parliament, but wrote to him anyway, on March 2, enclosing a copy of his printed statement regarding his application to Perceval. The main purpose of the letter was to suggest to Sheridan that there was no essential conflict of interests between them, in spite of Elliston's refusal to act at the Lyceum: "I apprehend it must be a matter of Indifference to you, & to others holdg patent Rights, whether the Dialge in pieces performed at my Theatre be perplexed by a piano forte accompaniment, or not."[28]

On March 5 Sir Thomas Turton presented Elliston's Bill in Parliament. Its main tenor was of complaint against the restriction under which Elliston was labouring. Permission was requested, not for regular drama outright, but for the use of dialogue. The Prime Minister was not pleased with the Bill's bluntness. Further explanation on Elliston's part proved fruitless, for on March 11 Perceval indicated by letter that the request "cannot be granted, except upon a ground which would go to alter the whole principle upon which theatrical entertainments are at present regulated within the metropolis and twenty miles round it."[29] Such a "principle," which was really a "practice," could not, of course, be changed as simply as all that; thirty-two years were to pass before such a radical move could be dreamed of. Instead, Elliston, who was unwilling to have his Bill read unless he had a reasonable chance of success, altered its import so that it did not so much complain of theatrical laws as claim that Elliston should be exempt from them. His respectability and that of his theatre were to be the grounds of such a claim.[30]

This version pleased Perceval no more than the last, apparently, for on March 21 Elliston wrote to him that because the Bill was thought "objectionable" he had "without hesitation, withdrawn his application from Parliament; although he had received the warmest assurances of support from many Members; & although, by such course, he leaves his property & Interests exposed to many inconveniences, from which he had hoped he might have been relieved, not only without injury, but with advantage, to the public."[31]

So ended Elliston's hopes of an extended licence. For a brief moment it almost looked as if insult would be added to injury by the Privy Council. When the members met on March 12 to decide on the Third Theatre petition Elliston was in Bath fulfilling an acting engagement. His solicitor Allen wrote him that, to everyone's surprise, the Privy Council had postponed its decision for several days, as if the matter were debatable. Allen tried to make it sound as if the Council was merely seeking to be absolutely fair, but that same day he revealed his anxiety to their mutual friend Warner Phipps: "I cannot imagine why these Dons should give to others in full what seems accordg to Mr. Percevals Acct, improper to be given to Mr. Elliston in part only."[32] It is possible Phipps alerted Elliston. At any rate, when the Privy Council convened on March 16 to hear objections to the Third Theatre petition, a counter-petition from Elliston, dated March 15, was among the many read. This document indicates a reluctance to pronounce on the "expediency or inexpediency" of a third theatre, merely intimating that if such was in fact needed, Elliston's personal experience and the immediate availability of the theatre be stressed. Rather grandly, Elliston offered "to take the whole burthen and responsibility of such an object" as establishing a third theatre, upon himself.[33]

Elliston found himself in the company of Greville, Arnold, Sheridan and others against the proponents of a subscription theatre. He did not employ counsel, as Greville did, emphasising his reluctance to enter the debate on a fundamental level. This was probably wise, for next to Sheridan's counter-petition, which was "very declamatory," Elliston's "was as persuasive as any."[34] Graham, indeed, of the Drury Lane committee, said Elliston was "a pretty fellow to petition the King, after violating the laws at your *Circus*: and that if you were brought before him, he should deem the utmost penalty under the Vagrant Act applicable in your case." This caused a great flurry, and much was said as to the illegality of Elliston's *Macbeth,* until Sheridan eased matters by observing that the greatest violation was to Shakespeare, in Elliston's attempting the role.

To keep matters going, Elliston wrote Allen a letter to be read at the next session (March 19), which did little more than repeat his position and claim protection for his property. Sheridan hardly did more. In a spirit of intransigent self-interest the Third Theatre movement was defeated, all existing theatres, major and minor, showing a united front against the intruder. Sheridan, for his part, refused to be drawn into the strict legalities of the monopoly maze, appealing instead to a sense of fair play for poor, threatened, Drury Lane. He, too, advanced the argument that if a new theatre were needed, his theatre could supply the want.

On March 30 Privy Council decided against the petition for a Third Theatre. Though the movement did not die immediately, this was a crucial moment in the history of the English stage; had the monopoly restrictions been broken at this time, with Drury Lane out of action and Covent Garden torn with internal strife, the future of English theatre might have been given a new shape. But on May 2 Sheridan got leave to bring in a Bill for the rebuilding of Drury Lane, and although a year passed before the actual building got under way, the wheels of establishment theatre, momentarily halted, were in motion again at this point, and the Third Theatre movement was doomed.

Elliston was disappointed at his failure to have the Royal Circus accepted as London's Third Theatre. In Manchester, at the close of an unhappy season, on March 24, he informed his audience of his intention never to tread a London stage again, "except a new Theatre should be built or Drury Lane should rise from its ashes."

During the following year, he continued, he would make a tour of England, Ireland, and Scotland, "with a view of concluding my scenic life." If the new manager of Manchester Theatre Royal should engage him then, he would "here have the melancholy honour of making you my last bow."[35]

Elliston was not really suited for this Richard-the-Second mood, however, and he had no real intention of quitting. In fact, since January 1810 he had thrown a lot of time and energy into altering the structure of the Royal Circus. Improvements had cost him in the region of two thousand pounds.[36] Having burned his boats as far as Drury Lane was concerned, he was hardly likely to let his hopes for the Royal Circus evaporate entirely.

When the doors opened on Easter Monday, April 23, Elliston was on stage armed with the inevitable address written by Busby. A loyal audience let him know he was appreciated. He came forward after the main piece—*The Beggar's Opera,* in which he did not himself appear—and advised the audience that he would not rest until he had made his theatre the most fashionable summer theatre, in spite of the efforts of his "opponents."[37]

That Elliston meant business the theatre itself testified. In 1809, there had been time only to add the idea of Family Boxes; now the whole structure was changed utterly, and the Surrey Theatre was born. Gone was the horse-ride: in its place was a large pit with seats. The contractor's specifications for these alterations have survived, and they indicate a complete removal of "the whole of the present pit, seats, floors, enclosures round ride, Orchestra, enclosure to pay place of pit & boxes & linings round underside of Centre boxes & every part described to be altered," etc.[38] The stables were converted into saloons, the mangers into fruit and lemonade stalls. Over all was a new air of style, even elegance:

Seats have been made with red covering, and a commodious passage in the middle [of the pit], which will prove convenient to the Public. The fronts of the Boxes, and the seats, have been fitted up in a style of superior accommodation, and the Lobby covered with matting. Chandeliers, and genteel rooms for refreshments, have also been added, making the entrance quite elegant and convenient.

  The draperies to the private boxes are crimson and gold, suspended with the greatest taste. The Royal arms, in gold, is placed over the box on the right side, . . . The *proscenium* is considered a master piece. Over the curtain, Apollo and the nine are finely painted by Gueta, of the Opera. The cieling is very finely ornamented with the story of Bacchus and Ariadne, done by Letilla, in the style of basso relievo. Other parts of the house are ornamented by artificial stone work, and the whole conveys an idea of taste and magnificence never seen before at this Theatre.[39]

The Surrey became in time one of the best-known theatres in London. Tom Dashall, whose bohemian adventures as told in *Real Life in London* probably reflect accurately enough the taste of the Regency buck, spoke well of the Surrey: "It is a neat building, and shows a good front to the road; is fitted up with considerable elegance, and is a very convenient theatre."[40] Thomas Dibdin is rather more technical, in finding the Surrey, "without exception . . . the best-constructed both for audience and actors in or near the metropolis: there is no part of the theatre from whence you may not see, nor any from whence you may not hear with the greatest facility: the audience part of the house is commodious, and as spacious, except in height, as either Covent-Garden or Drury Lane: the stage, its offices, green-room, dressing-rooms, and wardrobes on the first scale of convenience."[41]

Elliston was the first of the actor-managers to try to bring theatre to London's suburbs. The difficulties were staggering, even if one leaves the Licensing laws out of account. Audiences were unruly, uneducated, and loud; even the Tom Dashalls, the men about town, were more on the lookout for a tart than for art. The serious-minded simply stayed away, even from the patent theatres. In a place like St. George's Fields, theatre and debauchery were virtually synonymous. Thomas Dibdin says that the population there could be divided into three categories: one third were bankrupts, living within the Rules, one third were Puritans whose consciences forbade payment at a theatre (though not free passes), and among the remainder a small group, perhaps "a twenty-seventh part of the neighbourhood," who visited Astley's once a year.[42] The only hope was to leaven some of this ignorance by drawing in patrons from elsewhere. This Elliston seems to have been able to do. He offered subscription tickets at seven guineas for the season, and although he never outlined a season programme, he hinted enough about rational entertainment to make it clear that as manager he would continue to present dramatic performances, even if the law forbade them.

Although the present survey is concerned to stress this innovative aspect of Elliston's management, it ought to be said here that the Surrey by no means turned its back either on pageantry or on frivolity. One doubts whether this would have been possible at the time, even if Elliston were the man to do it. The fact is, the Surrey performances began at 6.30 p.m., and went on for four or five hours thereafter. This meant quite a full bill, which included gentlemen on the tightrope or, for variety, on the slack rope; popular singers, anticipatory of the music-hall artists of fifty years later; pantomimes; sketches; animal acts; little ballets, and so on. Oftentimes, the expense went into the pageantry, since Regency audiences had an insatiable appetite for spectacle. They would throng to see the Lord Mayor's show on Elliston's stage, having seen the real thing on the streets outside (Easter 1811). The same people would throng to Carlton House to catch a glimpse of the pageantry of the Prince Regent's way of life: and push and shove so violently that five women were trampled to death in June 1811, and dozens were stripped naked. "They were to be seen all round the gardens, most of them without shoes or gowns; and many almost completely undressed, and their hair hanging about their shoulders."[43] This appetite for spectacle had to be assuaged (one says nothing of the violence); and if the patent theatres were doing their bit, with dogs and horses and afterpieces, Elliston could hardly be excused from pageantry and pantomimes.

After the gala opening of the Surrey theatre, Elliston himself made his first appearance on May 11, playing Macheath. On May 21 he presented a three-act version of Farquhar's *The Beaux' Stratagem,* adapted by Dennis Lawler, who had been taken on as writer-under-contract in November 1809 (at a salary of one guinea a week). The principal feature of the adaptation were the songs, many of which were the work of Mrs. Elliston, by profession a dancing instructress. Books of the songs were on sale at the theatre, and no doubt members of the audience were encouraged to sing along with Elliston, who played Archer, Johannot, who was Scrub, and a blithe newcomer to the London stage, Sarah Booth, who played Cherry. A sample of the kind of thing offered is "Cherry's the Lass for Me," sung by Archer:

> O CUPID was surely my guide,
>   When we came to this inn to quarter;
> Where a sweet little lass I've espied,
>   'Tis Cherry, the Inn-keeper's daughter.

Cherry's the lass for me,
  In Cupid's net I've caught her;
Fresh as the rose is she,
  Although but an Inn-keeper's daughter.

How she cock'd up her nose with pride,
  When I to love besought her;
'You're only a footman,' she cried,
  'And I am an Inn-keeper's daughter.'
                                        Cherry's the lass, &c.[44]

"The Plague of a Drunken Husband," a descriptive ballad, and
"The Virtues of Ale," were two others for which Mrs. Elliston
was responsible. But the most popular of all was Condell's "Love's
Catechism," a duet between Archer and Cherry. This was frequently encored and the playbills spoke of it in scarlet letters,
a practice as yet unknown at the major theatres.

   The Beaux' Stratagem proved popular, and on June 4 was de-
creed "established," by the advertisements, and the large crowds
of nobility were requested, accordingly, "to order their Coachmen
to set down with their horses heads towards the Bridge, and take
up in the opposite direction." One week later, however, the play
was withdrawn, in accordance with Elliston's principle of supplying a constant change of production. A three-act serious piece followed, together with much activity in pantomime, before Elliston
launched another adaptation. This time it was *Three and the
Deuce,* Hoare's musical drama, in which Elliston played his well-
known triple part of the three Singles. He was joined in this
production by De Camp from Drury Lane. For the month of July,
the latter production, *The Beggar's Opera* and *Beaux' Stratagem*
formed the back-bone of the repertory, with a change of programme
every evening.

   A new production, however, was essential if interest in the Surrey
was to be sustained. On August 6, consequently, Garrick's *Jubilee*
was presented, adapted by Thomas Dibdin. John Cross had died
during the preceding winter, and Dibdin now took over as author
and stage manager at the Surrey. He was a big fish for Elliston
to have landed, since his pantomimes, operas, and comedies had
made his name a household word, while his hard-nosed view of art,
"The intrinsic value of a thing/Is just as much as it will bring,"[45]
made him peculiarly suitable for the tough audiences of St.

George's Fields. To lure him from Covent Garden, Elliston paid him three times his old salary.

The pageant was the main attraction in the Jubilee. Seventeen scenes from a variety of Shakespeare's plays were offered, each acted out with appropriate mime and music. Elliston gave extra assistance to his audience by filling his playbill with a synopsis of each scene—a practice he observed with regard to most new productions. The *Hamlet* scene, for example, in which Elliston himself appeared, was described as follows:

The solemn interview between the Shade and the Prince, who is called upon to revenge his father's murder. The distraction of Ophelia, and earnest determination of Laertes to see her wrongs redressed.

And the *King Lear* scene, in which Elliston appeared as Edgar, was described as:

The old King in the storm, attended by his faithful follower, Kent; his rage, imbecility, and distraction; meets with Edgar as Mad Tom, to whose habits and manners he appears to be wildly attached; the sudden entrance of his youngest daughter, Cordelia, and his eventual remembrance of her.[46]

Each scene, then, was a miniature ballet of action. The finale was set in a Greek temple, where Elliston recited an ode written for the occasion by the redoubtable Dr. Busby.

Elliston clearly had a high opinion of the Pageant, and of the role he was fulfilling in the community by making accessible Shakespeare without tears. *The Times* of August 15 echoed such a sentiment with remarkable fortuitousness:

Those worthy inhabitants of distant villages, who from daily occupation and difference of habits, have hitherto had no time or inclination to peruse the works of our immortal bard, SHAKESPEARE, have, on their coming to town and paying a visit to the Surrey Theatre, imbibed, from the sample exhibited in the Grand Pageant, such a taste for Shakespearian productions, and so much curiousity to peruse plays, of which they have just seen enough to make them wish for more, that the demand for pocket editions and other sets of the Poet's works is so great, that the booksellers have of late been obliged to reprint them in all forms and sizes.

Regardless of the turmoil he was causing in the printing industry, Elliston pressed on with his *Jubilee* through August, throwing in Hoare's *Three and the Deuce,* and *The London Hermit,* by

O'Keeffe, for good measure. A victim of his own integrity, however, he was forced on August 17 to tell the public that "although the unparalleled attraction of the Pieces now performing might warrant the Proprietor in continuing them much longer,"[47] new pieces must be given, such as *Harlequin Basket Maker* by Dibdin, and a new burletta, as yet undisclosed. What, one wondered, could the new burletta be—everyone understood the importance of the new pantomime—that might warrant an end to the educational *Jubilee,* if not to a printing boom?

On August 27 the mystery was solved. *A Bold Stroke for a Wife,* the early eighteenth-century comedy by Susannah Centlivre, condensed into three acts and versified into burletta form by Dennis Lawler, was to be presented that evening. The play concerns the efforts of Colonel Feignwell to win the hand of Ann Lovely by obtaining the unwitting consent of each of her four guardians, each of whom is a type character. Feignwell impersonates in turn a Frenchified fop, an Egyptian traveller, a Dutch merchant, and Simon Pure, a Quaker, in order to impose on each of the guardians; he gets some assistance from his loyal friend, Freeman. The play is thus largely a vehicle for the versatility of Feignwell, played by Elliston; Sarah Booth played Ann Lovely. As with *The Beaux' Stratagem* it was the new music and songs that won most attention.

But the crowning production of the season was yet to come: a melodramatic romance based on Scott's poem *The Lady of the Lake,* staged on September 24. As is well known, the novels of Sir Walter Scott were frequently dramatized during the Regency, suiting the taste of the time for action and melodrama. Thomas Dibdin anticipated this movement by adapting a romance that had much in common with the later novels.

Dibdin's version, termed a "melodramatic romance," was in two acts, with 183 lines in act one, 306 in act two: a total of 105 lines were by Dibdin himself.[48] There were six songs, all from the poem itself, one being turned from dialogue into song.[49] All in all the adaptation is a pretty skilful piece of synopsis. Dibdin's main addition was in the characterisation of Lady Margaret, the mother of Roderick Dhu, made into an out-and-out villain contrasting effectively with Ellen, who is in her clutches. Dibdin also introduced a little low comedy as another sop to the taste of the age, inventing two stage Scotsmen, Norman and Sandy, for the purpose.

Dibdin was also responsible for the direction, and seems to have achieved a remarkable sense of unity in the romantic mode. The scenery was Gothic-romantic, i.e. practicable and at the same time evocative of mystery and wonder. In this regard he was fortunate to have Marchbanks as artist, who painted some beautiful scenery "delineating his native country with the true amor patriae."[50] The costumes, according to the notes accompanying the printed text, showed a genuine effort at authenticity, all the Highland characters being dressed in strictly accurate tartans and accessories. The impetus for such accuracy may, perhaps, be attributed in the first place to Scott himself via John Philip Kemble,[51] but it is interesting to note its quick adoption by the minor theatres.

The staging followed the usual pattern of minor-theatre spectacle. There was a good deal of dumb-show, use of music for effect, use of a scroll (once), and two pageants. Then there was the obligatory scene, the finale battle scene, a single combat between Fitzjames and Roderick Dhu.

As Fitzjames, Elliston was the only actor advertised when the play opened, but the actor whose career was launched by the production was T. P. Cooke, who played Roderick Dhu. Cooke was to return the compliment many years later, by bringing fame to Elliston's last days as a manager, through his appearance in *Black-Eyed Susan*.

Elliston chose *The Lady of the Lake* for his benefit night, September 28, and it ran in repertory until the end of November. Dibdin quotes Elliston as describing the play as a "godsend" to the Surrey.[52] It certainly ensured a successful season, with a net profit of £3000.[53] Perhaps flushed with his success, Elliston issued a communiqué on November 23, announcing, with a laudable spirit of public concern, that the Surrey should remain open for a winter season.[54] Subscription tickets were issued at three guineas, and after much trumpeting about the heating and his service to the local inhabitants Elliston opened the new season on November 28, with *Love's Perils*, *The Lady of the Lake*, and *Sylvester Daggerwood*. The latter was a sketch by Lawler based on Colman's farce. It was rendered topical by the appearance of Elliston as a strolling player with a difference, namely Napoleon Bonaparte. Cruikshank caught the savage glee of this lampoon to perfection, in the print reproduced on plate 6 below. *Sylvester Daggerwood* proved a big hit, both prior to Elliston's departure for an engagement in

Bath and Bristol on December 10, and after his return to the Surrey on January 28, 1811. It was part of the bill of entertainment when he took his benefit on February 8. The season closed about the middle of March.

It appears that Elliston used Greville's licence for this (winter) season, his own being good for the summer season only. In November the two men negotiated again about a winter opera season, and Greville was supposed to withdraw his licence from the Lyceum for the purpose.[55] But on his playbill announcement Elliston specified that the entertainments at the Surrey would consist "as hitherto" of music, dancing and "other Entertainments of the like kind." This suggests he had a licence for burlettas, and the like, only. At the same time, there is evident in the fare offered a definite attempt to simulate opera. Dibdin brought out a new melodramatic romance, *The Harper's Son and the Duke's Daughter* on December 12, which was awarded the term "operatic" in the advertisements; and indeed the play itself relies heavily on music, songs, recitative and choruses to flesh out its slight, melodramatic plot.[56] On January 7 of the new year Dibdin brought out an adaptation of his own highly successful opera, *The Cabinet*, calling it *Secret Springs*. On January 31 another adaptation of Scott appeared, this time of *The Lay of the Last Minstrel*, and on February 11 Dibdin again obliged with an adaptation of another of his operas, *Il Bondocani*. To sing in these operas, billed either as melodramas or burlettas "founded on" their immediate sources, Elliston engaged several men from Drury Lane, Covent Garden, and the provinces. His big "find" this season, corresponding with his launching Sarah Booth the year before, was Miss Feron, then only in her early teens, destined to become one of the great singers of her time.[57] She first appeared at the Surrey for Elliston's benefit night, February 8, and was engaged for a few nights only. By February 18 her popularity was such that Elliston could use it as a vindication of his ever-active vigilance for the good of his theatre; since Miss Feron was popular at Bath and the provinces, Elliston informed his public he "conceived that he was affording to the frequenters of this Theatre, a specimen of British talent, worthy of their fullest support."[58]

The year 1811 was to be a year of decision for Elliston. His continuing to work at the Surrey was something which his friends were against. There were two main arguments, one moral, the other professional. Elliston, it seems, was having a gay old time, like any Tom Dashall himself, and acquiring a rather disreputable name. One of his closest friends, Warner Phipps, took him to task for his drinking, and also for his neglect of his family. Mrs. Elliston had twice called on Phipps, in "great, very great, mental anxiety. Once she called, after the day of your opening [November 28, 1810], and again about three weeks since. These were occasioned by your absence from home on the whole of the two previous nights, without either notice or the most careless explanation."[59] Had he met Elliston for the first time now, Phipps added, he should have shunned him. Among Elliston's other friends and correspondents was one in Bath who invariably signed himself "Mentor." He was, it seems, an admirer from the days of Elliston's career in Bath. He was convinced that acting at the Surrey was injurious. When the papers carried the story that Elliston was negotiating with Colman over a possible engagement at the Haymarket, (early in 1811), "Mentor" responded in the following, characteristic style:

I form no particular wishes as to *our* engaging at the Hay Market, yet I hope if *we* do so, it will prove to the London Public that *we* ought to take the lead in any theatre that may be erected in London. However well regulated the Surrey Theatre may be, yet the pieces that can be represented there are too trifling to give the proper scope to *our* talents, & if *we* perform *only there* in the Metropolis, what *we* can do will cease to be remembered. Colmans terms are certainly good, & will help to repay any loss *our* absence from the Surrey may occasion, where I should hope *showy* pieces would in *Summer* be productive without *us*.[60]

To Mrs. Elliston, who apparently was worried that the company of Colman "& his Gin" would be no advantage to Robert William, "Mentor" wrote that it would be wise for Elliston to move to the Haymarket. The Surrey, he told her, was "a Theatre elegant & commodious;—excellently conducted, the scenery & dresses grand," but it was remote, and had to meet a lot of competition. Elliston deserved credit for his attempt to "correct the taste & mend the morals of such Theatres as the Surrey," but this correction had not resulted, and Elliston should now withdraw.[61]

Elliston probably saw the wisdom of both of these arguments, for he began to pull his socks up. A couple of brief engagements at Bath got him good reviews, and he drove a hard bargain with

Colman for the summer season: forty pounds a week plus two clear benefits.[62] Following a successful petition to the Prince Regent, Colman had now authority to open in mid-May, for a five-month season.[63] With Elliston as spear-head, Colman used the situation to strike a blow against the patent theatres. No doubt this role coincided agreeably with Elliston's own attitude at present, and allowed him to address the Haymarket audience, in his capacity of acting manager, in a way that made some sort of bridge with his own theatre. For example, on opening night, May 15, he recited a versified address in which he compared himself to Napoleon, and spoke of fighting "with fury—near the Obelisk," winning "triumphs" described as "wonderful."[64] Likewise on closing night, October 15, he informed the audience that the season was an experiment to save the managers' interests from annihilation by the patent theatres. This polemic was not forced throughout the season, however, and in the present context it takes second place to the question of Elliston's individual problem.

"Mentor" had reminded him that the main purpose of the Haymarket engagement must be to prove that his acting ability had not fallen off. He must play as he did at Bath, by being *"always perfect & present to the business of the scene,"* and by paying attention to trifles; by avoiding too much rouge, and by taking greater care over his costume; and by abstaining from negus "or any substitute to encrease vivacity," including the company of Colman.[65] Whether or not he listened to these Polonian precepts, Elliston worked hard, playing a total of thirty-eight roles over the summer. The reaction of *The Examiner* (May 19) to his acting in Tobin's *The Honey Moon* may reflect the work he put into the engagement:

One might have thought that he would have brought away with him some of the vulgarity of his new subjects in Saint George's Fields, but his *Duke Aranza* was the same accomplished gentleman as ever,—his humour the same finished dryness, his gallantry the same emphatic tenderness.

He added one new role to his repertoire, i.e., Pierre in *Venice Preserved*. The critics were rather surprised at the result. *The Dramatic Censor . . . for the year 1811*, no friend to Elliston, conceded that he showed up the Jaffeir by displaying great energy. The *Morning Chronicle* (August 23) praised Elliston's "vivacious action, and masculine intonation," but may have been less than serious in finding him "peculiarly happy in the dying scene." In short, the season could be considered a vindication of Elliston's name.

In one other respect Elliston returned the laugh on his critics this season. On April 29 a quatrain appeared in the *Morning Chronicle* poking fun at Kemble's controversial introduction of horses onto the august stage of Covent Garden, in *Timour the Tartar*:

> Though Kemble and Elliston change their pursuits,
> Their Actors are at their old habits again:
> The men at the Circus still acting like brutes,
> The brutes at the Theatre still acting like men.

One of the new productions at the Haymarket was a burlesque of hippodrama, entitled *The Quadrupeds of Quedlinburgh* (July 26). It was compiled by Colman from a burlesque on Kotzebuean sentimentality by Canning and others in 1798: Colman updated the satire and provided a finale which was a send-up of *Timour the Tartar*. Elliston played the Manager of the Haymarket, "a very Poor Gentleman," the implication being that Kemble was cashing in on horse-dramas while other managers were sporting withers lean but unwrung. Meanwhile, the Surrey, without its "Chieftain . . . great Field-marshal ELLISTON!" to use his own terms,[66] could scarcely be blamed for joining the horse race. Thomas Dibdin was in charge in Elliston's absence. An attempt to get Charles Mathews to deputize, at a salary of fifty pounds a week, was sharply turned down.[67] After the opening production of *Industry and Idleness,* a dramatization by Dennis Lawler of Hogarth's "Apprentices," into which the Lord Mayor's show was incorporated, the most impressive show was a double bill by Dibdin called *What's a Stage Without Horses?* and *Blood Will Have Blood; or, The Battle of the Bridges.* The latter proved a big hit. The combined services of Davis and Ducrow were used, to horse twenty knights from four countries (one of Elliston's sons, Henry, was a Polish knight, along with Ducrow). Two suits of armour, one steel and one brass, which Elliston had had especially made for the Lord Mayor's pageant at a cost of almost seven hundred pounds,[68] were used for the big battle scene, "a simultaneous combat of cavalry and infantry, on four bridges, with the storming and firing the Castle."[69] This *The Times* of July 4 said was fought with "unprecedented fury." The troops were not engaged indefinitely, however, and audiences soon had to content themselves with an ending borrowed from *Lodoiska,* showing a castle in flames. In consolation, there was a procession in the first act, with two horses in armour, the two suits aforesaid, and an elephant, *"decorated in all the costly habiliments of the East."*[70] By January 1812 a stupendous white spotted camel was added, said by the playbills to be above ten feet high.

This is a hard act to follow, and further documentation of the 1811 season would add little of any import. It was a season that must have given Astley a few worries. It was too much even for Dibdin, who resigned from the Surrey at the end of the season.

Elliston's first appearance was on his benefit night, October 23, when he played Archer. In the inevitable curtain speech he apologised for his "seeming" neglect of the Surrey, assuring his audience, however, that he had watched the "progress" of his theatre "with unremitting care and solicitude," and that he had "not the slightest intention of quitting this concern."[71] He also referred to the role his theatre was playing in London, in providing performers with "an honourable passport" to the patent theatres. He did not refer here to horses or even elephants. The impression conveyed by the whole address, indeed, is that Elliston, recharged after his Haymarket experience, was determined to put a lot more work into the Surrey. He made a "last professional visit" to Bath in November, and reappeared for the last night at the Surrey, December 9.

As in 1810, Elliston reopened for a winter season some days later. The horse-pieces and a new pantomime were the main attractions. In an effort to get some better material he wrote to Walter Scott, told him of the success of *The Lady of the Lake,* and asked him to provide a new piece for the Surrey. This drew the following response:

Sir,
I was favour with your letter and am much obliged to you for the polite expressions it contains as well as your supposing me capable of advancing in any degree the Dramatic art or the advantage of its professors. As I am very fond of the Stage which is the only public amusement that I ever indulge in, I have at times from my own inclination or at the solicitation of friends partial like yourself to my other productions been tempted to consider the subject your letter proposes to me. But upon a mature consideration of my own powers such as they are and of the probable consequence of any attempt to write for the Theatre

which might fall short of compleat success, I have come to the determination of declining every over-ture of the kind, of which I have
received several. I have therefore only to express my regret that it is
not in my power to assist your exertions, which I have no doubts the
public favour & your own talents will render successful without such
aid. I am very glad I have been indirectly the means of supplying new
subject for your Theatre and am very much

Sir

Your obedient Servant
Walter Scott.[72]

Edin. Jan 7 1812
Robert Elliston Esq.
9 Stratford Place
Oxford Road
London.

Nothing if not pragmatic, Elliston made do with adaptations of
such popular plays as *The Blind Boy, Raymond and Agnes, A Tale
of Mystery,* etc. As the year went on, various original pieces were
added, of no real importance except that they reflect the taste of
the time. They included *America; or, the Colonists,* by Thomas
Dibdin, a version of the story of Pocohantas, "whose intervention
preserved an English Captain from a cruel death, and by whose
means, a mutual good understanding was created between the
British and the Aborigines of the Country."[73] Apart from the sensational and the jingoistic, there was an educational dimension to the
play, "respectfully offered," said the playbill, "as a practical description of the Ancient Customs, with respect to the ceremonies of
declaring War, making Peace, celebrating Marriage, among the
North American Tribes." Much the same description could be
applied to *Robinson Crusoe,* by Dennis Lawler. This was billed as
a serious pantomime, but it was in effect a full-length melodrama.
It had been usual to stage the Crusoe story with a Harlequinade;
Lawler broke with that tradition, and instead "humbly attempted
to engraft on the original matter, the supposed history of Friday."[74]
The exotic setting, the tense situations, the story of love and danger
which Lawler invented, were all likely to appeal to contemporary
sensibilities.

To replace Dibdin, Elliston attracted the actor Samuel Russell
to the Surrey. Besides being acting manager, he played opposite
Elliston in a variety of adaptations, for Elliston now acted frequently at the Surrey. The first occasion they teamed up was December 9, 1811, when Russell played Jerry Sneak opposite Elliston's

Major Sturgeon in *The Mayor of Garratt* (as adapted by Dibdin).
This was Russell's best role: as late as 1827, Oxberry called it one
of the "few faultless performances of the present day."[75] From
February onwards, Russell and Elliston played together as often as
three times a week, in such plays as Colman's *Battle of Hexham*
and Townley's *High Life Below Stairs.* The repertory was gradually expanded to include a wide range of comedy and melodrama,
as Elliston attracted several actors and actresses from Drury Lane
and Covent Garden. He did not join the Haymarket this year,
but built up a rival company at the Surrey. Included were De
Camp, Webb, Dowton, and Mrs. Edwin. The latter, in particular,
was of immense value, for she was admired as an imitator of Dora
Jordan, and thus made an excellent partner for Elliston in the
plays in which he had starred with Jordan, e.g., *The Honey Moon*
and *Matrimony.*

As usual, these adaptations were interspersed with other attractions. Sieur Sanches, for example, performed what had never been
attempted by any person but himself, viz., walking against the
ceiling with his head downwards. A one-act piece by Dennis
Lawler poked fun at Gothic ghost stories in *The Earls of Hammersmith,* the hero of which was nine years old, of extraordinary
talents and acquirements. In order to win the hand of Lady
Margaret Marrowbones he dares to sleep overnight in a cellar
haunted by the Dowager of Hammersmith. When the latter
appears, amid the usual thunder, trembling candles, and Hammer-
film horrors, the miniature hero pours the ghost a glass of gin, and
in turn is offered the informative scroll, "Wed not Lady Margaret,
she is your grandmother!"[76]

There was also the political scene to be considered. On Mrs.
Edwin's benefit night, August 18, the Surrey was deserted for the
streets, where civic illuminations celebrated Wellington's victory at
Salamanca. So Elliston got up a spectacle for August 31 which
would do justice to the occasion. Since February he had been
recording the capture of Ciudad Rodrigo in a *"petite* Melo-
Dramatic Spectacle . . . containing incidents and situations similar
and appropriate to the recent gallant and glorious achievement of
our victorious Army in the Peninsula";[77] he now extended this, to
include a correct and striking likeness in transparency of the immortal (*sic*) Marquis Wellington.

On October 9, Dowton, Russell, Elliston, and Mrs. Edwin

appeared together for the last time at the Surrey. The programme
was all legitimate: *Three Weeks after Marriage, Sylvester
Daggerwood,* and *The Wood Demon.* The next night marked the
opening of the new Drury Lane. All four, with De Camp, were now
members of this company. To Elliston, indeed, went the honour of
reciting Byron's occasional address and leading the cast in *Hamlet.*
In the course of the following few weeks this company treated the
Drury Lane audience to such Surrey pieces as *The Beaux'
Stratagem* and *The Honey Moon.*

Though he retained management of the Surrey until the spring
of 1814,[78] after he returned to Drury Lane Elliston appeared only
briefly at the Surrey himself. Samuel Russell, with the aid of D.
Grove as stage manager, carried on the good work in much the
same style as before. *Macbeth* was revived once (August 30, 1813),
and versions of *Richard III, Romeo and Juliet, King Lear,* and
Othello were staged. From the scant details that have survived, in
playbills and advertisements, it seems clear that the melodramatic
spectacle which had made *Macbeth* a hit in 1809 was a continuing
inspiration for the staging of these Shakespearean adaptations.
Adaptations of contemporary thrillers, such as *Ella Rosenburgh*
and *Timour the Tartar,* were matched by the occasional new piece
of note, such as the delightful *Hamlet Travestie,* by John Poole,
and the hit in which a dog was the star, *Llewelyn, Prince of Wales.*
The Surrey, in short, continued to be a theatre of surprises and
variety, a showman's theatre, some place larger than life, where
Shakespeare and Harlequin found common ground.

THREE

Olympic Success

Countess: Heavens! You need not squeeze my hand so
violently.
Rochester: Merely a form of law, madam, and you
know the law is at times very pressing.
William Moncrieff, Rochester

THOUGH leading actor at Drury Lane from its reopening in October
1812, Elliston by no means abandoned his managerial ambitions.
Indeed, in association with Richard Wilson, a member of the
board, he tried to lease the new Drury Lane, but it was decided to
run the theatre by committee. In January 1813 Elliston was negotiating for both the Olympic Pavilion in London and the Theatre
Royal Birmingham; he also considered Crow Street Theatre,
Dublin, the Theatre Royal Edinburgh, and the Pantheon Opera
House. He had a positive mania for real estate. In 1815 he just
failed to secure Vauxhall Gardens, but on securing some property
near Lambeth, he erected a sign on it, if a contemporary print (in
the Enthoven Collection) is to be believed, alerting the known
world to 'The Boundary of Mr. Elliston's Land, Vauxhall Walk—
1815.'

In the event, Elliston leased Birmingham and the Olympic
Pavilion. The latter, on the face of it, was rather a white elephant.
It was situated at the west end of Wych Street, in the Strand, "one
of the narrowest, dirtiest and most disreputable thoroughfares the
West End has ever known . . . inhabited by the dregs of the town,
the thieves, the informers, the harlots, the go-betweens and the
hangers-on of every kind of vice."[1] The Pavilion dated from 1806,
when Philip Astley, who was something of a royal favourite, got an

annual licence for equestrianship in Westminster. He opened the
Pavilion on September 18, 1806, and one of the first visitors was the
actor George Frederick Cooke, who described it as follows:

It is circular: the roof, with a small dome, is composed of sheets of tin,
and is supported by pillars—From the centre of the top a circular lustre
of cut glass, consisting of twelve separate parts, each containing four
lamps, has a very pleasing appearance. The stage is on a level with the
area for horsemanship, and the orchestra rather strangely disposed up
stairs, on the left of the stage. A tier of boxes go entirely round the house,
with the exception of the orchestra: the pit is underneath and behind it,
a small space between is the gallery.[2]

In 1811, when the craze for hippodramas in London promised
better days for the circuses, Astley overhauled the Pavilion. He
moved the gallery up over the boxes, which necessitated raising the
roof, and he converted the ride into a pit. The drawback of this
costly rebuilding lay in the difficulty of transforming the stage,
through use of heavy machinery, into a ride when needed. The
free movement of the horses was thus greatly curtailed. The New
Pavilion lost heavily for a number of years, and Astley decided to
get rid of it. "We'll throw the bone out," he said to John, his son,
"and let the dogs fight for it; one of them will snap at it."[3]

By January 17, 1813, Elliston had snapped.[4] The Olympic under
Astley closed on January 29, and by February 8 the deal between
himself and Elliston was clinched. On March 18 Elliston became
full owner of the Olympic, for the princely sum of £2,800, plus an
annuity of £20 to Astley for the rest of his life—one year, as it
happened. A house went with the theatre.

The question immediately arises whether Elliston was not a
complete fool to take over the Olympic when Astley could not make
a go of it. There were two major advantages to the acquisition, to
which Elliston was not blind. The first, and more important, was
that Astley had a licence for twelve months, for burlettas as well as
for horsemanship, and this licence was to be renewed by Astley on
Elliston's behalf, according to the terms of agreement. At the
same time, Elliston agreed "not to exhibit or perform in the said
Theatre any Exhibition or performance not conformable to the
Lord Chamberlain's Licence."[5] The second advantage was the
location of the theatre in Westminster. It was actually right behind
Drury Lane. The invitation to infiltrate the domain of the legiti-

mate theatre was therefore strong. Elliston's idea was to run the
Olympic in conjunction with the Surrey, in the manner which
Alfred Bunn later made notorious in managing Drury Lane and
Covent Garden—the same actors, stage manager, scene designers,
and repertory should serve both theatres. Matters did not work out,
however, as planned.

The theatre opened on April 19, under the new name of 'Little
Drury-Lane.' The opening productions were established Surrey
pieces, *Love's Perils* and *Punch's Festival*. Elliston did not appear
himself, the opening address being recited by one Mr. Barnard. On
May 5 Thomas Dibdin's horse-drama which had been such a hit at
the Surrey in 1811, *Blood Will Have Blood,* was brought out,
accompanied by *Harlequin Colossus,* also by Thomas Dibdin. If
they had been content to ignore Elliston's kind of theatre when he
was cavorting around St. George's Fields, the proprietors of Drury
Lane and Covent Garden were not going to allow him to set up a
quasi-legitimate theatre in their backyard. Whitbread and Harris
memorialized the Lord Chamberlain almost immediately to have
Little Drury-Lane suppressed. Letters were sent back and forth
between Elliston and these parties until May 10, when the daily
papers announced that the theatre had been closed by order of the
Lord Chamberlain, because Elliston had exceeded his licence. This
Elliston vehemently denied, in a letter to *The Times* on the following day, but rather darkly added that it would be "premature" to
explain why performances had now been "interrupted." Astley's
licence, which Elliston took over, did not expire until July 5, so that
a certain amount of mystery surrounds his leaving his theatre closed
from early May until December 27, after which it was called simply
'Olympic Theatre.' It may mean something that the prices then
went down from five to four shillings for boxes, and from two-and-
sixpence to two shillings for the pit: the former were legitimate
theatre prices. At any rate after December the Olympic was a
winter theatre only, with a season from Michaelmas to Easter.
Elliston's benefit night at Drury Lane, May 10, was reported to have
been a bumper, amounting to over seven hundred pounds.[6] It
cannot be said with complete confidence that this testimony to
Elliston's popularity did not also reflect an agreement reached
with the legitimate theatres over the Olympic licence.

Partnership with the Surrey theatre was continued only until

March 1814, after which Elliston relinquished the Surrey. In the meantime the Olympic presented burlettas and pantomimes, using Surrey material and personnel. Management was in the hands of Russell and Grove; Branscomb and assistants looked after the scenery; and Mountain, from Covent Garden, was in charge of the orchestra—if a band of nine or ten can be so designated. Elliston did not take a direct part. Indeed, he seemed rather at a loss to know what to do with the Olympic now. What with opening Birmingham Theatre Royal during the summer of 1813, and rushing back to Drury Lane in September his "business," as he put it, "has pressed so heavily upon me I have not had enough hours in the day for my wants."[7] From December 1814 he operated under his own licence, which meant he could sell at any time. By January 2, 1815, however, when the theatre newly opened, Elliston's affairs were such that he was obliged to make a real effort to make the Olympic a going concern.

There was one person who brought Elliston's affairs to a crisis, and that was Edmund Kean. Difficult though it may now be to believe, in October 1813 Kean accepted the post of acting manager and leading actor at the Olympic. Before the theatre opened, however, he had got a good offer from Drury Lane, which he quickly accepted. Elliston stubbornly refused to release him from his contract, until a few days before the Olympic opened, and then only on two conditions: that Kean pay the salary of his substitute as leading actor, Henry Wallack, and that he agree to act at Birmingham during the following summer.[8] Samuel Russell, who had been Elliston's right-hand man at the Surrey then became acting manager at the Olympic. Kean went on to become the star attraction at Drury Lane, making his debut on January 26, 1814.

At Drury Lane Elliston and Kean avoided each other for the most part, although Elliston played Othello to Kean's Iago twice during those frenzied months of Kean's appearance. Then, in November 1814, he was cast as Macduff to Kean's Macbeth. He refused the part angrily, and was fined £75. The following January he was Mercutio to Kean's Romeo; Kean got rave reviews, Elliston was not even mentioned. In March he played a watered-down Bolingbroke in an adaptation of *Richard II* which gave all the limelight to Kean's Richard. Once was enough. Elliston reported ill for the next performance. At the end of the season he resigned, convinced he had been victimized by the Drury Lane committee.[9]

There is no doubt but that Kean showed up glaring flaws in Elliston's ability. In tragedy his mannerisms now appeared entirely artificial. He had a habit of snatching his breath, or "sobbing," which broke up the natural rhythm of verse but became monotonous. His voice was considerably more rich and musical than Kean's, but in his attempts to be forceful he sometimes descended to rant. Many critics blamed the Surrey theatre for his growing negligence, and for a coarsening of his style. Others saw now that he was not really suited to tragedy: "His eyes are bright and quick," one critic said, "but their expression is altogether comic. Nor does he appear to have those mental qualifications, without which it is impossible to attain success—he has no feeling—no just conception of the tragic passions."[10] He was still conceded the palm in comedy, even by Leigh Hunt, but as it were grudgingly. Repeatedly, he received harsh words from the critics, so that there was no real alternative to resigning his position. That this must have galled there can be no doubt. That it was a wise decision time testified. When he returned to the London stage from Birmingham, in May 1818, he was welcomed at a prodigal son, and described then as "to Drury-Lane's comedy, what KEAN is to its tragedy; his name in the play-bill is a sufficient voucher that you will not want entertainment."[11]

In 1815, then, Elliston went to the provinces, leaving the London stage to the man he had almost engaged for the Olympic Pavilion. "It had become plain to me," he said later, "that if I was ever to cease to be the mere implement of other men's speculations, it was high time to set about the means."[12] Meanwhile, the Olympic had had its usual short season, from January to March, during which the only production of note was a farcical burletta by Charles I. Dibdin called *My Uncle's House*. It was time the house was put in order.

Because he intended to stay in the provinces himself, Elliston needed a reliable deputy at the Olympic. James Winston, currently manager at the Haymarket, agreed to be *locum tenens*—Elliston's expression—for one hundred pounds for the season. He took up office in September 1815, and thus began a relationship and a style of management by proxy that were to last for the rest of Elliston's career. Elliston deluged Winston with letters, sometimes twice or three times a day, with instructions on the rebuilding and redecorating of the Olympic. "You shall have a good Company," he advises

him, "if you astonish the town with the Theatre."[13] What Elliston
had in mind may be estimated from the description of the theatre
contained in the playbill for opening night, October 30:

The greater part of the Interior has been re-built; and the whole newly
painted and embellished. The Pit and Gallery have been much improved; and the Boxes have been rendered in every way elegant and
commodious, with enlarged Avenues and appropriate Lobbies.
    Several Boxes have been added; and so arranged as to hold from
six to twelve Persons. These are fitted up for the particular reception
and accommodation of Families; and may be engaged nightly.
    The Box saloon has also been newly constructed. The visitors at
Second Price will be admitted to this part of the Theatre at Eight
o'Clock.
    A Company of the best Performers that could be procured from the
London and Provincial Theatres has been engaged; and Novelties, and
New Performers, will be produced in rapid succession . . .[14]

The exterior, the saloon, and part of the auditorium was lit with
gas, for the first time in English theatrical history. The theatre
was renamed the 'Olympic New Theatre.'

After the theatre opened, Elliston kept in touch with Winston
as regularly as before, giving him instructions on every aspect of the
management, even down to the purchase of coal for the theatre's
furnaces. While these letters—written on the wing as Elliston
dashed from Birmingham, to Shrewsbury, to Worcester, etc., and
punctuated with such confidences as, "I am almost dead with
anxiety and fatigue"—say a great deal for Elliston's managerial
shrewdness, they no doubt struck Winston rather differently.
Elliston wanted both accountability and personal initiative from
Winston. Winston's patience soon ran out:

Your letter of yesterday vexes, perplexes me you ask me to do impossibili-
ties & for the *first* time seem dissatisfied with what I am doing—I am
dissatisfied myself with the receipts. but not with anything else I have
done because I never effected as much as I expected . . . and I believe your
most particular friends think I have done my duty towards your
Interests.[15]

"Retrenchment" was Elliston's favourite word to Winston. But in
spite of all admonitions the Olympic failed to make money: by the
end of February 1816 expenses were outstripping receipts by fifty
pounds per week. Good productions were presented, but the result
was the same. Among these were two quite adventurous burlettas

written by the successor to Dennis Lawler, who died in December 1815, namely William Thomas Moncrieff. *The Diamond Arrow,* presented on December 18, and *All at Coventry,* on January 8, were lively little musical farces, highly praised by the *Theatrical Inquisitor.* They marked the beginning of a successful career of a minor dramatist. Moncrieff was then only twenty-one, and he was to provide many a hit for Elliston in the years ahead. During the rest of this season alone he supplied two more pieces, *Joconde* and *Bamfyde Moore Carew.* The former, presented on January 29, was an adaptation of a French drama; the other piece was a pantomime, first presented on February 19. Both were well cast, and carefully mounted. Elliston had some trouble, however, from his scenic artist, Andrews, who, according to Winston, was "a mule & there is no way of keeping him to his work without being as great a blackguard as himself."[16] Kirby, the clown, was in charge of panto-mime direction, and he too, seemingly, was something of a scoundrel. Winston was unable to prevent even popular hits from running into heavy expenses for scenery, tricks, and costume.

There were other factors also which contributed to the difficulties of the season. Once again the major theatres harassed the Olympic. The immediate issue was Elliston's first production (October 30), *Another Maid and Another Magpie,* a burlesque of the melodrama by Caigniez and d'Aubigny. Kinnaird of Drury Lane accused Elliston of stealing their adaptation by Thomas Dibdin, which had been presented in September. This gave Elliston a bad fright, though, as he wrote to Winston, he was confident he was in the right: the translation was by himself, "entirely different from any that has appeared; and if there be any robbery, it has been com-mitted by the winter Theatres."[17] A couple of weeks later, upon learning that the Lord Chamberlain was due to visit the Olympic to see for himself whether or not the law was being infringed, Elliston struck an attitude of heroic endurance: "The more I con-sider the subject, the more I am convinced that my case is very strong, & I shall fight the cause to the last," adding, with more domestic than heroic relevance, "My stake is great & I have a wife & eight Children to support." He came up to London shortly after this, went to the Lord Chamberlain's office, and apparently con-vinced him of his spotless innocence. The tension created by this little affair, however, inhibited further experimentation for the

season, and condemned the theatre to more dog-shows and pantomimes than the exchequer could support.

There was also competition from the Sans Pareil, which had a
better location. The benefit nights at the Olympic were each thirty
to forty pounds less than those of its rival, although, as Winston put
it, "the Company & pieces are very far superior to the Sans Pareil."[18]
The Olympic was "out of the public Throughfare & that is
materialy injurious to its receipts." The audience it *had* captured
was not one that Winston admired. In November, for example, he
had to reject a little ballet from Mrs. Elliston, who took an active
interest in the theatre, giving as his reason its excessive refinement.
To please an audience at the Olympic, he adds, entertainments
"must be very broad (perhaps I might add vulgar)."[19] As a result of
all these drawbacks, Winston advised Elliston that "the Olympic
can never be made worth the attention of you or any respectable
Theatre Man . . . get rid of it by all means & as soon as you can take
the first good offer."[20]

This latter suggestion was in confirmation, seemingly, of
Elliston's own deliberations. Among the Elliston Papers is a document in his hand dated February 28, 1816, which describes the
conditions under which the Olympic and a house adjoining would
be leased: these included a seven year contract, and payment of
£130 *p.a.* ground rent to Lord Craven; on the other hand, the
theatre was stocked with new scenery, and was "most complete"
as to boxes, chandeliers, and so forth; it had a six-month licence,
and possessed the copyright and "regular Licenses of a great number
of excellent pieces"; and the possibility of purchasing five houses
in front of the theatre "is not very remote, and may by industry be
easily effected." The rent was not specified. Elliston had no luck
in leasing the theatre, however, and re-opened for a short season in
February 1817. He then considered acquiring the five houses
mentioned above, in order to build a theatre on a large scale. On
March 17, accordingly, he petitioned the Prince Regent for permission to build a new Olympic, to be "externally ornamental to
that part of the city of Westminster, and shall, internally, afford
proper & suitable accommodation to the Public."[21] Though he
hedged his request with all sorts of disclaimers, Elliston plainly
wanted to acquire full rights for such a theatre: this was implied in
the very name the theatre was to bear, "the Royal British Theatre,"

under the patronage of the Prince Regent. This petition had no
positive result. How Elliston proposed to finance the scheme is not
clear: the cost of the houses was to be £25,000.

It was on this stop-go basis that the Olympic opened for business
again on November 20, 1817. It appears that Winston dropped out
at this point—the name appearing on letters of applications for
licences, according to Dougald McMillan's *Catalogue of the
Larpent Plays*, is that of D. Grove, who was also acting manager
for Elliston at Birmingham. Almost immediately, things began to
go better. The opening productions were *The House that Jack
Built*, a pantomime, and *Love and Poverty*, a burletta. An adaptation of Milman's *Fazio* and a revival of *The Lady of the Lake*
followed. These were well cast, with singers and dancers such as
Hill, Ellar, Miss Perry, and Sloman, and new performers such as
Lee, from Birmingham, and Mrs. Pincott, who received high praise
from the *Theatrical Inquisitor*.

Before the performances started on November 20 there was a
monologue, written by Moncrieff, in elegy for the recent death of
the much-beloved Princess Charlotte. Its seventy lines are well
represented by the following:

> We mourn the pattern of domestic life,—
> The faithful daughter, and the virtuous wife;—
> The gentle mistress—all our hopes could paint;
> The Friend, Protector, Christian, and the Saint.[22]

The public mood was despondent, at this time. The time was ripe
for a show that would allow the public to let off some steam. With
the first stroke of luck he had since taking over the Olympic Elliston
now produced an extravaganza which sounded a healthy blast of
frivolity. *Giovanni in London*, written by Moncrieff, was first presented on December 26.[23] It was not so much a burlesque of Mozart
as an anticipation of Shavian impertinence. It begins in Hell,
where Giovanni's philandering proves too much for demonic inter-
relations: he is unceremoniously sent back to earth in the company
of three of his lady loves, and arrives in London where Dona Anna
is now married to Leporello. He sets about upsetting as many
marital applecarts as possible, a theme eminently suited to the
pantomimical format of the play, which provides a tour round all
the notorious Regency haunts of gambling and entertainment. The
audience could really have its cake and eat it, for Giovanni's essays

in libertinism were set in a frame of general condemnation of his profligacy. The whole thing was given a new dimension when, after the first few performances, the part of Giovanni became a breeches role, played by Miss Burrell, familiarly known as "Joe."

This show put the Olympic on the map as no former production had. On December 31 it was announced that it would play for the remainder of the season. Crowds thronged to the Olympic all through January and February 1818, necessitating frequent instructions in the playbills regarding reservation of seats by servants. All "orders" were cancelled. Several important productions were unavoidably held back. The songs of the play were published, for the convenience of the public. Elliston was rolling again.

The success drew him to the theatre himself, though he did not act there this season. January 10 was a big night in the history of the Olympic for on this night the Lord Mayor of London, his Sheriffs and their wives favoured the theatre with a formal, much publicized, visit. Elliston was on hand, in full dress, to wait on the august company, in a box specially prepared for the occasion; he was determined to make a good impression. All went well until act two when Leporello, waiting to assist Giovanni's retreat after a visit with an alderman's wife, rendered the song:

> Giovanni's leading his usual life,
>   Hey, Randy Dandy, oh!
> He's come here to make love to another man's wife,
>   With his galloping randy dandy, oh!
> I've brought him a ladder, I've brought him a lamp,
>   Eh, Randy Dandy, oh!
> For a notion I have when he means to decamp,
>   That he'll find them both devilish handy, oh! &c., &c.[24]

An undeniable hiss was heard from the pit. Elliston, knowing the Lord Mayor to be a devout man, prominent in religious tract circles, sprang up and stormed off to lay hold of the playwright, Moncrieff. The latter, run to earth in the greenroom, was inclined to make light of the affair, firstly because Elliston had laughed as much as anyone at this song during the seventeen nights previous, secondly because Elliston's outrage, he guessed, was the product, not unusual, of intoxicating stimulation. "You'll find," Elliston stormed, "this is a very serious matter. . . . His Lordship shall soon see that I will have none of your 'randy dandy' proceedings here; this is a respectable house, sir!" Adding, as the final incontrovertible argument, "I am a father, sir!" "Yes," retorted Moncrieff, "and a very miscellaneous one!" "Silence, sir!" thundered the paternal manager, and led his uncontrite writer off to the Lord Mayor's box. There he informed the company he had disowned Moncrieff's disreputable song, substituting for it an emended form which he would now read in their presence, regardless of their protests. Acting out the new version, which consisted of a deletion of "randy" and "devilish," Elliston's eye fell on the shapely wife of one of the Sheriffs, and warming to the verse he gave her a huge wink and several signs of unmistakably amorous advances. The shapely lady was in actual fact a prude, and took instant alarm, crying "save me from that terrible man!" and, quite naturally, fainted away. The emendations, however, were thereafter retained: the purity of Elliston's house was as secure as its fame.

No sooner was the Olympic on its feet, however, than the major theatres moved against it once more, this time for the kill. The pretext was Elliston's staging and adaptation of *Fazio,* a five-act tragedy in blank verse. This tragedy had been published in 1815 by its author, Henry Hart Milman, in the hope that publication would lead to production. It was ignored by the major theatres. Then in December 1816, Thomas Dibdin brought out an adaptation, called *The Italian Wife,* at the Surrey theatre, of which he was then lessee. It was, surprisingly, an immediate success, so much so that at the start of his 1817 season Elliston borrowed the piece from Dibdin and staged it at the Olympic, starting November 29. He had not done this without submitting the script in advance to the Lord Chamberlain's office and receiving the usual written licence. On January 6 the Bath Theatre Royal, inspired, no doubt, by the success of the play at the Olympic, where it was still running, put on the full five-act tragedy of *Fazio.* One month later Covent Garden staged the play with Charles Kemble and Eliza O'Neill in the leading roles: it made a huge impact on the town (enthralling even that reluctant theatregoer Percy Bysshe Shelley). But the Licenser of plays, John Larpent, politely asked Harris, the Covent Garden manager, where *his* licence for the play was, since even the patent theatres had to comply with this (censorship) aspect of the Licensing Act. Harris referred Larpent to the Bath manager. The

Bath manager turned out his pockets in embarrassment, having thought the play was already licensed in London.[25] Covent Garden was thus in the serious position of having staged a play which had not been officially licensed.

In anger, Covent Garden, enlisting the support of Drury Lane, turned round on the immediate source of this embarrassment, Robert William Elliston. A joint memorial was submitted to the Lord Chamberlain on March 14 asking for the complete suppression of the Olympic theatre. The Sans Pareil was included in this attack, but the Olympic was the real target. It is clear, the memorialists say, that the Lord Chamberlain does not realise the limitations of the burletta licence possessed by the Olympic. He is not clear on the nature of 'burletta' itself, a deficiency the memorialists attempt to repair by sending him copies of certain burlettas and by supplying him with a definition: "A PIECE IN VERSE, ACCOMPANIED BY MUSIC,"[26] like *Poor Vulcan, Midas,* etc. The late Lord Chamberlain, Dartmouth, never intended Astley's licence to sanction "such a tragedy as *Fazio.*" It is time to enforce the law against such pirates as the Olympic and Sans Pareil, for the public good.

The nature of burletta, then, was the principal issue in the attack against Elliston. At the Surrey, it will be recalled, Elliston had construed burletta as any drama or melodrama cast in rhymed verse, cut to no more than three acts and accompanied by music. At the Olympic however, especially after 1815, he had gone further, dispensing with rhymed recitative, and using instead prose interspersed with songs and dumbshow. He was always careful to protect himself by giving the material a certain guise. *Another Maid and Another Magpie,* for example, was almost entirely in prose: of a total of 1356 lines, apart from 9 songs, only 16 lines were in rhyme, according to the MS text in the Larpent Collection; but Elliston warned Winston that music, "little comic snatches of odd out of the way, and some mock majestic, airs" ought to introduce the characters. "This is indispensable," he continued, "as it is to denominate all we do by the name of 'Burletta.' I mean of course every thing but Spectacle or Pantomime."[27] This precaution, with the additional one of avoiding the adaptation syndrome which geographical displacement (from St. George's Field's to the Strand) now rendered unwise, enabled Elliston to stage Moncrieff's farces, *The Diamond Arrow,* in one act, and *All at Coventry,* in two acts, both in prose, and *Giovanni in London,* also in prose. In presenting *Rob Roy,* on February 16, 1818, however, Elliston was trailing his coat: this piece was an adaptation of Scott's novel that anticipated those at Covent Garden and Drury Lane by several weeks.[28] The *Italian Wife* production went too far. Elliston carefully wrote an opening scene altogether in dumbshow, and thereafter put in stage directions (in his own hand, in the Larpent MS) for melodramatic music. But his text was in blank verse, 702 lines as compared with 1707 in the original, with 10 lines of prose; the solitary song in the original was omitted. No attempt was made to make the play comic or burlesque; the production was a brazen attempt to out-Surrey his Surrey style by simply cutting a five-act play down to three acts.

The Lord Chamberlain, the Marquis of Hertford, sent a copy of the memorial to Elliston and invited his reply. This Elliston supplied in brief on April 12 and at great length on May 2. He then published the whole affair, the joint memorial, his initial reply, his long defence, with various documentary evidence. An Advertisement put the whole affair into the widest context, i.e., as a battle royal for free theatrical competition.

In his reply of April 12 Elliston divided the attack of the memoralists into fifteen separate charges, or "pretences" as he termed them; over one hundred and twenty pages, on May 2, he refuted every one of these "pretences" in turn. Of most importance was his reply to the tenth, concerning the definition of burletta.

First, in a rather facetious manner, he gets rid of the charge that *Fazio* had been illegally acted at the Olympic. No licence for such a play was ever granted the Olympic; a licence was granted, however, which Elliston reproduces with appropriate capitalization, for *The Italian Wife.* This licence was signed by the Lord Chamberlain himself, not by Larpent, under the words "in pursuance of an Act of Parliament in that case provided,"[29] meaning in effect, that *The Italian Wife* was licensed as a burletta.

Taking the definition supplied by the memorialists, "a piece in verse accompanied by music," Elliston makes clear, as devil's advocate, that by 'verse' is meant rhyme and by 'accompanied by music' is meant recitative. Burletta, then, says the opposition, is rhymed recitative only. With the relish of a true performer Elliston produces several definitions from Italian and English dictionaries and shows that there is nothing in the term itself that prescribes rhymed recitative. Then, as to practice, the form had changed over the years. Recitative has now no part in burletta, and even at the major theatres rhyme is not essential. His trump card for this statement is a burletta which the memorialists had omitted from their list, though it was the most popular of all and had been presented at Covent Garden as recently as March 20. This was the burletta of *Tom Thumb*:

My lord, the 'burletta' of 'Tom Thumb' has, notoriously, neither rhyme nor recitative. It never had either. Still, it has not only been considered a 'burletta,' strictly within the meaning of the word; but it always has been, and always now is, advertised as a 'burletta,' by the Theatres of which the memorialists are the conductors.[30]

By the usage of the major theatres, as well as by definition, therefore, rhyme and recitative are unnecessary to burletta.

The Olympic theatre, Elliston asserted, had kept well within its licence by observing the above interpretation of burletta. He did not stop to explain how it was *The Italian Wife* was subtitled "A Melo Dramatick Romance," although he himself defined burletta as comic in content: according to the argument he was advancing, burletta and melodrama were synonymous formal terms. As a red herring he suggested that the memorialists, in attacking the production of *The Italian Wife*, were really attacking the authority of the Lord Chamberlain: they were implying that he did not know his job. If the memorialists could advance the terms of the Licensing Act against Elliston, let them do so. If not, they should desist from harassing the innocent. For his part, Elliston would "not yield one atom."[31] From this embattled position Elliston turned the attack on his adversaries. The memorialists had complained of competition from the minor theatres, and of the ruin this was wreaking on their theatres. If repression of the repertory of the minor theatres were called for, this would not eliminate competition, but keep it at a low level. The minor theatres, "instead of supplying, at a moderate price, a diverting and rational entertainment," would have to adhere altogether to the kind of mindless spectacle now being peddled by the legitimate theatres:

Posture-masters must be found who should writhe themselves into more contortions than Mr. Pack was employed to do, on the stage of the Theatre Royal, Drury Lane:—dogs must be found, who should bark more eloquently than the 'Dog of Montargis' was engaged to do, on the stage of the Theatre Royal, Covent Garden . . .—horses must be found, to prance, if possible, more classically than those who sustained the 'regular' and 'national drama' of 'Timour the Tartar' . . .[32]

This was to put the ball right back into the court of his opponents. If they were having trouble at the box-office while staggering to uphold that entity known as the national drama, the fault may lie not with the malignant intentions or even practices of such minor devils as the Olympic or Sans Pareil; the fault, Elliston did not hesitate to declare, with as much force as was at his command, lay with ineffectual management. This counter-argument was unanswerable. As the *Theatrical Inquisitor* put it (August 1818), "For acuteness and justness of reasoning, force of argument, keenness of satire, and brilliancy of style, we have scarcely ever seen any thing to excel it." The Lord Chamberlain found in Elliston's favour.[33]

During the summer of 1818 Elliston wound up his affairs in the provinces and prepared for the next season at the Olympic when, for the first time, the theatre would be under his "immediate direction and superintendence." He followed his usual practice of renovating the theatre and gathering a good company, and worked so hard at the preparations that a few days before opening date he physically collapsed. This was the first in a series of attacks culminating in a serious stroke in 1825; but Elliston himself quickly denied the report that it was "apoplexy," stating himself to be exhausted "from the unremitting attention I have been compelled to give in the reconstruction of my theatre, which I pledge myself shall open on Monday next, the 16th, with *unrivalled attractions*."[34] Showing now, as later, remarkable powers of recovery, aided no doubt by copious draughts of brandy and water, Elliston was as good as his word, and the Olympic New Theatre opened for business on November 16, 1818.

Elliston's renovations were extensive, costing between three and four thousand pounds.[35] The pit was enlarged, and, containing sixteen rows of seats, had a capacity of just over six hundred.[36] There were sixteen private boxes, ten more than in 1815, each to hold upwards of ten people; public boxes brought capacity to three hundred and fifty. The gallery had been "rendered so capacious, that every person can see the stage with the most perfect ease";[37] there were four rows of seats there, to cater for over three hundred people, thus bringing the total capacity to just over thirteen hundred, about half that of the Surrey.

The rest of the house was decorated in Elliston's usual elegant manner. There was a gala preview of the theatre before it opened at which newsmen attended and were inspired to furnish a full, if slightly glowing, account of the theatre's attractions. By all accounts, the interior was luxuriously decorated, by Lethebridge of Drury Lane, and was a long way from Astley's dingy pavilion. *The Times* found it "equal to the proudest" of Elliston's rivals,[38] while *The Examiner* said it was "just what play-houses should be."[39] To the *European Magazine* it was almost as if Harlequin's wand had transformed the theatre from the old, "dull, heavy, and uncomfortable," to the new, "which for elegance and comfort may vie with any of its rivals."[40]

When the curtain went up at 6.30 on Monday evening, November 16, Mrs. Edwin came forward to recite the address written by Moncrieff. This was a veritable crow of triumph. The legitimate theatres were attacked, for peddling only "*Melo* trash of Gallia . . . gaudy show . . . empty noise." Elliston, spoken of as "One, who spurns such base neglect," was given credit for making good the deficiencies of these theatres. With the purpose of nurturing the drama and providing an "asylum" for acting talent, the Olympic "rears its simple unassuming dome," in the teeth of "the obstacles of thousand foes."[41] This self-congratulatory note set the tone for the ensuing season. Every effort was made to put on productions that might thumb the nose at the major theatres. To assist this purpose, Elliston gathered around him an impressive company. Besides Mrs. Edwin and himself, "in their line, unexceeded, if equalled, by any performers now before the public,"[42] there were Wrench, Oxberry, and De Camp, all refugees from Drury Lane; the singers Pearman and "Bell" Stevenson from the English Opera House; together with the pick of Elliston's Birmingham players, and some old reliables at the Olympic. Among playwrights now interested in the Olympic were Moncrieff, Poole, Oxberry, Beazley, and James Robinson Planché. The orchestra too was improved, under the conductorship of Ware from Covent Garden. Greenwood was in charge of scenery, which was quite extensive: according to an inventory (dated September 6, 1819) in the Harvard Theatre Collection there were 39 pairs of flats, 25 pairs of wings, 4 drop cloths, and a number of setpieces, totalling just over £2000 in value. An earlier list, perhaps compiled at the time Elliston was trying to lease the Olympic, makes clear that the scenery took the form of landscapes, sea-views, villages, Gothic interiors, etc., with "setting pieces," which must have been cloths, of London or rustic bridges, and a castle piece stretching the whole width of the stage, i.e., thirty feet.[43] There were a lot of practicable pieces for use in pantomime—sliding windows and doors, shops, flaps, etc. One remarkable feature was the height of the scenery, which was only eleven feet, or half that at Drury Lane, although the stage was quite large for a minor theatre. The wardrobe, finally, was quite extensive, being valued at £500.

On opening night the programme matched the note of defiance struck in the address. Besides *Giovanni in London,* which was revived, there was a new play, a burletta in three acts by Moncrieff, called *Rochester; or King Charles the Second's Merry Days.* This was a fully-fledged comedy in prose, with eight songs scattered through its three acts. From the point of view of form it is a landmark in the history of the English theatre. It went a step further than Elliston had formerly ventured, for it abandoned the musical introductions to each scene. As Moncrieff himself said, "Rochester is remarkable for being the first regular drama produced at a minor theatre, without an accompanying tinkle of the piano."[44] In applying to Larpent for a licence for *Rochester,* Elliston behaved as if content were now the only possible grounds of objection. "Be assured," he said in his application, "as heretofore there is not an objectionable line in it."[45]

Rochester was a comedy, "founded," as the advertisements liked to say, "on an historical fact, related by St. Evremond to the Duchess of Mazerine," and discovered a surprising affinity between the spirit of the Restoration and that of the Regency. The plot concerns the eccentricities of John Wilmot, Earl of Rochester, and Sheffield Villiers, Duke of Buckingham (played by Elliston and Pearman respectively), who, banished from court, have set up an inn in Newport, on the road to Newmarket. The first scene introduces Rochester as landlord, extravagantly treating some farmers to free fare, in language obviously referring to Elliston's role as victorious manager: "Your presence here amply repays me all, and while you meet pleasant company, a good bill of fare, and rational entertainment—let me presume to hope, my humble house, may again and again be gladdened by your coming."[46] Thereafter many changes are rung on the love-chase theme, with the Countess of Lovelaugh (Mrs. Edwin) adding zest as a seventeenth-century Life Force in appropriate disguise.

That the play was "uncommonly well got up," with historical costumes and scenery by Greenwood, and "acted in all its parts with a perfection seldom witnessed on the modern English stage," Moncrieff himself testifies. Elliston was outstanding, since he was "by nature the Rochester he represented."[47] One may fancy the unction with which he delivered such lines as, "A rake, my dear, is a thing that tumbles and tosses other things about" (II, i). Although *The Examiner* had recently commented that he had grown quite fat, and a little stiff, there is little reason to believe his powers had fallen off. Be that as it may, the death of Queen Charlotte on November 17 unhappily cut off immediate critical response to the play, and closed all theatres, in fact, until after the funeral on December 2.

On December 3, however, Elliston himself described the opening night in the newspapers as "so auspicious, that the Proprietor dare not trust himself in the expression of his Feelings, in the fear of incurring the charge of the 'Puff direct,'" preferring to leave *Rochester* "to the judgment of the Public." The playbills carried similar marks of restraint. Crowds of notables then began to frequent the Olympic, and Elliston published a sort of Who's Who in the daily papers. By December 14 he announced plans for further expansion of the theatre during the Christmas recess. Adjustments would also be made to the steam heating apparatus,[48] of which Elliston was justly proud.

After Christmas *Rochester* ran right through the holiday season, which was unusual, since this time of year was usually given over solely to pantomimes and stock pieces. A new pantomime was indeed added as a further attraction, and this too had its novel aspect. It was written by James Robinson Planché as a melodrama and converted into a speaking pantomime employing prose. Usually of course, pantomimes were silent, except for songs and occasional rhymed recitative; but in *Rodolph the Wolf,* first played on December 21, 1818, all the characters, except one, speak prose.[49] The exception is Harlequin. (Columbine, it might be remarked, makes up for him.)

The success of *Rochester* continued all through the season; it played approximately eighty nights. The play was published as quickly as possible, with a dedication from Elliston to the public for its "Approbation of the general Conduct of the Performances" at the Olympic, which he regards as "the most flattering Reward" for his "anxious Endeavours." Not his only reward, however. Elliston is said to have cleared three thousand pounds this season on *Rochester*.[50]

As indicated, Elliston did not rely on a single production to keep his theatre full. This practice continued through the season. On January 15 *Giovanni in London* returned as afterpiece, and thereafter alternated with *Rodolph* nightly. Other novelties, usually comic sketches, were added as time went on to provide a full programme without recourse to minor-theatre tumbling, tightrope walking or the like, so that by January 18 *The Times* could say, of the afterpieces alone, that they did not fall "below the standards of more splendid establishments." Such pieces included *Actress of all Work* on January 28, which was originally written (by Oxberry) for Miss Kelly of Drury Lane. Mrs. Edwin played the six parts called for. *Where Shall I Dine?* on February 17, was a slight piece by Beazley which gave Wrench the role of Sponge, a hungry London buck. Elliston himself had formed the habit of diverting the audience with extempore material, but on March 11 he got Moncrieff to provide him with a two-act farce, entitled *The Three Singles in London,* as vehicle for his versatility. The *Theatrical Inquisitor* found it quite ingenious, and Elliston "as vivacious and spirited as could be desired." As the season drew to a close, those farces were sometimes combined to form an alternative to *Giovanni in London* or some other afterpiece.

The theatre closed on Saturday April 3. In a curtain speech Elliston referred once again to the radical element in the Olympic's programme: "Persons interested in a monopoly were most anxious to repress the endeavours of their less aspiring neighbours: the effort failed; and thus a measure intended to oppress, produced an increased exertion to merit your favour." Both on economic and on artistic grounds, the Olympic had done the state some service and they should know it, or it would not be the fault of Elliston.

"It is needless to add, the success of the season has more than equalled my expectations."[51] With a promise of unstinting devotion, and a re-opening of the theatre in September, Elliston took his farewell. But when September came the Olympic was leased out. Elliston, with supreme irony, had become lessee of Drury Lane. But before this happened, Elliston had to sever his connection with Birmingham Theatre Royal, which is a story in itself.

FOUR

Birmingham Theatre Royal

'One has not great hopes from Birmingham. I always
say there is something direful in the sound.'
Jane Austen, *Emma*

PERSONIFICATION seems permissible where eighteenth-century
culture is under review. Thomas Gray might have called Birmingham, had he the occasion to wax Pindaric under its inspiration,
the Child of the Industrial Revolution; Edmund Burke certainly
called it "the great Toy-Shop of Europe," perhaps to emphasize
its importance to a nation of shopkeepers. Because of its thriving
iron, steel, and brass industries, Birmingham progressed from a
country, even pastoral, town of some eight thousand swains in
1730 to a manufacturing centre supporting eight times that number
by 1800.[1] Yet its theatre did not have a royal patent until 1807. A
major reason behind this surprising deficiency (since at least fifteen
of the provincial towns had patents by 1800) was the religious
and political conservatism of an expressive segment of the local inhabitants.

There was a permanent theatre in existence since 1774—in New
Street—and many efforts were made to obtain a royal patent, and
put the town, so to speak, on the theatrical map.[2] Full use was made
of the fact that the Lord Chamberlain, Dartmouth, was a native of
Birmingham. But, as emerged when a poll of citizen opinion was
taken, there was a greater body against than for a theatre, a matter
which must have arrested the drive for a patent. Moreover, the
riots of 1791, while they were mainly against dissenters and political
liberals, spread to an attack on the theatre. For four days following
Bastille Day, 1791, a mob roamed the streets of Birmingham, chant-

ing the catch-cry "Church and King," and destroying the houses of
well-known dissenters, the most famous of whom was the philo-
sopher Priestley. On August 7 the theatre was burned to the ground,
not, it would appear, because it was a bastion of either radicalism
or Voltairean defiance; but because the theatre was somehow associated with Methodism.[3]

Rebuilt in 1795, the New Street theatre was leased by an experienced and capable man of the theatre, William McCready. Up
to the year 1807 McCready succeeded in making the theatre pay;
but after the obtaining of the royal patent matters altered, the
town being either unwilling or unable to support a year-round
theatre. Things got steadily worse, until by the end of 1812
McCready owed considerable arrears in rent. It was hardly with a
great deal of regret that he passed the theatre over to Elliston at
this point, as, indeed, he had passed over Manchester Theatre
Royal to him in 1809.

If the conceit be permitted, the very geographical position of
Birmingham supplies a convenient image of the place of this
management venture in Elliston's career: it is the hub, the centre.
From the time he leased Manchester, for one winter season, until
the collapse of his financial affairs in 1825, Elliston had an active
interest in provincial management. He purchased a theatre in
Croydon[4] in 1810, leased Birmingham in 1813, added Worcester
and Shrewsbury[5] to it in 1815 to make up a circuit, tried for Bristol[6]
in 1817, leased Lynn[7] 1817–18, Leicester[8] and Northampton[9] in
1818, Leamington[10] in 1819, and Coventry[11] in 1821. Even on his
becoming lessee of Drury Lane, Leamington, Croydon, and
Coventry remained in his possession as summer retreats during the
1820's. The question naturally arises, what was there to attract
Elliston to provincial management?

The provincial manager was in business, it need hardly be said, to
make a living, not to be a patron of the arts. Elliston was a gambler
at heart; there was undoubtedly money to be made by a man of his
national reputation. In addition, he was a man of extraordinary
energy, who delighted in the endless bustle of theatrical affairs; he
was a man, in short, who *enjoyed* managing, even where the risks
were great. "If thrown overboard in rags," as Francis Wemyss said
of him, "from one side of a ship, he would appear before his
tormentors could turn round, upon the other side of the deck,

Engraved by Ridley from a Picture by Drummond.

1 Elliston, from a portrait by Samuel Drummond, 1796.

2 & 3 The Theatres Royal, Bath (top) and Birmingham (bottom),
from James Winston, *The Theatric Tourist*, 1805.

Mr. ELLISTON

Has the Honour to acquaint the Ladies and Gentlemen of Birmingham and its Vicinity, that he shall have the Pleasure of presenting himself to their Notice THIS PRESENT MONDAY, in the Character of OCTAVIAN. From the very limited Vacation of the Winter Theatres this Season, and the consequent Inability of some of the principal Performers to fulfil many of their provincial Engagements, Mr. ELLISTON has had some Difficulty in arranging his own Nights, so as to meet the Convenience of several Persons whom he had engaged ; anxious however to complete the particular Pledges he made at the Commencement of the Season, he has, with some Labour and some trifling Alterations in his original Plan (which the Urgency of the Occasion will, he trusts, justify) so contrived it, that his liberal Patrons will be gratified with some of the first Talent of the Metropolis, but their Stay will necessarily be reduced to short Periods.

This present MONDAY, July 12, 1813,

Will be presented Mr. Colman's operatic Play of the

MOUNTAINEERS.

Octavian, Mr. ELLISTON,
(His first Appearance this Season)

Virolet, Mr. BARNARD,　Kilmallock, Mr. DOBBS,
Bulcazin Muley, Mr. MIDDLETON,　Ganem, Mr. WILSON,
Lope Tocho, Mr. MEREDITH, - - - Roque, Mr. RICHARDS,
Sadi, Mr. MALLINSON,

Goatherds, Messrs. Walton and Benwell, jun.
Muleteers, Messrs. Payne, Stebbing, Bland, and Hollingsworth.
Floranthe, Mrs. PAYNE,　Zorayda, Miss HOLLAND,
Agnes, Mrs. BROOKES,

The Vocal Parts by Miss Donaldson, Mrs. Weston, Mrs. Richards, Mrs. Stebbing, Miss Francks, &c.

After which will be produced (fourth Time) a new Melo Dramatic Romance, called

Aladdin;

OR, THE

Wonderful Lamp.

As acted FORTY NIGHTS this Season at the Theatre Royal, Covent Garden, with the most unbounded Attraction and Applause. With entirely new Music, extensive Scenery and Machinery, and superb Dresses and Decorations.
The Machinery partly prepared in London and partly on the Spot, from accurate Models.
The Scenery designed by Mr. SMITH, and executed by him, Mr. WALTON, and other Assistants.
The Whole of the Dresses made in London, and in the same Costume as at Covent Garden.
The Action of the Piece, Processions, &c. under the Direction of Mr. SMITH.

Aladdin, Mr. BARNARD,
Tahi Tonluck (Cham of Tartary, Mr. MIDDLETON, Karar Hanjou (his Vizier) Mr. RICHARDS,
Kalim Azack (the Vizier's Son) Mr. SMITH,
Abanazer (the African Magician) Mr. BARTLEY,
Kazrac (his Chinese Slave) Mr. BRISTOW,
Mandarins and Officers of State, Messrs. Hollingsworth, Benwell, jun. Stebbing, Williams, &c.
Citizens of Cham Tartary, Messrs. Walton, Bland, &c.
The Princess Badroulboudour, Miss DONALDSON,
Amrou and Zobyad (her chief Attendants) Miss HOLLAND and Miss GREEN,
Chinese Dancing Girls and Ladies of the Court, Mrs. Richards, Mrs. Stebbing, Miss Francks, &c.
The Widow Ching Mustapha, Mrs. GROVE,　Genii of the Ring, Miss WESTON,
Olrock (Genii of the Air) Mr. MEREDITH,　Genii of the Lamp, Mr. PAYNE,

With the WHOLE of the new and splendid SCENERY.

On WEDNESDAY, the Drama of the THREE and the DEUCE ; the three Singles by Mr. ELLISTON, his second Appearance.
On THURSDAY, for the BENEFIT of Mr. DUNN (the Treasurer) a favourite Play, in which Mr. ELLISTON will appear, with a FARCE, and other Entertainments.

JONATHAN KNOTT, PRINTER, BIRMINGHAM.

4 Elliston's first appearance as actor-manager at Birmingham, 1813.

THE

HISTORY,
MURDERS, LIFE, and DEATH
OF

Macbeth:

And a FULL DESCRIPTION of the
SCENERY, ACTION, CHORUSES, and CHARACTERS
OF THE

BALLET
OF

MUSIC and ACTION,

OF THAT NAME,

*As performed, with enthusiastic Applause, to over-
flowing Houses, a Number of Nights, at the*

ROYAL CIRCUS,

St. GEORGE's FIELDS, London;

WITH THE

OCCASIONAL ADDRESS,
Spoken by Mr. Elliston ;

And every Information, to simplify the Plot; and
enable the Visitors of the Circus, to comprehend
this matchless Piece of *Pantomimic* and *Choral*
Performance.

London:

Printed by *T. Page, Black Friars Road,*

For STEVENS & Co. St. George's Circulating Library, Borough
Road: and W. KEMMISH, King-Street, Borough.

T. Hughes, Ludgate-Hill; N. & I. Muggeridge, and Wilmott and Hill,
Borough; Perks, St. Martin's Lane; Aldo, and Mather, Hol-
born; Evans, Gerrard-Street, Soho; Brown, Drury-Lane, Barfoot,
Norton-Falgate; &c. &c.

Price only 6d.

Engraved by E. Ealing.

Mr. ELLISTON as MACBETH.
ACT I. SCENE VII.

Macb. Who's there? what! ho!

5 Elliston as Macbeth.

BONAPARTE.

Written by Mr. LAWLER; introduced by Mr. ELLISTON, and Sung by him, with unbounded Applause, in the Character of SYLVESTER DAGGERWOOD, at the Surry Theatre.

6 Elliston as Bonaparte.

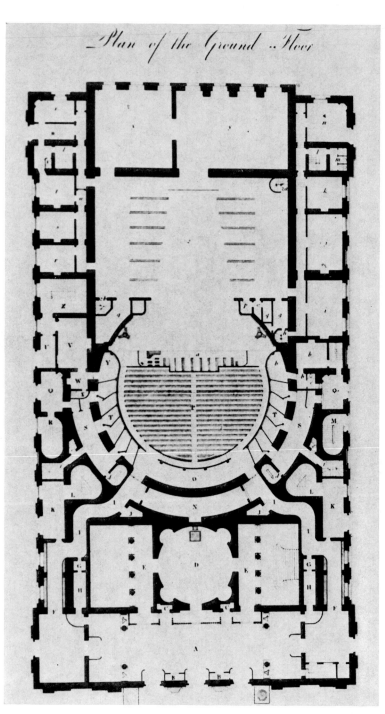

Plan of the Ground Floor

7 Drury Lane, 1812.

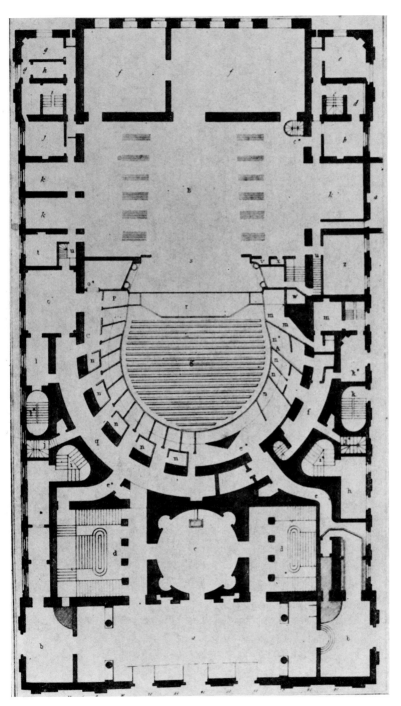

8 Drury Lane, 1825.

9 The Olympic Theatre, 1814.

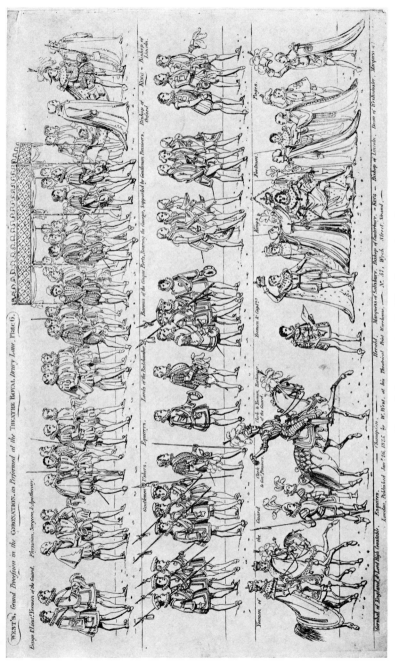

10 Part of the procession in *The Coronation*, 1821.

Mr Elliston, as KING GEORGE the IV.th in the Coronation, at Drury Lane Theatre

11 Elliston as George IV.

12 Elliston as Falstaff.

The Singles. *tale the Thus of the dust.*

'The first is Pertinax, a lad of parts'
'Wise, learned, Grave & Bachelor of arts'

'The next is Peregrine a Buck indeed'
'Sings, Dances, Fights, does every thing but read'

'The third poor Percival a thimple Thoul'
'Travels beneath a tutors strict controul'

The characters are *Prazas* the Actor *one*
And each illimmitable Elliston.

13 Elliston in a triple role.

14 Madame Vestris in *Giovanni in London* at Drury Lane.

15 *Black-Eyed Susan* at the Surrey.

16 Master Burke, child star at the Surrey.

17 Elliston, a portrait by G. H. Harlow, *c.* 1808.

dressed as a gentleman, ready to begin the world again.'[12] But of course neither of these qualities, the gambling instinct and natural buoyancy, would be of the slightest value without talent. Of his acting talent there was no question, and it proved perhaps Elliston's greatest asset through the six seasons of his Birmingham management. If managerial talent is to be assessed in terms of winning an audience and keeping a good box-office, then, as we shall see, Elliston's encounter with the formidable Brummagems provides much testimony of his abilities.

Elliston had been in negotiation with the proprietors of Birmingham Theatre Royal some time prior to mid-January 1813, offering himself as lessee. On January 25 at a committee meeting of the proprietors a letter from Elliston was read, enquiring to know what had happened to his application. The committee immediately drafted an apology for delay in communicating with him, assuring him that since they wished the theatre placed "in the most respectable hands," they were in fact inclined to treat with Elliston "on the most liberal terms," and consequently "could have no motive or excuse for anything but the utmost openess [sic] of negotiation."[13] The only point of dispute the proprietors had with his proposals concerned the basis of reckoning weekly expenses: they considered three nights a week the optimum for keeping the theatre open, and on this basis the committee would calculate its share of the profits. This was not to be a restraint on the number of nights Elliston might keep the theatre open; nevertheless it was the unanimous opinion of the committee "that the Town does not require and may not support a more frequent exhibition" than three nights a week.[14]

Elliston's reply was read at a meeting on February 2, and on March 5 an agreement was sent him. This differs slightly from the agreement signed by Elliston on March 23, the differences being in his favour.[15] He was declared lessee for five years at £300 *p.a.*, liberal terms indeed when one recalls that McCready had paid £500 plus half profits in 1795.[16] It was stipulated that Elliston himself must act a minimum of twelve nights per season of twenty weeks. Expenses of £52-10s were allowed nightly, up to sixty nights. The theatre was to be open "at least" three nights per week. Since capacity receipts were in the region of £270,[17] a handsome profit was a distinct possibility on these terms; Elliston was to get the first £300, the balance to be divided equally.

The question of audience clearly lay at the heart of any attempt at making Birmingham Theatre Royal a going concern. Elliston's plan was to get at the town's prosperous middle class, the landed gentry, the respected families, the army officers and the city fathers: if these could be persuaded to support the theatre such happenings as the history of conservatism and the growth of Methodism and Quakerism might be offset. With characteristic attention to method, not to be dissociated from his flair for advertisement, Elliston issued a grand manifesto outlining his aims.[18] Dated May 20, 1813, eleven days before the grand opening, this address to the people of Birmingham was couched in Elliston's characteristic style of confidence and appeal commingled. Unusually, it was in the first person, betokening Elliston's whole approach here. Bare facts were given first: the theatre would be open for twenty weeks; star actors would be engaged whenever possible; plays would be "carefully selected, and diligently superintended" with a view to presenting "the very best example of the British Drama." Then followed the appeal, based on Elliston's basic aim, which was "to place the theatrical entertainments of Birmingham on a par with those of other great commercial places." A little flattery was called for here: in a town "so large and populous" as Birmingham, with a "neighbourhood so crowded with opulence and distinction," a theatre was a necessity, "in point of policy" as well as "of rational recreation." But even in such a case, a theatre needed protection and patronage by "those who lead and govern the public taste." Otherwise, the "best efforts of the Manager must be enfeebled, and, in the end defeated." Elliston proposes that of the three evenings a week on which the theatre would be open, Friday should be dedicated as a Fashionable Night. "On this evening . . . an expectation might be held out that the best company . . . of Birmingham and its neighbourhood, would be collected at the Theatre. An elegant place of periodical assemblage might be thus established." In this manner, Elliston would be enabled to do full justice to his ambitions "and to satisfy the wish the public are always entitled to entertain, that what is done on stage at all shall be done well."

The theatre opened under Elliston's management on May 31,

1813. Being himself still at Drury Lane, Elliston had obtained the services of Bartley from Liverpool as his acting manager and temporary substitute. Bartley it was who delivered the opening address, written by Eyre, and led the cast for the first six weeks: Elliston did not appear until July 12, when he played Octavian in *The Mountaineers*. He took this opportunity also to confess that he was having a certain amount of difficulty in engaging first-rate actors. He blamed the extended London season for this, for it made difficulties in arranging "his own Nights, so as to meet the Convenience of several Persons whom he had engaged."[19] Since he was anxious, nevertheless, "to complete the particular Pledges he made at the Commencement of the Season," he had "with some Labour and some trifling Alterations in his original Plan (which the Urgency of the Occasion will, he trusts, justify) so contrived it, that his liberal Patrons will be gratified with some of the first Talent of the Metropolis," even though "their Stay will necessarily be reduced to short Periods." Miss Booth, the actress-singer discovered by Elliston at the Surrey, and Charles Mathews, were named as among the stars to be expected. Mrs. Edwin and the "American Roscius," John Howard Payne, were among others who appeared briefly during this season. The resident company was made up of actors and actresses from Liverpool, Derby, Nottingham, and other provincial theatres.

Legitimate drama, whether Shakespeare or well-established contemporary tragedies and comedies, formed the backbone of the bill of entertainment this season, with perhaps most emphasis on comedy, in view of Elliston's own particular talents. Besides stock dramas, recent London successes such as Coleridge's *Remorse* (in which Elliston had appeared at Drury Lane[20]), were transplanted with similar hopes of success before a Birmingham audience. But since the programme was a four-hour one or more, from seven p.m. on, recourse was necessarily had to melodramas, afterpieces, and pantomimes as was the practice at the London theatres. The criterion in this regard was the degree to which the Birmingham afterpiece emulated its London prototype. Along with *Mountaineers* on Elliston's first night, for example, was presented *Aladdin*, a new melodramatic romance "as acted FORTY NIGHTS this Season at the Theatre Royal, Covent Garden, with the most unbounded Attraction and Applause."[21] It was now presented "with entirely new Music, extensive Scenery and Machinery, and superb Dresses and Decorations." The machinery, the public was further informed, had been "partly prepared in London and partly on the Spot, from accurate Models," while "The Whole of the Dresses" were made in London, "and in the same Costume as at Covent Garden." The local critic was obviously awed by these sturdy references. "Our spirited manager," said that worthy, "determining not to be outvied by the London proprietors, has taken our senses by assault, and we will venture to say that, in the memory of our oldest inhabitant, no piece has ever been brought upon our boards where the success has been more unqualified, and where the splendour has in any degree been parallel to this. We understand that the dresses and properties alone have cost a thousand guineas."[22] Needless to day, *Aladdin* ran through the summer.

Though the theatre did not close until November Elliston gave an air of finality to the season when he addressed the audience on his benefit night, September 2, prior to his return to Drury Lane. It is clear that this first season was not all it might have been, mainly due to Elliston's failure, already mentioned, to capture London stars for any worthwhile length of time. Regarding the Fashionable Night idea, however, he was pleased to say that it had proved popular this season and consequently he had hopes that the future would enable him to realize his aims more fully. The main focus was to be on a theatre offering "the greatest variety consistently with the decorum and taste that ought to prevade [sic] a regular stage."[23] His theatre was to be neither a minor theatre nor the ape of any particular London theatre. It would proceed "on a plain, unobtrusive scale," not in mechanical obedience to a set system, but seeking to achieve the focus mentioned "without the quackery of mere pretension."

These aims bear the stamp of sincerity, even if a certain vagueness surrounds the question which is at the heart of the matter: how to give the best without mimicking London; how to achieve local identity and still attain high standards. It was not a question Elliston managed to solve. His whole belief was that if an environment were carefully fostered, good theatre would grow as it were organically. To this end he invariably paid a good deal of attention to the physical aspects of the theatre building, aiming at a shaping elegance, even opulence. On February 28, 1814 he persuaded the proprietors to authorize his plans for renovating the theatre; Cabanell was the architect, the cost £1330, to be borne by the proprietors.[24] What structural changes Elliston made in the 1795 design is hard to say. The description by *Aris's Gazette* of the alterations, when the theatre opened early in May, fails to be specific. The auditorium is declared " 'second to none in the Kingdom' whether we refer to the classical effect of the designs, the magnificence of the proscenium, the convenience for sight, or the incomparable construction of the theatre for hearing."[25] It would appear that sightlines were improved, probably for the two tiers of sixteen boxes which gave the auditorium a semi-circular form. There were also new chandeliers, both for stage and auditorium. Since the stage lighting was praised for its brilliance, it seems likely that the scenery was renewed for the occasion also. Elliston was loudly called for on opening night, and received a standing ovation.

This auspicious start led into a successful season, with Elliston's share of the profits topping one thousand pounds. He was able to draw to Birmingham a great many star performers, opposite whom he himself appeared. These included Mrs. Jordan, Miss Booth, Joseph Munden, Charles Mathews, and Edmund Kean. The latter was bound to appear this year at Birmingham, in accordance with the terms under which Elliston had released him from the Olympic to Drury Lane in 1813.[26] Fresh from his London triumphs, Kean received a wildly enthusiastic welcome in Birmingham in September 1814. The local critic was inspired to offer an interesting account of the impact Kean made on the audience through force of passion, naturalness, absorption in the character, and so on; but as can happen with the best impressionistic reviewers he omits to mention the roles actually played. One may assume he repeated his Drury Lane successes, particularly Shylock and Richard III.

The temptation now was to assume that the Birmingham audience had been won over, and that legitimate drama was the answer. With this understanding, perhaps, Elliston took his leave, playing opposite Mrs. Bartley in *Every One Has His Fault* on his benefit night, September 2; after a conventional speech of thanks to his supporters he left for London for his last season at Drury Lane. Word soon reached him that Birmingham was sick of his theatre. "When do you mean to close the Theatre?" a friend wrote to enquire. "Every body thinks you kept it open too long . . . in fact the Town seems quite sick of it and if you were to send Angels to perform the people would not go to see them." Elliston's name has become a slogan: "There is hardly a blank wall that has not something written upon it against you."[27] On the theatre itself was scrawled the unfortunate phrase, "Mangling done here."[28] After September, he is told, only horse spectacles, acrobats, and the like, stand the least chance.

The Brummagems got their wish with a vengeance in 1815. Bartley was gone, and in his place Elliston had two men, John Brunton as acting manager and John Ashley as treasurer, who ran the theatre for him. As always in such circumstances, Elliston directed matters by post; where such letters have survived, as between himself and Winston, they provide useful evidence of his acumen: where the correspondence to him has survived, as in this instance from Brunton and Ashley,[29] it throws a certain amount of light on theatrical conditions of the time. Both of these assistants had a shrewd knowledge of the provincial market; both were dedicated to providing the cheapest form of entertainment possible. The season began badly, with nightly receipts no more than £50. A tightrope walker by the name of Godeau was all that stood between Elliston and ruin. Brunton was a great believer in pantomime and spectacle, and rather gifted, it seems, in looking after the complicated scenery they demanded. When Elliston transferred a speaking pantomime, *Broad Grins,* from the Olympic to Birmingham on May 18, Brunton altered the stage grooves to facilitate scene changes: formerly, according to him, it took four men to pull off one pair of flats, "& that very imperfectly done."[30] In consequence of this success, and in the firm belief than only pantomime fare would answer, Brunton had hopes that the season would mend.

There was a craze current at this time for performing dogs on stage. Initially, these heroes held the stages of the minor theatres— "Moustache" starred at Sadler's Wells in the 1780's—but they beat the horses to it in capturing the legitimate stage. 1803 has gone down in the annals of Drury Lane as the year of Carlo the dog. In the climactic scene of *The Caravan,* just as a child was sure to drown in a real tank of real water, Carlo it was who leaped nightly from a high rock into the tank and brought the child to safety. This stunt packed the theatre for forty nights, virtually rescuing Sheridan himself from drowning. Ten years later the craze was still in

vogue. Elliston had a big hit at the Surrey in 1813 called *Llewellyn*.
In 1814–15 two versions of a Pixérécourt piece were enormously
popular at the Surrey and Covent Garden respectively. In each
version a dog was the prime attraction. While waiting for Godeau
to raise the box office at Birmingham, Brunton pondered the implications of a dog piece. If a troupe of dogs were to be engaged for
pantomime, it seemed appropriate to present *The Caravan* and the
Pixérécourt piece as well. But as it was done in the provinces, *The
Caravan* did not call for real water, rendering the climactic scene,
to Brunton's mind, a failure. "The Scene is the painted Still
Water," he wrote Elliston, "a Child is thrown behind a Rock &
caught by a Man (which must be seen by the Audience) it is then
drawn across the Stage on a truck as if in the act of swimming, the
Dog then jumps *over* the painted Water, & is drawn back across
the Stage standing on the truck with the Child hanging about his
Loins—there is no deception in it it is palpably evident how it is
done as the dog is motionless on the Truck without the least
appearance of swimming." In the event, Elliston decided to have
real water. A victory here for Brunton and illusionism. He may
also have saved Elliston on dog food. The troupe of dogs would
want twenty pounds a week, but "there is not one thing their best
dog does that mine wont do in three days & you are perfectly welcome to him." As for the Pixérécourt piece, *The Dog of Montargis*,
Brunton was sent the two London texts and he made an amalgam
of them; he had great hopes for a big hit with this spectacle. But
here Fate held up her hand and said Brunton nay. For June was
the month of Waterloo. On June 25, the eve of *The Dog*, Brunton
wrote, "There is every Reason to expect a good House . . . but I am
almost afraid to think so till I see it—The news on Friday set all
the People mad & materially injured our House at Night." His
worst fears, indeed, came true. The theatre was virtually deserted:
"this news is the making of the Public houses but the ruin of us."
July was as good as a write off. A lesser man would have despaired.

But Elliston himself was never one to let a thing like Waterloo
stagger him. When he arrived on the Birmingham scene, on July 28,
it was as a free spirit, his ties with Drury Lane now severed. In a
businesslike manner, he set about winning his audience back. He
dedicated a Fashionable Night to a fund in aid of a Waterloo subscription, "now raising in the Town." He held a masquerade in

honour of the English victory. The theatre exuded jingoism. The
audience returned. The caravan, so to speak, moved on.

Now that he was committed to, and indeed dependent upon
Birmingham Theatre Royal, Elliston made every attempt to make
it a going concern. He extended the season by chopping up the
year into little festival periods, each meant to have its own distinction, and perhaps to cater for different audiences. Thus from October 23 to December 9, 1815, he initiated a season of hippodrama,
engaging the equestrian Davis on a share-of-receipts basis. This
seems to have worked well financially; receipts averaging over £160
weekly allowed Elliston to pocket £230 in lieu of "expenses."[31]
From Easter Monday, April 15, until May 2, 1816, there was a brief
season of drama, in which Elliston himself starred; once again the
idea paid off. To keep the customers interested, he made a speech
re-affirming his basic aims and promising a "Scale of Expenditure
equal to the Bath and Liverpool Theatres."[32] Such rhetoric may be
tested with reference to two concrete proposals Elliston also made.
Firstly, to engage personnel from the provincial circuits. He named
the actors and actresses involved, who did in fact appear thereafter.
They came from Dublin, and his own theatres at Worcester and
the Olympic, and they provided him with the nucleus of a permanent company. He lost the inestimable Brunton and Ashley
at this time, but he gained T. P. Cooke, who, at a salary of two
pounds a week was placed in charge of all melodramas and spectacles, for which he had a special touch. Secondly, Elliston promised
to present all the most popular London hits. This tended to mean
the plays in which he himself had made his reputation; but it also
took into account the contemporary taste for melodrama. Indeed,
during the summer season, June 3 to October 25, what is most
striking is the popularity of essentially minor-theatre fare. On the
Fashionable Nights a particular favourite was *The Maid and the
Magpie*, the tear jerker which Elliston had recently staged at the
Olympic. Not far behind was *The Blood-Red Knight,* staged "with
all the horses," as it had lately thrilled audiences for some one
hundred and seventy nights at Astley's.

All in all, Elliston was successful in winning support from the
Birmingham middle classes—for a time. Even the army participa-
ted in the Fashionable Nights, supplying a band and treating the
audience to selections from popular operas. Financially, Elliston

netted around £50 per week himself; receipts remained steady. The proprietors renewed his lease for three years from April 30, 1816, allowing him to lease the adjoining Tavern and Assembly Rooms also at the reasonable total of £500 *p.a.* Although slow to pay up arrears, Elliston was clearly regarded as a good investment.

There are many stories dating from this time which may be said to illustrate Elliston's technique of sustaining audience interest. Some of these are of the shaggy dog variety, such as the one about the strong man. Apparently, Elliston advertised as a novelty the appearance of a Bohemian of "unexampled Strength and Stature" who would lift up a stone weighing one ton, and handle it like a tennis ball. This strong man had, it seems, been received with favour in numerous Rhenish states and, to entertain a German princess of interesting tastes, was said to have felled an ox with one blow of his fist. On the night, the play itself, *Pizarro,* was scarcely heard, so great was the local excitement over the strong man. A hush fell as an obviously affected Elliston, still recognisable as Rolla, appeared before the curtain. Jack Worthing in crêpe could hardly be more solemn. "The Bohemian has deceived me," was his message, when grief allowed him utterance. What affected him more than this unforgivable circumstance was that "the faithless foreigner" had deceived his audience. Elliston had voluminous correspondence in support of his own spotless innocence in the matter. When this declaration was greeted with less than enthusiasm, he actually produced the letters and asked for a volunteer to translate from the German. The ensuing uproar Elliston construed as a vote of confidence, rendering translation unnecessary; with a magnificent gesture he told his friends that even if he was not in a position to exhibit the strong man, he was nevertheless able to show the stone he ought to have lifted. With that, up went the curtain to discover a large object bearing a scroll, which made all plain with the words, "This is the stone."[33]

Though he did not always fail to deliver the man as well as the stone, Elliston's technique remained that of an effective impresario. When he had a star attraction, he gave him or her enormous advance publicity, and squeezed the last ounce of notoriety out of the most ordinary hitch in proceedings. Invariably, the effect was to promote himself as a selfless worker on behalf of a highly regarded public. The manner in which he handled the engagement of Eliza

O'Neill, the darling of Covent Garden, in October 1816, is an object lesson in theatrical public relations. Playbills and broadsheets and paragraphs in the newspaper all traced the efforts of Elliston to win this pearl for Birmingham. The result was an enormous sense of excitement, with the town actually en fête for the week of her appearance. Elliston brought in two other provincials, Conway and Bartley, to assist himself in the company, but stoutly refused to raise admission charges. The theatre was packed out, with hundreds turned away. Many people settled for a glimpse of the adored actress coming or going at the Royal Hotel. As for the performances, Miss O'Neill played Juliet, Mrs. Oakley in *The Jealous Wife,* Belvidera in *Venice Preserved,* Mrs. Haller in *The Stranger,* and Mrs. Beverley in *The Gamester.* She lived up to all expectations. The Oldest Inhabitant did not feel called upon to make any comparisons with Mrs. Siddons, but the local critic found praiseworthy not only her pathos and bursts of passion, but also her "undeviating" attention "to the scene."[34] Determined to make as much mileage, in every sense, out of the occasion, Elliston followed her to London and sought to extend the engagement. Though he failed, the Birmingham audience felt the comfort of knowing, as they were certainly reminded, that their manager was indefatigable in serving their interests.

When he took his benefit, on October 27, Elliston presented to the audience his two eldest daughters, Eliza and Frances Maria; in a ballet *divertissement,* perhaps the work of Mrs. Elliston. The gesture was typical. At Birmingham Theatre Royal they were all one big happy family.

So long as Elliston was content to continue with the unremitting attention shown to Birmingham in 1816 his success seemed assured. When the next season opened, May 26, 1817, it was with the best auguries. Elliston appeared during the first week, and the high receipts, almost £350, indicate his continuing popularity. It was a matter of some significance, also, when the theatre was noticed by the prestigious *Theatrical Inquisitor* in July. The company was given serious attention in this review, and in general described as "numerous and well-selected." Every department was found "excellently arranged," making the critic pleased to remark that the "very improved system" on which the theatre was now conducted "under the superintendence of Mr. Elliston" met the patronage "it so justly deserves."

From June 30 until August 8 Elliston was able to keep the theatre open five nights a week. During that time visiting stars helped swell the box office, e.g., Grimaldi, Junius Brutus Booth, Miss Somerville, and John Liston. After the regular summer season followed the horses, as was usual now, in October, and Elliston pronounced himself to his treasurer, Lee, as "as gratified that Mr. Davis is well pleased, as I am with our success just at the end of the Season."[35]

But in this same letter Elliston rather startlingly reveals his true attitude towards conformist Birmingham society, intimating that all was far from well in the bosom of the family: "It is a disgusting Town in its chattering & interferences, & we must give them no handle that can be properly avoided." It may be that in extending his immediate interests beyond the Birmingham circuit at the end of this season, Elliston was unwittingly providing the "handle" of disaffection he wished to avoid. This winter he became lessee of Lynn Theatre Royal on the Norwich circuit, assisted by his old friend John Brunton.[36] If William Oxberry is to be believed, Elliston's behaviour at Lynn was hardly what the Birmingham city fathers would approve of, "a race of drunkenness and profligacy."[37] At the A. G. M. of the proprietors of Birmingham Theatre Royal Elliston had a rent balance of £353 unpaid. When on January 12, 1818 he offered £300 in clearance of this debt, he excused himself with the declaration that his other engagements had kept him from attending to Birmingham affairs.[38] His offer was declined.

It seems likely that when Elliston opened Birmingham Theatre Royal on or about March 23, 1818, he was rather under a cloud. He had become somewhat notorious as a man-about-town, and had even been attacked from the pulpit.[39] The acid test was whether or not the public would continue to support him. For his part, Elliston presented the best his theatre was capable of, in melodrama, pantomime, and regular drama. He himself went through his popular roles, such as, Charles Surface, the three Singles, Dr. Pangloss in Colman's *Heir at Law,* Young Rapid in Morton's *A Cure for the Heart-Ache,* etc. And he had more than his usual stream of visiting stars to parade before the public and repeat their London-established roles. These included the child star Clara Fisher, Mrs. Charles Kemble, Miss Somerville, Miss Kelly, and, making his first appearance at Birmingham since he was a schoolboy, William Charles Macready. The town remained uninterested. On the benefit nights of the visiting stars the neglect was obvious. The season was a financial disaster.

Elliston was indignant at this sudden lack of support. In a published address, which he termed an "Exposé," he adduced the dismal receipts for the season as evidence of a serious problem. The tone of the address is quite remarkable. It is candid without malice, accusatory without self-pity; it is a document of character. Quite frankly, the loss for the season would, "without an effort from the public," amount to £1500. Elliston refuses to accept the implications of this as regards the quality of his company. "Experiments upon new talent must be made, and will often fail; yet engagements for the Season must be honourably fulfilled."[40] The lack of support on benefit nights[41] indicated that even visiting talent had gone unrewarded: the fault, surely, lay not in the stars. For himself, he had no reason to feel reproach. "Mr. Elliston's whole mind has been employed in promoting the interests and respectability of the Drama in this town, and from the period he first undertook the management of this concern, his time, his purse, his personal efforts, have been devoted to it." Clearly, the Birmingham audience had not kept faith. All he can say now is that three days remain during which some amends might be made. On two of these evenings some gentlemen of the town, amateurs, were to participate in the plays. A special effort was requested for one of these nights, a so-called Fashionable Night, September 4. Elliston himself appeared also on these nights, playing Pangloss, Walter (*Children in the Wood*), and Young Rapid (*A Cure for the Heartache*). No doubt he enjoyed the rich irony implicit in his appealing for audience approval on the basis of his supporting cast of townspeople, but it is doubtful that he went as far as the late Anew McMaster in a somewhat similar situation. In 1953, after a lifetime of touring the Irish countryside with a Shakespearean and classical repertory, McMaster came face to face with the burgeoning amateur drama movement. His annual visit to Athlone coincided with the first national amateur drama festival, and he was ignored. On his final night, he came forward after *King Lear*, still in full cos-

tume, and castigated the town for the insult paid him. Then, taking
off his spectacles, which he had rather incongruously donned to
read his statement, he delivered his marvellous exit line, "I will
leave you to the amateurs!"[42] However much Elliston may have
been tempted to a similar gesture, he could ill afford it. He had one
more night to go, and this was his benefit night. For the occasion,
September 7, he presented a new comedy called *The Green Man*.[43]
If there was a joke here, it was a quiet one about nonconformity;
but how green the green man was prepared to be, in view of the
green stuff he wanted to line his pockets with, is hard to say.

Because of the lack of a receipts book for this period, it is likewise
hard to say what precise effect Elliston's "Exposé" may have had.
It could have shamed Birmingham into making good half the total
loss declared by Elliston. The fact that the theatre reopened on
September 21 for a brief engagement with the singer Braham,
accompanied by the comedienne Mrs. Humby, suggests the melting
mood. The wording of Mrs. Humby's appeal for her benefit night,
moreover, indicates that the engagement had been successful:
she speaks of the "liberality of sentiment which has hitherto so
much encouraged her efforts" as emboldening her to ask for a benefit although her stay was a short one.[44] It seems not unlikely that
Elliston was able to extricate himself without any enormous deficit
on the season.

He made no attempt thereafter, however, to disguise his con-
tempt for the way he had been treated. The victories he had recently won elsewhere gave his future a new and more promising
shape than that of a provincial manager. In May 1818 he had made
a brilliant return to the London stage. During the summer the
Lord Chamberlain had upheld Elliston's defence of the Olympic
Theatre, thus opening the door to 'Little Drury Lane' and success.
Elliston was now finished with Birmingham. As for the full year's
arrears in rent, for which the proprietors howled, he coolly suggested that they mortgage his house and property in Bristol as
surety, although he had no real intention of allowing this. At the
A. G. M., on December 21 he failed to appear, and for the first time in
years no dividend was declared. On January 9, 1819, the proprietors
registered their lack of faith in Elliston, and resolved to prosecute.
The theatre was also advertised to be let. But Elliston refused to
hand up the keys until his valuation of scenery and effects were

accepted. He was then threatened with double rent, which enraged him. "You will pardon me," he wrote in reply to the solicitors for the proprietors, "if I say you are here as deficient in law, as your phrase 'flimsy pretense' is repugnant to politeness."[45] He well knew that his lease did not expire until the end of April 1819. On this rather sour note Elliston terminated his management of Birmingham Theatre Royal.[46]

Apart from the financial aspect, two points remain for final comment. Although standards are difficult to assess, it seems fair to assume that Elliston worked to make them as high as circumstances permitted, since his overall aim was to make a good case for theatre in a rather indifferent community. He was certainly successful in establishing the theatre as a fashionable centre of entertainment. In a tribute one hundred years after Elliston's death a writer in the *Birmingham Post* said: "As a manager Elliston did more than any of his predecessors or successors to impress upon the social life of Birmingham the claims of the drama. His 'Friday nights' were an immense success. The performances were invariably under the patronage and often in the presence of 'the High and Low Bailiffs, the Churchwardens and Constables.' "[47] Other local supporters and patrons, named on the playbills, stretch across a wide social spectrum, and this fact alone testifies to Elliston's salesmanship. If the product did not stand up to scrutiny he would neither have lasted six years nor have taken the tone he did in his "Exposé."

On the negative side, he had had pointed out to him the need for consistency. Lack of concentrated effort, of personal attention, may account for the unevennesses in Elliston's achievement. There was a grim warning here which he failed to take. Elliston was always inclined to spread himself too thin over too many projects. He also experienced in Birmingham the precariousness of contemporary audience taste, something which was becoming a grave problem all through the theatre and making the manager's task a nightmare. In the revelation that good legitimate theatre presented by good acting was not enough any more, the Birmingham management thus served as an ominous prefiguration of the state of things at Drury Lane, when Elliston assumed management of it in 1819.

FIVE

Drury Lane

'Bilgewater, I am the late Dauphin!'
Mark Twain, *Adventures of Huckleberry Finn*

FROM OLYMPIC, not to say Olympian, heights Elliston, it will be recalled, had administered some home truths in 1818 to the managers of the patent theatres. Regarding Drury Lane, his strictures in *Copy of a Memorial* were unanswerable. From its brilliant opening in 1812, with Elliston himself as leading actor, the graph had gone mournfully downward, as the theatre, even after the arrival of Edmund Kean, failed to make ends meet.[1] In 1817–18, box-office receipts were half of what they had been in 1812–13, and the sub-committee of bumbling amateur managers admitted to a debt on the theatre of £84,800.[2] A good deal of pettifogging followed this announcement to the shareholders, and an effort was made to get George Colman to take over the management. The sub-committee survived a coup attempt, however, and Colman was unwilling to undertake management under either a controlling committee or an enormous debt. It was decided by the proprietors to try again under the old system, but the combination of Stephen Kemble, Kean, and the sub-committee made no improvement. On June 5, 1819, after Drury Lane closed abruptly, the debt was stated to have climbed to £90,922.[3] It was clear that the principle of a joint-stock company, on which the theatre had been based since 1812, was unsuitable for theatre management. The sub-committee resigned, and a Select Committee was formed to raise £25,000 to clear pressing debts. On Monday June 7 an advertisement appeared in the *Morning Chronicle* announcing that the Select Committee was ready to receive proposals from any prospective lessee. The significance of this shift in theatrical policy was not lost among the cups, the marmalade, the tea of one London household, at least, on that morning. The Ellistonian response is unrecorded, but it can have been little short of high glee.

He wrote to Ward, the secretary, that very day, asking a barrage of questions regarding conditions of renting.[4] There were applications from Kean, Arnold, and Thomas Dibdin also. Kean, in his cocky manner, volunteered to "cleanse the Augean stable" at a rent of £8000 *p.a.*, independent of all committees.[5] Although he raised this sum to £10,000, it seems Kean was not wanted. The real battle was between Elliston and Dibdin. Elliston offered only £8500 at first: his final figure was £10,200, to beat Dibdin by £100. In between came a good deal of politicking. On July 5, for instance, Elliston had a letter from a member of the committee, Wathen, advising him that since Dibdin's security seemed very sound Elliston should make over his own property "to some one rich person who would be substantial security for you."[6] He should also canvass the members of the Select Committee. "I need not tell you a little flummery & flattery goes a great way." In the end, Elliston was able to produce security of £25,000 and to pledge £7000 for renovating the theatre.

On September 8, at a general meeting of the proprietors, Elliston was confirmed as lessee, for fourteen years.[7] The Select Committee was now dissolved, and a new sub-committee was formed. From now on, committees took a back seat. For the first time since it was rebuilt, Drury Lane had an autonomous manager.

Elliston was in his element. His life-long ambition had been achieved. Charles Lamb tells how he met him in the street at this time. "Grasping my hand with a look of significance, he only uttered, 'Have you heard the news?' Then, with another look following up the blow, he subjoined, 'I am the future Manager of Drury Lane Theatre.' Breathless as he saw me, he stayed not for congratulation or reply, but mutely stalked away, leaving me to chew upon his new-blown dignities at leisure. In fact, nothing could be said to it. Expressive silence alone could muse his praise. This was in his *great* style."[8]

There was too much to be done, however, for Elliston to bask for very long in his new-found glory. As a first step he enlisted James

Winston as acting manager, a move of doubtful wisdom, for though Winston was conscientious and had proved reliable at the Olympic, he was unpopular among actors for his meanness. But he was loyal to Elliston and had qualities of steadiness and sobriety which helped, as time went on, to cover Elliston's personal lapses. Regarding the company, Elliston's policy was, first that the theatre was not a hospital for invalids, and secondly that Drury Lane should have the best talent available. He purged more than forty from the payroll. He picked the best members of his Olympic and Birmingham companies, including Robert Keeley, M'Keon, Mrs. Harlowe, etc., and toured the provinces for the best he could find there. Edmund Kean, furious over his failure to obtain control over Drury Lane, wasted a lot of Elliston's time by refusing to act under his aegis, although he was bound by Articles. Mrs. Siddons declined Elliston's request that she make a return to the stage. Apart from Kean, Elliston had hardly any actor of merit in tragedy. In comedy he was in a happier position, having Dowton, Harley, Gattie, Miss Kelly, Mrs. Edwin, besides himself. For opera, Elliston persuaded John Braham to return after an absence of four years, but until Eliza Vestris joined him in February 1820 this side of the company was only mediocre.

As to playwrights, Elliston had his hacks of former days, who graduated with him to the status of the legitimate. He was eager also to attract good writers to the theatre. Both Walter Scott and Thomas Moore refused his overtures, however, and though he received scripts from Keats, Shelley, and Leigh Hunt, they were not suited to the stage.[9] Byron had left England, and a year had yet to pass before he wrote his first play. Elliston was thus faced at the outset of his Drury Lane management with one of the insurmountable problems of the Regency theatre: the failure of the greatest literary talent of the age to produce stageworthy plays.

Time did not permit the overhauling of the theatre itself, as Elliston had promised. Instead of rebuilding, Elliston concentrated, for the time being, on redecorating Drury Lane. From the provinces he wrote to Winston as regularly as he had of old written over Olympic affairs, and plied him with instructions for Beazley to have the theatre finished as soon as possible. Inventories revealed a healthy stock of scenery, costumes, and properties,[10] but the painters must be put to work immediately, "for the whole of

the Scenery must be refreshed."[11] Among his scene designers he had
engaged two men of talent, Dixon and Marinari. The former he
had come across in the provinces, "pining in solitude over his
neglected merit & consoling himself in dignified pride." Marinari
he considered " a great card," and when he arrived Winston was
by no means to confine his efforts to scenery but to "consult him
as to the Ceiling, for there will not be wanting Critics, who will
arraign & condemn our taste, & classical knowledge."

Winston was responsible for all sorts of arrangements, with con-
tractors of many kinds. Of most interest, perhaps, is the contract
for lighting. Elliston dictated the terms he would pay for chandeliers: the arrangement made was to hire sixteen lustres for the
front of the 'dress circle' and proscenium for twenty pounds per
week; after twenty-one weeks, they would be Elliston's property.[12]
John Gardner contracted to light the other, "fixed," lights for
thirty pounds a week, to include lighting "Fourteen Hundred occasional single lights for the Scenery alone."[13] Arrangements also had
to be made over the free lists. Elliston consulted Harris of Covent
Garden, and together they came to an agreement as to which
newspapers and magazines should receive free passes, and how
many. These were distributed according to circulation and estimated influence of the newspapers. At the same time, the two
managers agreed to advertise in the same papers only, and on the
same terms.

As a final bit of advertising, Elliston announced a preview of
the theatre on September 30, to which the nobility as well as
members of the press were invited. The theatre was much admired
—especially the colouring—and the lighting and scenery.[14] Afterwards, dancing and refreshments were provided. Elliston, aided by
Winston and Samuel Russell (whom he had taken on as stage
manager), was on hand to see after the comfort and convenience
of all. He felt he had done all that could be expected. Opening
night was set for Monday, October 4.

The house was packed out. After the usual loyal anthems, lustily
sung by all the company and enthusiastically received (a feature
of Regency theatre which comes as a constant surprise to the
phlegmatic twentieth-century theatregoer), Fanny Kelly was led
forward to deliver the opening address, written by Busby. She spoke
of Elliston as Atlas, the people as his support; the honour of drama,

Elliston's dedication thereto; the matter of talent, and Elliston as patron. The play presented was O'Keeffe's sentimental comedy, *Wild Oats,* which had held the stage for twenty-five years. Besides the fact that Rover was one of Elliston's most popular roles, the play was chosen, apparently, for its theatrical imagery, since it concerns the attempts of a country player to 'make it' on the London stage. Certain lines probably received special appreciation from their application to Elliston's management, e.g., "Do you know, you villain, that I am this moment the greatest man living?" —spoken by Rover in II, i; or Rover's devil-may-care utterance, in the next scene, "Why, I may fail, and gods may groan, and ladies drawl, 'La, what an awkward creature!' But should I top my part, then shall the gods applaud, and ladies sigh, 'the charming fellow!' and treasurers smile upon me as they count the shining guineas!"[15] Not only the gods, but the whole theatre applauded as soon as Elliston appeared, and after the play he was called for and given a huge ovation. Immensely pleased, Elliston made his first speech before the curtain. He ran over in prose all that Miss Kelly had gone into in verse earlier in the evening, emphasizing once again his general purpose of keeping the theatre open "at all times to the offerings of genius" and "devoted to the legitimate drama of our country."[16] Little did he suspect the difficulty of achieving this purpose. "If it falls now, it falls, probably, never to rise again," was the way *The Times* put it next day, speaking of the desperate plight of Drury Lane.

During his first season Elliston made a real attempt to stage Shakespeare with the kind of splendour made famous by John Philip Kemble. Before embarking on Shakespearean production, however, he had to await the arrival of Edmund Kean on November 8—for Kean always timed his annual entrances for maximum effect. In the meantime, Elliston himself led the cast in the tried-and-true comedies which supplied him with his most popular roles. His appeal in these sentimental comedies was as great as ever. But with his first new production, on October 20, came the first setback of his management. *Fisherman's Hut,* a tragi-comedy left unfinished by John Tobin, author of *Honey Moon,* had been reworked by George Soane and set to music. The theatre was closed on October 19 while final rehearsals were held. Though strongly cast, with Munden, Dowton, Harley, Miss Kelly and Mrs. West, it was poorly received on opening night, stormily received on the second and entirely damned on the third. Elliston, who had obviously pinned a certain amount of hope on *Fisherman's Hut* was forced to come back himself again on October 23 in *Wild Oats*. From then until the end of the month he was on stage nightly, repeating his stock roles.

He planned to make an impact with *Richard III*. In his Advertisement to the prompt-copy, published to coincide with the production on November 8, Elliston paid tribute to the advances made by Kemble and placed himself in that tradition. His own conception of staging Shakespeare, however, was less scholarly than Kemble's. As in 1809, when he staged *Macbeth* at the Surrey, he wished to give Shakespeare the advantage of modern stage techniques and to devote to the plays some of the attention lavished on melodramas and pantomime. In *Richard III* this aim was confined to lavishness of costume. In this regard Elliston steered a path between antiquarianism and meretriciousness. He even supplied the sources of his historical accuracy, thus anticipating Charles Kean by a good forty years. Among these were Strutt's *Antiquities,* Charles Hamilton Smith's *Ancient Costume,* every volume "of the same nature" in the British Museum, "together with a multitude of old engravings." At the same time historical accuracy was sacrificed, when required, both to "the words of the poet" and "to stage effect."[17]

The critics were unimpressed. "Kean jumped about in an iron skull cap and a close-bodied gown," said one reviewer, "the sleeves curiously cut, looking more like a Tartar Amazon than the Richard of our idea."[18] Elliston as Richmond appeared "in a new suit of shining armour, and strutted about the stage, grasping a terrific pole axe and a bright shield, very much to his own delight, Kean's annoyance and the amusement of the audience." The *Theatrical Inquisitor* sneered at Henry VI (Pope) and the princes because they wore silk stockings, "though queen ELIZABETH, almost 80 years afterwards, figured away with the first pair that was sent to this country." *The Times,* while admitting that "the dresses are in good costume, as well as of a superior description," carped at a tentative and obviously under-rehearsed attempt at a crowd scene. Whatever the critics might think, the Elliston-Kean combination served to boost the lagging receipts to over £561 on November 8. Receipts held steady at about £250 as *Richard III* went into repertory, to be staged a total of eight times before the end of the season.

Kean on his own, however, was no longer an attraction. Receipts fell steadily before Christmas as he ran through Sir Giles Overreach, Macbeth, Hamlet, Bertram, etc. Elliston pinned his hopes on a new five-act comedy, *Gallantry,* on January 15. Once again it was strongly cast, with himself, Munden, Dowton, Harley, Mrs. Edwin, Miss Kelly and Mrs. West. It was also carefully costumed. A large audience turned out, but found the play confusing and hackneyed. Elliston had listed only the actors on the playbill, without indicating the role played by each, which added to the confusion. The play was noisily received. Mrs. Edwin's epilogue, pleading for indulgence, went down just as badly. Elliston was called for, consoled the audience by assuring them the play was to be withdrawn, and then commenced to lecture them on their inability to pronounce judgement, a measure which led to a virtual riot. *Richard III* was hastily substituted for *Gallantry.*

Some days later Elliston announced his second major Shakespearean production of the season, *Coriolanus.* This time he added to historical accuracy of costume the aim of textual restoration. The version of *Coriolanus* then on the stage was a hodge-podge of Shakespeare and James Thomson made stageworthy by John Philip Kemble.[19] Elliston daringly broke with the great Kemble tradition and favoured the original over the amalgam. In his Advertisement to his own version, he admits that to present *Coriolanus* on stage in its complete form would be impossible, because of its length, "but though we cannot bring upon the stage all that the great poet has written, there yet appears no just cause for interpolating his text with the works of others."[20] His playbill for January 25 rather ostentatiously announced that "His Majesty's Servants" would perform "*(for the 1st time at this Theatre)* SHAKSPEARE'S CORIOLANUS." The only "deviation" from the "genuine Text" would be in omissions, "and that done solely with a view to reduce the whole within the limits allowed by custom to an acting play." There would be, however, a new Ode of Triumph in act 2, written by George Soane, set to music by Thomas Cooke and sung by the operatic corps.

Together with textual restoration, Elliston wished to present *Coriolanus* as accurately as possible as regards costume and scenery. But he was quite willing to bend "truth" in order to satisfy "stage effect": contemporary taste was his real guide.

Elliston did not play in the production himself, building it instead around Edmund Kean, who proved a huge disappointment in the leading role. The *Theatrical Inquisitor* went so far as to say Kean played Sir Giles, or Richard III, or Sir Edward Mortimer in the part, but certainly not Coriolanus. This failure set all of Elliston's preparations at naught. *The Times* (January 26) discounted the restored text as much less suited to theatre and actors than Kemble's version. To the *New Monthly Magazine*, Shakespeare's play was itself faulty: the battle scenes were unstageable and the interest at the end lacked a culminating point. In the *London Magazine,* Hazlitt inveighed against the spectacular aspects of the production: "One would think there were processions and ovations enough in this play, as it was acted in John Kemble's time; but besides these, there were introduced others of the same sort, some of which were lengthened out as if they would reach all the way to the Circus."[21] Hazlitt also took exception to Elliston's minor-theatre style of staging the battle scenes, finding it melodramatic and noisy. *Coriolanus* was popular with no segment of the audience, and played a mere four times during the season.

On January 30 George III died and the Regency was at an end. This had two effects that concern us here. The theatres were closed until February 19, and the way was now open at last for a production of *King Lear,* long banned from the stage because of George III's insanity. Elliston decided to try once more with a lavish production of Shakespeare. He could certainly do with a box-office hit, for receipts were miserable, both before and after Easter.

Not encouraged to restore Shakespeare's text, Elliston decided to make do this time, for the most part, with Nahum Tate. In his Advertisement to the printed text he excused himself with the observation that "the public taste long ago decided against the sublime, but terrible, catastrophe of the original, and even the critical Dr. Johnson has sanctioned that decision."[22] For the moment then, Cordelia's life continued to be spared on the English stage. But though Elliston adhered, in the main, to the text then current on the stage, he made two slight but important restorations. Shakes-

peare's language was restored at the beginning of Lear's raving on
the heath, and at the recognition-of-Cordelia scene.

He did not settle the historic period of the play's action any more
satisfactorily than he had that of *Coriolanus*. Kean had certain
thoughts on the costume, i.e., that both Garrick and Kemble were
wrong in their ideas for Lear. In a letter to Elliston on March 31,
Kean went into some detail on the question, and decided "to blend
Dramatic effect with Traditional Simplicity."[23] Elliston obviously
was guided by Kean's meditations, for he virtually quotes his
scholarship in his Advertisement. He felt bound, nevertheless, to
plump for some definite historic period, and against Kean's judgment he decided upon the early Saxon. His aim then became to
"adhere to it with fidelity," by making the costumes "fac-similes of
engravings from the best authorities." A similar line of argument
guided Elliston with regard to the scenery. Truth to antiquity
would involve ugliness, where colour and splendour were more in
accordance with public taste; he therefore eschewed accuracy for
stylization. For the storm scene, however, he was entirely guided
by Kean, who was enthusiastic in having it staged realistically.
With Elliston's permission he brought some friends into the theatre
to assist Marinari in setting up the storm after the manner of De
Loutherbourg's *eidophusikon*.

After a massive build-up in preliminary playbills, *King Lear*
opened on April 24. Once again, Elliston did not himself appear
with Kean, and the role of Edgar was taken by Rae. More and more
he was content to cling to his comedy roles, and to supervise rather
than participate in experiments. For Kean the production was a
triumph, though Lear was perhaps not one of his best roles. Neither
the costume nor the scenery, however, escaped censure. Kean was
"well dressed for the part, in a Saxon robe of crimson, and the
Saxon cap, which looked extremely becoming," but "he was enveloped in the same *Nimbus* of white hair which had proved so
nearly fatal to his predecessor, JUNIUS BRUTUS BOOTH. This absurd
accumulation of wig totally spoils the physiognomy."[24] The meanness of the ladies' costume was also commented on. The storm scene
made anything but a good impression. So realistic were the thunder
and creaking trees [*sic*] that Kean could not be heard. When a
blackout was followed by billows of smoke which all but suffoca-
ted the front rows of the audience, Shakespeare by flashes of light-

ning met with something less than enthusiasm. The effect of the panorama, based on De Loutherbourg's picture, "Storm on Land," was a most colourful King Lear, "one instant . . . a beautiful pea-green, and the next sky blue, and in the event of a momentary cessation of the rotary motion of the magic lantern, his head would be purple and his legs Dutch-pink."[25]

However unreceptive the critics were to Elliston's production, the public was impressed. The announcement in the playbill for April 25 may have represented a slight exaggeration—"Nothing on the British Stage has been more powerful: reiterated peals of Applause accompanied the whole performance"—but *King Lear* packed them in for twenty-six performances. After May 30 it had the support of *Giovanni in London,* which Elliston now revived (and revised) for the laudable purpose of presenting Eliza Vestris in a breeches role.

Giovanni in London had once saved the Olympic Theatre. Now it went far towards saving the season at Drury Lane, for it was the most popular afterpiece of Elliston's management. Crowds thronged just to see the fascinating Madame Vestris in the breeches role. "What a breast—what an eye! what a foot, leg, and thigh!" enthused one of her many admirers. There were those who complained that this parading of Madame Vestris' advantages was not reconcilable with the aims of the national drama, but the majority seemed to approve Elliston's taste. When the theatre closed on July 8 receipts had reached £44,000, or some £10,000 more than the catastrophic season of 1818–19, although with expenses amounting to roughly £200 a night for the 199 nights profits were still pretty slim.

As he was accustomed to do at the Surrey and at Birmingham, Elliston wished to extend his season beyond the regular limit. To this the Drury Lane committee had no objection, provided he paid a stipulated security for each night beyond the two hundred agreed upon. Elliston intended to re-open at the beginning of August and, making use of the fact that Kean was about to leave for the United States, build everything around Kean. He also persuaded Junius Brutus Booth to join the venture. If Booth would act seven nights with Kean, Elliston would engage him for the following season at Drury Lane and the Olympic together.[26] Booth was to get £20 a night; Keen got his usual £30 for three nights, plus £10 a night thereafter, thus giving him as much as £60 a week. The rest of the Drury Lane cast that Elliston persuaded to forego their usual provincial engagements, eighteen actors, and eight actresses altogether, including Elliston himself, were given a pro-rata amount of their regular weekly salary, depending on the number of nights each played.

The season opened on August 15 and ran until September 16. Kean played a total of twenty-five nights, running through all of his best parts; to him Booth played Richmond, Pierre, Iago, Macduff, Edgar and Milford. Elliston himself played Macduff, Pierre, and Richmond on nights when Booth was not engaged. Receipts were quite good, and Winston says that Elliston cleared £2000 on the venture.[27] The sudden and unpopular case against Queen Caroline redounded, strangely, to the credit of the experiment. The public, avidly on Caroline's side against George, who was seen in a melodramatic light as a tormentor of hapless innocence, insisted on reading into theatrical productions allusions to the Bill of Pains and Penalties then in its second reading. *Othello* was the favourite in this regard. The audience would applaud Emilia wildly, at her outburst in defence of Desdemona. Sometimes they stood up and cheered at the line, "What place? what time? what likelihood?" and at the end of the speech the applause, with waving of hats and handkerchiefs, would go on for several minutes.

In order to work out his summer season without running into the competition of Covent Garden, which usually opened early in September, Elliston made an agreement with Harris, the manager, whereby the latter should not open until September 18; in return, Elliston should not reopen until October 16.[28] Elliston used the intervening time to slightly decorate the theatre and erect a portico outside, in front of the box entrance in Brydges Street, now Catherine Street, and did not in fact reopen until October 30.[29]

To make up for the absence of Kean, Elliston engaged Junius Brutus Booth, John Cooper and James William Wallack. The latter was returning to Drury Lane after three years, but Cooper, a provincial actor of some note, was making his London debut. Together, these three actors tried to offer an alternative to the star system. But the audience simply was not interested in Messrs. Cooper, Wallack and Booth in *Romeo and Juliet, Hamlet, Julius Caesar,* or even *King Lear*. Receipts for Booth as Lear on November 17 plummeted to a rockbottom £57. Each of these actors was admitted by the critics to be good, with reservations. The reservations all added up to the fact that none of the actors was Edmund Kean in his prime. When Eliza Vestris appeared as Macheath and receipts leaped over £300, Elliston had his answer to the problem. Having lost Braham this year, and having no male singer, he coolly slipped Vestris into this slot. *Giovanni* was brought back, followed by *Midas* with Vestris as Apollo, in which she was declared to beat love hollow, since "Love has not legs to play Apollo."[30]

Doubtless taking his hint from Vestris' popularity, while a wide variety of well-cast stock plays and a couple of new melodramas proved unwanted, Elliston decided, when the new year arrived, to concentrate on opera. On January 12 he used red lettering for the first time at a major theatre in announcing another bright young thing, soon to be revealed as a Miss Mary Ann Wilson. Her debut on January 18 in *Artaxerxes,* in which Vestris played the male lead, was, according to *The Times's* reviewer, the most striking debut ever witnessed. "Her success," continued *The Times* of January 19, "has determined the managers to make the musical drama the prevailing feature of the theatre, and it was announced yesterday evening by Mr. Russell that three nights in the week are in future to be devoted to operas." Miss Wilson was engaged for forty nights at £21 per night. Her complete success led to a further twenty-five-night engagement after Easter.

Miss Wilson was really only a seven-day wonder, but while she lasted her success was phenomenal. She sang in only three operas, *Artaxerxes, Love in a Village,* and *Duenna,* all three of which were standard English operas; but she drew receipts of from £488 her first night to £695 when the King came to see her on February 6.[31] Hunt in *The Examiner* wondered if her attraction was not a sign of sudden change in taste, away from legitimate drama. Inasmuch as receipts fell to one-third of those on opera nights whenever Elliston appeared in *A School for Scandal, Road to Ruin, The Dramatist* etc., in January and February, Hunt clearly had a point.

The change in taste is also seen in the contrasting reception of two new pieces. The first of these was a melodrama, *Thérèse,* the origin of which is a melodrama in itself. John Howard Payne was languishing in prison in London when one day a mysterious package arrived from France. Inside were two French melodramas, one of which was *Thérèse*. Payne translated the latter in four days, brought it to Elliston on January 27, and saw it on the Drury Lane stage on February 2.[32] Payne got out from prison in disguise to appear at rehearsals. So rushed was the whole thing, lest Covent Garden or even the minor theatres should bring out a rival version, that the last rehearsal was a scene of despair. But in true rep. fashion, all was well on the night. Indeed Elliston was prompted to declare in his playbill next day, "No Piece, however successful, was ever received with such extraordinary Applause"; by February 5 *Thérèse* was emphatically "the most successful Piece that has ever been produced." It ran, in fact, for thirty-one nights. An important effect of the play's success was that when Payne went to Paris shortly afterwards he persuaded Elliston to employ him as agent there, with the task of sending to London other likely French melodramas. The correspondence between them indicates how closely the English was now following the French stage.

On the other hand, Elliston's production of Byron's first play, *Marino Faliero,* on April 25, was anything but a good omen for the future of tragedy. In October 1820 Elliston had written to Byron for details on the play, just finished.[33] He did not get permission to stage it, for Byron knew all too well the mauling a dramatist's work had to undergo in the public theatre, and he had no intention of exposing himself to it. He did not know Elliston—or rather, he knew the actor and not the manager. As the play was in press, Elliston got a copy, page by page, secured the approval of the play from George Lamb, a Drury Lane committee man,[34] and had copies made for rehearsal early in April. He did not scruple to cut the play considerably, nor did he waste any time over rehearsal; in fact, casting was not complete until one week before opening.

Marino Faliero went on under an injunction secured by Murray, Byron's publisher, barring a second performance before April 30. Since Elliston had obtained a licence for production from the Lord Chamberlain, he was in a very strong position. In one of his famous handbills (April 30), he virtually rubbed his hands in glee at the sensation he had aroused, while within the strict letter of the law. He gained his point, and *Marino* was staged for five nights after April 30. He lost public support, however. Receipts averaged less than £140 over the seven nights of production, and the critics, to a man opposed in principle to the staging of the play contrary to the author's wishes, had little good to say of the acting of Cooper as Marino, Wallack as Bertuccio, or Mrs. West as Angiolina, wife of the Doge. The general verdict was that Byron's own view was right: the play was not suited to the stage. This was clean contrary to Elliston's boast in his handbill: "Of the fitness of Lord Byron's Tragedy for Representation, as performed at this Theatre on Wednesday last, the effect produced on the Audience of that Evening may sufficiently speak. No impression could have been more forcible: no applause more genuine, or perfect." To this *The Times's* critic responded on May 1: "the piece was received coldly, let the play-bills say what they please." An anonymous pamphlet, *A Letter to R. W. Elliston, Esq.*, summed up the general view: Elliston was not guilty of illegality, but his cleverness in this instance smacked of injustice. Yet if Byron emerges from this incident the moral victor, one is tempted to observe, it can only be because everybody wished he had not written a boring play.

About this time (April 1), Mrs. Elliston died suddenly, and her husband's attention was momentarily diverted from *Marino Faliero.* He was left with nine children, ranging from Eliza, twenty-four, to Mary Ann, not yet four. Undaunted, Elliston drew up the details of the funeral procession, in which the place of every child, as well as every friend and relative, was clearly marked out. Afterwards, Elliston withdrew to Leamington, where he was trying to establish his three eldest sons, William Gore, Henry Twistleton, and Charles Robert, in theatrical management. It was from Leamington that Winston received at Drury Lane his instructions about the costumes[35] for *Marino,* and about the extraordinarily shrewd procedure he was to follow over the licence.[36] The letters were edged in black. One could rely upon Elliston to look to the trappings and the suits of woe.

When the season came to a close, on June 15, legitimate drama had lost ground over the year before: opera and melodrama out-numbered the nights drama had played by two to one. Financially, this fact meant higher receipts, amounting to a total of almost £42,000. At the meeting of Drury Lane proprietors the original debt of £92,000 was declared reduced to £39,800.

The summer season was launched with a commemoration of the victory of Waterloo, involving masquerade dancing and a supper as a special feature. The pit was boarded over for the occasion, making an enormous stage. The entertainments took the form of five bands, acrobats, strong men and other variety artists dear to Elliston's heart, plus the talents of Miss Wilson and Madame Vestris in farces and a concert. Elliston secured the nobility as patrons—he even wrote to Queen Caroline asking for her patronage (in return she would receive vouchers bearing the king's portrait . . .). It was a gala occasion, and it netted Elliston £300 profit.

On the day of the coronation of George IV, July 19, Elliston announced a facsimile representation of the ceremonies; the sudden return from the United States of Edmund Kean postponed it until August 1. The purpose, according to Elliston's playbill, was "as far as the Stage limits will allow, to give a tolerably faithful Delineation of the various Local Points, Dresses, Paraphernalia, and Decorations Which were beheld" on coronation day itself. Traditionally, the major theatres would stage *Henry VIII* or *2 Henry IV,* with the coronation scene given elaboration. Both Garrick and John Rich had so celebrated the coronation of George III, with Rich's production being especially noted for its splendour.[37] Covent Garden, indeed, had staged just such a pageant, tagged on to *Henry VIII,* on June 25. Elliston's was a novel idea. Having been granted permission to have drawings made of all the original costumes, accoutrements, and paraphernalia, he was in a position to offer a mimetic coronation. The text for his show was reality, as described in the three-page account of the coronation in the *Morning Herald* (July 20). The latter found Elliston's attempt not only a "tolerably" faithful reproduction, as he claimed, but "a very faithful one" (August 2). Over a period of ninety minutes, the procession to the Abbey, the ceremonies there, and the banquet afterwards in the Hall (with the ritual of the Champion on horseback), were reproduced with complete accuracy. When Elliston entered as George IV the Drury Lane audience rose to its feet, for he "was dressed in what seemed the exact regal costume, and . . . looked extremely kingly."[38] Some notion of the splendour of the spectacle may be grasped from the toy theatre prints issued by West, which are reproduced.

Whether flanked by stock pieces or accompanied by a new farce, the coronation spectacle projected the season without pause into the new theatrical year. By December 18 it had run for 91 nights. King Robert William was himself again. But not for long. Stretch-

ing the season through the summer had meant lack of planning
for the next year: the company was depleted through the defec-
tion of Wallack, Booth, and Miss Wilson, and although Madame
Vestris and Kean appeared in November they failed to raise the
general quality of performance. A year's absence, indeed, had done
nothing to recharge Kean's appeal. A staleness had crept into Drury
Lane that resulted in the worst season so far in Elliston's management. Nothing signified this staleness so much as the Christmas
show, *Giovanni in Ireland.* Even with Vestris in a new breeches
role, and with Elliston as George IV being installed in St. Patrick's
Cathedral as the first king of Ireland and England, the audience
remained unsympathetic.[39] Receipts fell drastically, to under a
hundred pounds on the fifth night, and yielding to the protest
Elliston withdrew the piece, which he had hoped would prove a
lasting hit.

It was time to make a change of policy. Since becoming monarch
of Drury Lane, Elliston had shown nothing but scorn for minor
theatres, an attitude replete with all sorts of ironies. His practice
of keeping the theatre open during the summer months was a
decidedly reactionary one, which the minor theatres, backed by the
Haymarket, resisted as vociferously as total shock would allow.
Elliston, in response, merely appended to his playbill a refusal "to
enter into a competition of scurrility, which is only fitted for minor
theatres." But early in 1822 the Haymarket and other theatres were
successful in obtaining a decree from the Lord Chamberlain for-
bidding the encroachment being practised by Elliston on the traditional season of the summer theatres.[40] Elliston, accordingly, closed
Drury Lane on June 14. Because of the length of the season,
receipts had been high, totalling £50,000, and the proprietors,
collecting an extra £1100 in rent, pronounced themselves pleased.
But for Elliston the writing was on the wall. Shakespeare was already beginning to spell ruin and Byron bankruptcy.

First of the spectacles which characterize Elliston's management
from 1822 on was the theatre itself. In mid-July plans were submitted to the king, outlining the projected alterations. One month
later the whole theatre was stripped to its outer walls. Elliston's
proud boast, inscribed for posterity on a brass plate sunk into the

foundation stone, was that "in the space of fifty-eight days" the interior was entirely rebuilt.[41] The cost was £20,000,[42] or three times the sum he was obliged under his lease to expend on the theatre.

A comparison of the groundplan of the original (1812) structure with that of the theatre after 1822 (see plates 7, 8), will serve to make clear the changes Elliston made. By cutting six feet from the apron of the stage, and moving the boxes forward ten feet, Elliston changed the shape of the auditorium from three-quarters of a circle to horseshoe.[43] The dress circle, nominally in existence since he had assumed management in 1819, was made permanent by alterations in design (section C); the king's box, newly built and sumptuously decorated, was in this circle ('p'). Many new family boxes (marked 'n') were made. With the removal of the stage doors extra private boxes were added. Thus, though the capacity of the theatre remained much the same, at about 3100, there were less people in the pit and more in the boxes. At the same time, comforts and conveniences for the boxes were vastly improved, marking an obvious attempt to entice back to the theatre the lost upper-middle class.

Besides replacing the stage-doors[44] with boxes, Elliston brought the stage closer to the audience by shortening the apron. At the same time, he made possible a wider use of spectacle by removing many of the obstructing walls backstage and making scenerooms instead (sections 'k' left and right of stage). Communication with the scenerooms ('f') was also facilitated by a new archway twelve feet in diameter. Reynolds tells us that before Elliston's time the space behind the Drury Lane stage was so constricted that competition with Covent Garden on a spectacular level was severely hampered.[45] That was all changed now.

The theatre was ceremoniously reopened on October 12, the Duke of York attending the occasion. Elliston proudly showed his Grace around; the Duke was pleased to order a box fitted up for the first time. Also in attendance on this historic day were members of the committee and the press, and those others on whom the refulgent manager scattered a little of his own assured immortality, Winston, his acting manager; Thomas Dibdin, who now joined him as stage manager (replacing Samuel Russell); Dunn, the treasurer and successor to Ward as secretary; Samuel Beazley, the architect; and Henry Peto, the builder. All of these could be proud of the theatre which Hunt was pleased to call, in *The Examiner*, "the most finished theatre in Europe."

On October 16 Drury Lane was shown to the public. A newcomer, Daniel Terry from the Haymarket, recited the address written by George Colman, which ran through the principal improvements made in the theatre. When Elliston came on as Charles, in the opening play of *A School for Scandal*, the audience loudly registered its appreciation, the whole pit standing up, and the whole theatre astream with hats and handkerchiefs. Deeply moved, Elliston laid his hand on his heart "and made several obeisances in return for their reiterated plaudits." He repaid their enthusiasm by turning in a performance lively as ever.

Besides the theatre itself Elliston had one more stratagem to employ, short of actual pageantry on stage. This was the spectacle of a star-spangled cast. From this season dates the practice of enormous salaries being paid to leading actors; in order to build his theatre far above its rival, Elliston did not scruple to entice Covent Garden's top actors and actresses to Drury Lane at salaries twice or three times what they had been receiving. That this meant riding roughshod over a law, unwritten until 1824, which said that no actor could cross from one major theatre to another without the intermission of a full year, meant nothing to Elliston. Financially, Elliston could afford such high salaries because he hired these stars by the night, at so many nights per season. This was exactly his practice at the Surrey or Olympic, whenever he wanted the attraction of a big name to fill his house, and, of course, his habitual practice at Birmingham.

Chief among those so captured in 1822 were the tragedian Charles Mayne Young, the singer Katherine Stephens and the comedian John Liston, each at the top of his field. Elliston's idea was to play these newcomers off against his own stars, Young against Kean, Stephens against Vestris, Liston against Munden, thus creating a spectacular show of histrionic pyrotechnics. To the newcomers themselves, dissatisfied with the efforts of Charles Kemble to keep expenses down by either cutting back on, or refusing any raise in, their salaries, Elliston appeared as a munificent patron. Writing to Charles Mathews on October 17 Young looked on Elliston's move as an abandonment of "the cheap and nasty System" for "the Liberal one"; Covent Garden, he considered, was now foolishly trying the cheap and nasty system of scrimping which had failed with Elliston. The result was "Drury Lane is playing to enormous Houses and Covent Garden to empty Benches."[46]

This policy, maintained through 1825, was a huge success in its first year. In particular, audiences were thrilled by the Young-Kean combination. It took all of Elliston's charm to coax Kean into the duel, for Kean was almost pathologically sensitive to his dwindling reputation, and would brook no rival. Young, however, was willing to begin with Iago to Kean's Othello, on November 27, and thus accommodated, Kean could not back out. Following *Othello,* the pair appeared together in *Venice Preserved* on the 29th, *Othello* again on December 2, *Cymbeline* on January 22, 24, 29, and *Othello* twice more before the end of the month. These performances excited a lively interest, and drew receipts of twice what Kean on his own had been drawing. In other respects, Elliston's policy paid off also. Liston and Miss Stephens brought with them their own roles, adding a freshness and variety to the repertory, while a certain amount of "cross-grafting," as with Liston's playing Gobbo to Kean's Shylock or Elliston's playing Count Almaviva to Liston's Figaro in *The Marriage of Figaro,* had a healthy galvanic effect on both audience interest and receipts.

Inherent in all of this reliance on a star-spangled company was an obvious bit of nose-thumbing at Covent Garden. This is not to say that Drury Lane had not been in rivalry with Covent Garden ever since Elliston assumed management. Production for production, literally, the two had contested in 1819, with Macready's Richard III and Coriolanus vying with Kean's,[47] Elliston's latest French melodrama vying with Harris' latest French melodrama, etc. On the whole, this sort of rivalry was harmless before 1822. With the elevation of Charles Kemble, whom many considered a better comedian, to the management of Covent Garden, Elliston began a determined and perhaps unscrupulous campaign to make his theatre supreme. Eventually, Kemble made a bid to limit the effects of Elliston's policy by persuading him to sign an agreement in July 1824, according to which salaries and extent of seasons were to be controlled, but it was by this time rather too late to arrest the effects of cut-throat competition.

When the theatre closed on June 30, Elliston thanked his audience for their support, and explained his policy of *laissez-faire.*

Although receipts had been good, totalling over £60,000, Elliston had not all that much to feel smug about. He was himself doing little work, beyond churning out his old roles in *Wild Oats, The Dramatist, A Cure for the Heartache,* etc. There was, indeed, something superficial about his policy.

It soon was revealed to be so. Young returned to Covent Garden in 1823, and when Macready crossed over in his place Kean refused to do battle. The result was that for two years the greatest trage-dians of the age came and went at Drury Lane, like estranged lovers, at different times. Thus divided, their appeal was minimal, though their cost was very great. This practice spread to the other stars, who all tended to come and go like provincial visitors, on limited engagements, going through their standard roles mechani-cally, without ever a thought of teamwork or a fresh approach. Indeed, Elliston himself gave bad example in this regard; he too came and went periodically, and left the day-to-day business to Winston, Dibdin, and the other managers who succeeded Dibdin after 1823. A star-studded cast represents potential only; Elliston failed entirely, after 1823, to realise that potential.

But there was one area he did not neglect, which paid him ample return. Drury Lane had been notoriously behind Covent Garden in the area of spectacular pantomimes; with his new stage area, new scenic artists with new ideas, and new managers experienced in spectacles, Elliston made up the difference in a short time and went on to make Drury Lane renowned at least for its scenic wizardry.

The turning point was the failure of a pantomime at Christmas 1822. Thomas Dibdin's *Gog and Magog* was so bad that it had to be withdrawn immediately and a new pantomime put in its place. The importance of *Harlequin and the Golden Axe* is that Clarkson Stanfield, then only twenty-five, painted five of the fourteen scenes.[48] At the end of January 1823 he was joined by David Roberts, aged twenty-seven. These two young artists led Drury Lane to new heights of scenic beauty. Elliston also captured William Barrymore, whose skill in pantomime contrivance had been proved at Covent Garden.[49] During the summer of 1823 Elliston employed Stanfield and Roberts, assisting Marinari, to freshen up the scenery for a big splash in the autumn.

To replace Dibdin, Elliston engaged two men as assistant mana-gers. Frederick Reynolds was to be Elliston's personal agent and adviser. A playwright of considerable reputation, Reynolds also had experience, while associated with Covent Garden, as a contriver of pantomimes: it was in this latter capacity he was to prove most helpful to Elliston. Alfred Bunn, who had succeeded Elliston as manager of Birmingham Theatre Royal, had no clear office. Winston, rueful at the introduction of the two chiefs into his domain, says that Bunn spent most of his time sleeping on Elliston's sofa.[50] But Bunn, too, had that flair for spectacular production which Elliston was now determined to promote; and he did not hesitate to add his advice to that of Reynolds.

Reynolds certainly knew the theatre. A new melodrama by Moncrieff was to coincide with Macready's debut at Drury Lane in October 1823. This melodrama was to involve horses and a cataract; as September began, Reynolds fussed Elliston (on tour in the provinces) with the dread tidings that Moncrieff had produced nothing, and that neither horses nor a cataract had as yet been fixed upon. "Nothing but a Horse piece can support Macready," he warns Elliston.[51] His general fussiness about getting "*material*" ready well in advance was useful, since spectacles took a long time to prepare. Elliston, on reaching Birmingham, engaged Davis' troupe of horses from Bunn, was sent the scene plot of the melodrama from London, and had the horses practise at Birmingham.

The Cataract of the Ganges did not accompany Macready's debut on October 13. It did not in fact appear for a further two weeks, when it accompanied a revival of *Fazio*. It was made instantly welcome. The season had opened on October 1 with Elliston and a first-rate cast in *The Rivals,* only to be told by the critics to shelve the play, "for it is un-rivalled in dulness, and in its lack of incidents and of comic situations." Macready in *Virginius* was only slightly more popular. But with the advent of *The Cataract* receipts shot up over £400, and thereafter, no matter what the show, it pushed receipts way up: even Kean's threadbare *Richard III,* which everybody must now have known by heart, drew £370 with the aid of *The Cataract,* on December 15.

The Cataract provides a good example of the direction in which drama was beginning to move. In two acts, it told a simple story of love obstructed by a villain who seeks to tear a daughter away from her loving father. All the emphasis is on this thoroughly domestic feeling. Or nearly all. As everybody knows, *The Cataract* has one

of the best *deus ex machina* finales since *Medea*. An exit on horseback up a cataract, with fire raging all around, is a tough one to
beat. The critics, who at this time divided their time between
lugubrious prognostications of the death of the drama and castiga-
tion of what they could only label meretriciousness, hooted at the
"vileness of the plot and dialogue" of *The Cataract*,[52] but could not
gainsay the brilliance of the setting. The *London Magazine*, indeed, did not think much of the cataract itself: "It was something
like the pouring of a good tea-pot, only flatter; it was, in truth,
no broader than a yard of sixpenny ribband. . . . We ourselves could
have walked up the fall in pumps, and not have wetted the upper
leathers."[53] But most reviews gave full credit to the spectacular
aspect, on which Elliston had spared no expense. He relied to a
considerable degree on Clarkson Stanfield for the style, both of
architecture and of costume, because Stanfield had travelled in
Hindustan. The big scene in act one was set in a Grand Hindu
Temple, with a splendid bridal procession, featuring a magnificent
car drawn by six horses, plus two military bands, countless soldiers
with banners, slaves, dancing girls, etc. This was matched by the
finale, which combined the cataract with a full-scale pitched
military battle. Besides the scenic artists, some credit must also go
to James Wallack, who directed the show as well as playing the
lead. In the playbills, Elliston practically burst a bloodvessel trying
to do justice both to the merits of the piece and to posterity by
recording public enthusiasm. The *Morning Chronicle* probably
put the matter most accurately by prophesying (October 28) that if
The Cataract succeeded it was adieu to Shakespeare, "and welcome
noise, and nonsense, and all the tinsel and trumpery, with their
splendid delusions, to gratify the grown children of the metropolis."

Succeeding months held productions in which Macready, Elliston, and Kean individually appeared, but it was not until the
Christmas pantomime arrived that a sequel to *The Cataract* (which
flowed until December 22) was found. *Harlequin and the Flying
Chest*, written by Frederick Reynolds, is noteworthy as incorporating diorama for the first time on the English stage. Dioramas were
huge moving pictures in which light and shadow came and went
realistically, with cloud effects, storm effects and the like. The
principle was the same as De Loutherbourg's *eidophusikon*, but on

a much larger scale. Invented in Paris in 1822, diorama was brought to England the following year by A. C. Pugin, who opened a new building in Regent's Park on October 6.[54] Here two large paintings, seventy-two feet by forty-two feet, were displayed before spectators who were slowly revolved in the auditorium to experience the illusion of a moving picture. When transferred to the theatre, of course, the pictures rather than the auditorium moved. For the Drury Lane pantomime the diorama, by Clarkson Stanfield, comprised several scenes in succession, all painted on a transparent backcloth some two hundred and seventy-two feet in length,[55] which was drawn across the stage to give the illusion of movement. The scenes, in illustration of the Plymouth Breakwater, included a Vessel in Distress off the Mew Stone, with the Effects of a Storm. Stanfield's paintings were done from drawings made on the spot by W. S. Reynolds—this was to become a well-worn cliché in descriptions of scenery as the nineteenth century wore on. As with the dioramas at Regent's Park, people were urged to look upon the pictures as altogether authentic, as if that were their *raison d'etre.*

Stanfield's work won immediate admiration. At first, however, the glare of lights hampered the display. Since non-theatrical dioramas relied on natural light it took a little time to adjust the technique to gas lighting. But to a public hungry for show, the diorama was a godsend. Long after the pantomime itself had palled, Stanfield's illustrations continued to appeal, and were shown, on their own.

At Easter Moncrieff came up trumps again with a new melodrama, called *Zoroaster.* As he himself pointed out in the Advertisement, the play had to be chopped and cut to "suit the capabilities of carpenters and scene-shifters."[56] It had for hero a sort of Regency Peer Gynt, Eastern style, whose adventures provided Stanfield and Roberts with great scope for illustration. A diorama was once again used, this time a massive representation, billed as four hundred and eight-two feet in length, of Egyptian and other wonders. It was accompanied by "appropriate national, vocal, and instrumental music." The popularity and critical success of *Zoroaster* confirmed what recent productions had all implied: a romantic plot to hang a series of paintings on, with music and effects, was the way to interest the public. A musical version of *The Merry Wives of Windsor*[57] had been approved since February, but when Macready appeared in brave revivals of *Measure for Measure* and *The Winter's Tale* the response was ominous. "All must turn," said *The Times* of May 3 in condemnation of *Measure for Measure,* "with disgust from the circumstances out of which the action arises."

As if to show its appreciation of the direction in which Elliston was taking the theatre, the audience turned out for his benefit night, June 7, to make it the best night of the season, topping six hundred pounds in receipts. Though Elliston let the season drag out, as in former times, to July 26, which overextended his welcome somewhat, the season on the whole was a resounding success, resulting in receipts of over £61,115. Even with expenditures standing at over £45,000, this was a more than healthy turnover.

The formula found to be so successful in 1823–4 was, of course, used again the following season. The first spectacular, however, on October 28, got the season off on the wrong foot. The fact that this foot was equine was not quite enough. Elliston engaged the equestrian Ducrow and his troupe for a piece by George Croly called *The Enchanted Courser.* The play was wretched, even as melodrama, and the spectacular side was botched and under-rehearsed. It was impish of Elliston, who had so gleefully attacked Drury Lane in 1818 for allowing horses on stage, to let Ducrow's whole stud gallop all over the legitimate drama now. He was not let get away with it. "ASTLEY's gone mad," was the unenviable reputation he gained for his theatre during the first month of the 1824–5 season.[58] Later on in the year Elliston went so far as to place Kean on horseback, in a new tragedy by Soane, *Masaniello*: it was hissed off the stage.

More acceptable to the Drury audience was Soane's adaptation of Von Weber's opera, *Der Freischütz,* first staged on November 10.[59] This was the fifth adaptation London had so far seen, and it proved to be the most successful of all. A good deal of the success is attributable to the spectacular staging Elliston gave to the opera, especially to the incantation scene, considered the last word in the horrific. The production ran right through the season, and was commanded by the king on May 2. It became, indeed, the smash-hit opera of the decade.

It was probably the popularity of the diabolism of *Der Freischütz* that prompted Elliston to follow up with *Faustus.* This marked the first production of Goethe's play on the English stage. George Soane was again responsible for the adaptation. Educated at Cambridge, Soane (son of the well-known architect) had a good knowledge of German, and in 1820 was the first to give the English public some idea of Goethe's *Faust*.[60] In 1822 he set about a full translation, but managed only a fragment—of which Goethe approved.[61] The 1825 version, in three acts, was a far cry from a literal translation: it was closer to a corruption to suit the taste of the time.

Two prompt copies of Soane's text are in the Beinecke Library of Yale University, from which a full reconstruction is possible.[62] Since the present writer has already provided this reconstruction, in the article referred to, it would be superfluous to attempt it here. The Prologue, indeed, gives an adequate notion of what to expect:

> The author this evening has ventured once more
> Superstitions wild reign on the stage to restore
> A childish attempt perhaps—yet, let him say
> He intrudes not upon you a regular play
> 'Tis a holiday season, so he timidly stops
> At the Drama's high Claims and to Opera Drops
> Machinery, Scenery, music and song
> And all that to Melodrame Muses belong
> He culls to contribute their dazzling aid
> And by charming your senses, your judgements evade . . .[63]

The text was of minimal importance; everything hinged on production techniques.

Faustus first played on May 16, 1825, with James Wallack in the lead, Daniel Terry as Mephistopheles, Katherine Stephens as Adine (Soane's Gretchen), and John P. Harley as Wagner. The music, with an overture from Weber, was by the Drury Lane composers Bishop, Horn, and Thomas Cooke.[64] The scenery was by Stanfield (six scenes), Roberts (five scenes), and Marinari (five scenes). The critics were severe on the adaptation itself, although *The Examiner* considered that in avoiding Goethe as much as possible Soane was wise, in that *Faust* could not be staged, "so subtle and metaphysical indeed is it in its essence." The panto-mimical structure of the play was noted, with Mephistopheles as the magician, Faustus and Adine as Harlequin and Columbine, etc.[65] Taking it on this level no praise could be found high enough for the scenery and effects. Crabb Robinson, an excellent guide to the London theatre of the 1820's, could recollect no piece "of equal splendour and beauty—The scenery sweetly painted and the machinery better contrived than in any pantomime."[66] An important element in the execution of the effects was the skilful use of the vampire trap, facilitating the sudden appearances and disappearances of Mephistopheles. The *a vista* scene-changes were also commented on for their effectiveness.

Faustus played twenty-four nights before the end of the season, exceeding in popularity another new play, *William Tell*, in which Macready was starring. *Faustus* marks the culmination of the move towards spectacle which began with the reconstructed theatre of 1822. Elliston had found a formula. Foolishly, however, he pressed his luck, in an attempt to knock Covent Garden for six. For several years he had been in close contact with the French theatre, both he and Winston making several trips to Paris during the 1820's to keep a close watch on the latest developments. Now he decided to stage his homage to the French *mise en scène*, a sort of Giovanni-in-Paris incorporating the coronation of Charles X. James Robinson Planché was known to be working on a similar production for Covent Garden, with all the meticulous detail in which Planché prided himself. On July 5 Elliston got there first, by five days, slyly entitling his piece *Five Minutes Too Late*. The story-frame was quite pantomimical, and the peregrinatory structure offered Stanfield the opportunity of displaying a diorama of the crossing from Brighton to Dieppe, and the scenic beauties of the Seine. The playbill made much of the fact that Stanfield had spent several weeks on the Continent, "collecting appropriate Views." The coronation was staged with great detail of costume and setting, and used the novel effect of a platform going all around the auditorium, so that the great procession passed over the heads of the people in the pit.[67] After the Covent Garden version appeared, Elliston's playbill grew to two pages, placing side by side details of the actual and the simulated coronations, with all the appropriate sources. The town remained strangely indifferent. While the critics expressed admiration for the spectacle, they were out of sympathy with the subject, than which *John Bull* could not imagine anything in worse taste. Politically, this coronation apparently held no interest. First night receipts were only £150; within ten days, in spite of all that publicity could do, receipts were less than one third of this figure.

Elliston had over-reached himself. With the greatest reluctance he was forced to close Drury Lane on July 21.

Though receipts for the season were the best to date, totalling almost £67,000, expenses were abnormally high at £56,000. Here it has to be conceded that Elliston's judgement had become suspect, and his general behaviour such that he was in grave trouble with the proprietors.

Winston's view of the situation, as described in his Diary, is that a life of debauchery brought upon Elliston an inevitable downfall. Winston also recognized other factors besides the moral one in Elliston's failure, e.g., his involvement in the management of other theatres, the interference of the Drury Lane committee in management, etc. Winston's cataloguing of Elliston's sins is indeed shocking, as much for the coldness of the diarist as for the evidence of Elliston's weakness, but it is necessary to place it in the context of Elliston's whole career. As early as 1811, Warner Phipps, one of Elliston's closest friends, warned him: "You are publicly—you are universally known as intemperate. . . . You have not a moment to lose—your respectability is expiring—your energies declining—your estate wasting—and your very hopes are themselves becoming hopeless."[68] It did no good. Elliston continued to enjoy the good life. Yet the effects of this on his career were not great, prior to around the year 1823–4; perhaps it could be said that he did not realize his full potential as an actor, but it could not be said that he was anything like incompetent before 1824. He now displayed mental lapses and hallucinations, from which he recovered with extraordinary rapidity, giving him a reputation for eccentricity rather than for alcoholism. He began to show an uncontrollable tendency to kick whosoever caused him annoyance, actor, playwright, or member of the public. Such incidents landed him in the lawcourts with notorious frequency. As did Kean about this same time, Elliston got a very bad press, something that probably embarrassed the strait-laced Winston.

The relationship of Elliston's debauchery to his managerial affairs is a complex one. All through his career, he thrived on multiple management; as Raymond put it, "excitement was his element." In itself, the fact that he was manager of several provincial theatres while lessee of Drury Lane is of less damaging import than it might be with a different personality. But he does seem to have given rather too much time to Leamington. He took out an eighteen-year lease in December 1819 on considerable property in Leamington—including a library, assembly rooms, lodging houses, and a theatre. The idea seems to have been to provide security for his sons, who were to have managed the business, but in fact Elliston became more and more involved in running the place himself. Each autumn found him working in Leamington instead of planning the Drury Lane repertory. This might have been all right had he established a chain of command by which to delegate authority at Drury Lane. He never did this. He relied heavily on Winston in settling the repertory and hiring staff, but Winston always showed a lack of initiative that really made Elliston's own presence essential. Moreover, packing the theatre with assistant managers, such as Alfred Bunn, Frederick Reynolds, etc., was of no use since at the same time Elliston did not organize them into a clearly defined structure. When he himself was weakest, the plenitude of assistants served only to increase the impression of administrative chaos. And his use of the Drury Lane treasury to assist his other theatrical concerns led inevitably, in conjunction with the image of wastrel which he carelessly projected, to the charge of mismanagement.

The year 1824-5 was the critical one in Elliston's management of Drury Lane. Already the sub-committee was getting anxious; Calcraft, the Chairman, had gone so far as to chastise Elliston publicly in May 1824, and to threaten his removal as lessee. Three days before the opening of the new season, Winston complained, Elliston had still not cast any of the plays, and was "avoiding all Business, except writing long unnecessary letters."[69] When the theatre opened, on October 23, Elliston was on hand "in a muddled state," stayed for the main production, *The Marriage of Figaro,* and was not seen again for days. As the season wore on he grew unsteadily worse. He acted only twelve times, ten of these before Christmas. This was unusual, because Elliston, in spite of his other interests, acted an average of sixty nights a year at Drury Lane from 1819 to 1824, and had appeared sixty-four times during 1823-24, if the playbills are to be believed. He also borrowed large sums from the treasury during the year. Poole, the playwright, successfully brought the law on him for kicking him downstairs. One more paternity case was lodged against Elliston. The season, "successful but unprofitable," in Winston's words, was brought to an end only when the treasurer, Dunn, insisted that a bank loan was necessary to pay the salaries. Elliston, enthusiastically insistent that the costly *Five Minutes Too Late* should run on, although the theatre was losing two hundred pounds a night, was forced to give in.

In an attempt to recapture his lost popularity, and no doubt to put himself in funds again, Elliston now determined to go to the United States. His plan was to withdraw his eldest son, William Gore, from Cambridge and place him in charge of Drury Lane. (In 1822, at the age of twenty-four, William Gore had given up an attempt to manage the Leamington theatre, and instead had gone up to the University.) Calcraft, racking his brains for a legal method of getting rid of Elliston, refused permission for the trip to America. He knew he could not oust Elliston before November, since the deposit for the next year's rent had, by the grace of Dunn and Winston, been paid; but he was unwilling to let him off indefinitely.[70] At the Annual General Meeting, as was customary, a façade was presented. Calcraft underlined the good fortune of Drury Lane in having Elliston as manager. His colleague, George Robins, went so far as to recommend that Elliston be presented with a piece of plate. Some of his poppycock must have been aimed at placating, if not at reclaiming, Elliston, who played along but asked that the presentation be deferred a year until building expenses (for a colonnade) were defrayed, "and then the plate will be heavier."[71]

But then disaster struck Elliston. On August 5, 1825 Winston called at Stratford Place and found "Mr E in a state of imbecility melancholy to look at & shocking to contemplate—the curse of— I found a man who a few weeks ago was in health vigour [*sic*] & dwindled at 51 into a decrepid old man, in my opinion his existance will shortly terminate, or he will live in a state of Idiotism—."[72] He had suffered what seems to have been a minor stroke in 1818, but now the damage was far more severe. In spite of Winston's pessimism, however, Elliston appeared at Drury Lane on August 10. He was anxious to forestall any move by the proprietors to squeeze him out. William Gore arrived two days later, and Elliston made him his legal representative, his doctor testifying that Elliston had lost use of his hands, "but that he is in a perfectly sound state of mind;

and of course competent to transact any business requiring the faculty of reason."[73]

This move caught Calcraft and the sub-committee by surprise. Elliston, apparently, was legally entitled to make his son his deputy. The only hope of the sub-committee now, in their determination to break Elliston's lease, was to have him declared bankrupt, when Elliston, his executors and administrators would, according to a clause in the lease, "be barred & foreclosed from all relief or remedy in Law or Equity." The opportunity for this move, however, would not arise until November when further rent-payments were due. Meantime, accompanied by William Gore, Elliston went down to Ramsgate, on August 13, to recuperate, and to come up with some plan to outwit the sub-committee.

With William Gore as amanuensis, he communicated daily with Winston, urging him over theatrical affairs as in days of old. He got little satisfaction. Making Wallack stage-manager did not please Winston, and he, who the year before had complained bitterly about Elliston's having no details settled by October, now seemed reluctant himself to get matters moving for an early start in September. He complained, in his records, that the theatre was due to open "as backward as heretofore." This cannot have been Elliston's fault, though this impression was one the sub-committee held on to all year.[74] The obvious attraction to start off the season was *Faustus,* but both Terry and Miss Stephens had left him, and it was some time before old Samuel Russell and newcomer Miss Graddon were settled in the parts of Mephistopheles and Adine. Macready was not available; Kean had gone to the United States again; Eliza Vestris had gone to Covent Garden, whither Cooper had defected already; Munden had retired. The only hope was an impressive spectacle before Christmas. Elliston urged the production of *Aladdin,* a new opera by Soane for which he wanted Bishop to do the music, Stanfield and Roberts the scenery. He supplied hints himself for the *mise en scène,* along the lines of *Faustus.* But neither Soane nor Bishop would consent to an early production, and on September 14 Elliston ceased to press the matter.

The result was that when Drury opened on September 24 with *Faustus* there was little hope of a new money-spinner before mid-season. William Gore, in Elliston's place as manager, knew nothing of the business, according to Winston, "but, rather than be found out, did nothing."[75] There were plenty of other chiefs, how-ever. Dunn, Wallack, Obi Smith and James Kenney all had some administrative duties, besides Winston himself, who now seems to have been relegated to director of machinery. Stock comedies were staged, with Wallack in the lead, taking over Elliston's old roles. On October 10 Sheridan's *Pizarro* was revived with an attempt at spec-tacle; it was accompanied by a revival of Dibdin's *Valentine and Orson,* with new scenery by Stanfield and Roberts. On October 20, *Love for Love* was revived, with Wallack as Valentine; two days later Cibber's *She Would and She Would Not* was revived. London yawned in complete boredom. Receipts were poor.

Elliston watched anxiously from the sidelines of Ramsgate, urging retrenchment of expenses, hoping for a new opera, wishing Fanny Kelly would agree to play Giovanni, pressing commence-ment of work on the Christmas pantomime by mid-October, watch-ing Covent Garden for signs of its streaking ahead, as it had done the year before. On October 24, although still without the use of his hands, Elliston returned to London to face the music. Hopes of a brilliant season had faded.

On November 10 Calcraft called a special meeting of the sub-committee to discuss Elliston's affairs. It was announced that Ellis-ton had surrendered Stratford Place and had agreed to take lodg-ings in Temple Place, St. George's Fields: in short, he was now living within the Rules. It was decided to keep Drury Lane open, closely superintended by Calcraft and Robins, who fancied them-selves as managers. The real intentions of the sub-committee remain obscure. On November 16 Robins addressed Elliston's creditors and persuaded them to sign a licence giving Elliston six years to clear his debts, which amounted to twenty thousand pounds, from annual profits at Drury Lane.[76] This may have implied a proba-tionary period, yet when this season ended unprofitably Calcraft cancelled Elliston's lease forthwith.

In the meantime, Elliston spent a year of great anxiety, which was not helped by the simplistic notions on management held by his overseers. As soon as the box-office showed signs of recovery, after Christmas, Robins lectured Elliston on the need for sustained vigilance. "Can you for an instant suppose," replied Elliston, with a return of his old spirit, "that I am so utterly unfit for my station as to relent in my endeavours in consequence of present success? Have

I not had sufficient experience of John Bull's caprice to keep me constantly on the alert? or can I forget (altho you, my fine fellow do) that I have heretofore had the united names—of Miss Stephens, Madame Vestris Mr Liston, Mr Braham, M^rDowton & Mr Harley, —& *all would not do*? What! as Falstaff says—would you make a Younker of me? no, no, I am (I confess the fact) too old in these matters."[77] On January 28 a new ballad opera was produced, which ran seventeen nights and then went into repertory with *Faustus* to take the gloomy look off the box office. It was called *Malvina,* and in his Advertisement to the printed text the author, George Macfarren, attributed much of its success to the advice and corrections of Elliston. The committee relented and voted Elliston three thousand pounds to cover arrears of rent. He sold the Olympic Theatre for £5103, much less that it was worth.[78]

But the fortunes of theatre management are poised on a knife edge. The operas which Elliston hoped would turn the tide in his favour began to fail one after another, Kenney's *Benyowsky,* a version of *Oberon,* and finally *Aladdin,* with Kitty Stephens persuaded into a breeches role. Macready and the notorious Maria Foote scarcely made any difference. Elliston himself made a return to the stage, as Rover, on April 25, to no avail. The public was against him.

He had one more card to play. As the above quotation shows, he had been studying the part of Falstaff, for a production of *1 Henry IV* in mid-May. It was a role to which he was every way suited, and ought to have been one of the triumphs of his career. The final rehearsal, according to Macready, who played Hotspur, was such a triumph: Elliston "made the nearest approach to the joyous humour and unctuous roguery of the character that I had ever witnessed."[79] On the night, although the critics were impressed, the town at large stayed away. Receipts were a disappointing £166. The Drury Lane committee, incredible though it seem, took this opportunity to demand their pound of flesh: Elliston was ordered to pay his arrears or sacrifice his lease. On May 15 he was to repeat Falstaff. In the greenroom, before going on, he complained of feeling ill, and smelled strongly of ether. On stage he began well, but as the evening wore on, in Macready's words, he "gave signs of extreme weakness, was frequently inaudible, and several times voices from the front called to him to 'speak up.' There was not on this occasion even the semblance of an effort at exertion, and in the fifth act he remained silent for some little time, then, in trying to reach the side-scene, reeled round and fell prostrate before the foot-lights." The audience was unsure whether or not this was a new reading, of which Elliston's interpretation was replete. Wallack, as Hal, adlibbed to cover up,[80] but in this nightmare situation Elliston was unable to reply, and had to be carried off. The audience let him know what they thought of him. As Thomas Hood put it in *The Atlas* (May 21), "The Whitsuntide rabble, that had perhaps quaked before thee at the Surrey—holyday butchers, that had scrambled down from thy benches at thy bidding—men that had bowed to thy Olympic dignity—beheld thee prostrate! They hooted and hissed thee to scorn." The committee, waiting virtually in the wings, declared the lease cancelled, and advertised Drury Lane to be let.

Since Elliston was unable to take a benefit performance himself, William Gore was authorized to hold one on his behalf. On June 22, accordingly, the combined companies of Covent Garden and Drury Lane acted in as full a bill as London had ever known, in a farewell tribute to the Great Lessee. Samuel Russell appeared as Jerry Sneak, as he so often had to Elliston's Major Sturgeon at the Surrey; Charles Kemble appeared in *Charles the Second,* reminiscent of Elliston's Olympic days; Braham, Sinclair, Miss Stephens, Miss Graddon, etc., sang in concert; Monsieur Charles Vestris and Mme. Pauline Rossignol of Vauxhall Gardens gave a *pas de deux;* and the evening concluded with a comic opera, *The Wager,* starring Russell and Wallack. The critics pointedly ignored the event. On June 24 the theatre was declared leased to Thomas Bish, M.P., for fourteen years at an annual rent some twelve hundred pounds higher than that paid by Elliston.[81]

At the Annual General Meeting on July 3, held in the saloon of Drury Lane theatre, the details of Elliston's default were officially made public. The actual loss of the season was (wrongly) given as three thousand pounds;[82] added to Elliston's arrears, this meant a debt of £5,700. An inventory of the scenery, wardrobe, etc., showed an increase in value over that in 1819, though the exact amount could not be stated. Calcraft, as chairman, moved that in view of the increased rent to be paid by the new lessee, for which Elliston must be given credit, part of this increase should be paid annually to his creditors, for the remaining duration of his original lease. Deep sympathy was expressed, to loud cries of stout-hearted agreement, with Elliston's unhappy lot.

Elliston then stood forward and made his *apologia*.[83] He spoke of the low state of Drury Lane upon his assuming management, and of the efforts he had made to satisfy public taste. He justified his notorious expenditure, invoking the scenic artistry of Stanfield, Roberts, and Marinari. Proper economy, not parsimony, was the key to theatre management. He criticized the Press for lack of understanding and support, and likewise criticized the poets of the age for failing to keep the theatre supplied with good plays. He deplored the fact that the creditors' wish that he continue as lessee had not been honoured, just as he valued the support of his own men, Winston and Dunn in particular. Perhaps he should yet find in America the independence and patronage England had denied him.

All that remained was to undergo the indignity of bankruptcy. At the end of November, his effects were sold at Stratford Place, and on December 10 Elliston was declared bankrupt. Final examination before the Commissioners took place on March 2, 1827, when Calcraft proved a debt of £5670–16s–8d due to the proprietors of Drury Lane. It was established that on assuming management of Drury Lane Elliston had property amounting to twenty thousand pounds, and that he had sunk between thirty and forty thousand extra into alterations, i.e., independent of current expenditure.[84] His debts were declared to total forty thousand pounds, his available property fifteen thousand. He was sworn, signed the examination, and the assignees, having returned to him his watch, his gold seals, and his rings, said that they were perfectly satisfied. It was all over. Winston had a word or two to add in his Diary. "Thus," he said, "a very clever man has fallen through ambition and the love of drink, for I do not think after the repeated and very serious trials he has experienced (which have not prevented his return to his old habits) that anything can reclaim [him]."[85] Written off even by those closest him, Elliston would seem to have reached the end of the line. It is one of the most cheering pieces of real-life improbability that the man bounced back after this collapse and finished his career in something akin to glory.

SIX

"Last Retreat and Recess"

'What thall it be, Thquire, while you wait? Thall it be
Therry? Give it a name, Thquire!' said Mr Sleary,
with hospitable ease.

Dickens, *Hard Times*

IT IS DOUBTFUL if Elliston had any serious plans for a trip to the
United States. No details of an engagement have come to light, and,
so far as is known, he had no connections there. Of course, he
would have been welcomed in that most hospitable city, New York,
and, indeed, he had admirers and imitators elsewhere in America.
Yet the memory of Kean's inauspicious visits were still green enough
to be an obvious deterrent to one touched so nearly with the breath
of scandal. The question is, perhaps, academic, since Elliston was to
be confined for some time to come to the precincts of St. George's
Fields. But it may be stated that America, if it was ever a real
prospect, faded on the horizon of Ellistonian dreams as the year
1827 swung round, and never loomed up again.

Instead, Elliston became interested almost immediately in a new
theatre. After the Royalty burned down, in April 1826, some residents of East London approached Elliston and asked him to head a
scheme for building a new theatre, using the Royalty licence.
Elliston flung himself wholeheartedly into the venture. The new
theatre should be built by public subscription, should be designed
by his son, Charles Robert, who was something of an architect, and
should be called the Royal Brunswick.[1] The better to ensure its
success, Elliston should be manager. A site was obtained, in Cham-
ber Street, and it was hoped the new theatre would be ready for
opening by October 1827.

Early in 1827 a hitch developed, when it was suspected that the subscribers would have unlimited liability. The matter was referred to legal authorities, at which point Elliston offered to be lessee at £1200 *p.a.*[2] When it became clear that the subscribers would indeed be liable both during the building and afterwards, Elliston was still willing to go ahead provided Maurice, who held the site of the old Royalty, was willing to take the risk. Maurice was not. Yet, while the question was pending, he went behind Elliston's back and began rebuilding on the old site.[3] This concluded Elliston's direct involvement with the Royal Brunswick.

On May 18, 1827, an advertisement appeared in the *Morning Post* announcing that the Surrey theatre was to be let once again. It seems that Elliston could not resist such advertisements. He applied as lessee, offering £1300 *p.a.* rent. Since he was still within the Rules, until June 1828, he agreed to take the theatre in the name of Charles Robert, his third eldest son. This arrangement was supposed to continue only until Elliston got his certificate of release, but it was, in fact, never changed. Elliston also agreed to take the scenery, costume, and properties then in the theatre, in appreciation of which the proprietor, Temples West, knocked three hundred pounds off the rent.[4]

There was just time to make the inventories,[5] from May 28 to 31, and hastily to scramble together a company for the opening on Whit Monday, June 4. Characteristically, Elliston kicked off with a theatrical commentary on his own affairs, called *Sink or Swim*. When he came on to speak the prologue to *Three and the Deuce*, appearing before a Surrey audience for the first time in twelve years, he was received, according to the *Lady's Magazine*, "with as enthusiastic applause as perhaps ever marked the entrance of any performer." He had lost none of his old comic powers. The *New Monthly Magazine* (July 1827) praised "the art by which one face is made to serve three persons, all finely individualized by characteristic traits only. How sturdily pragmatical is he as the collegian! How vacant as the fool! How light and airy as the Frenchman, dancing with all the spirit of eighteen, and singing with as much glee and effect as if he had the best voice in the world!" After the third piece, *The Mill of the Lake,* a melodrama in four acts, Elliston reappeared to thank his audience and make the accustomed address.

Although it was back to square one, in a sense, this period of Elliston's career is not without interest. The critics expressed the hope that he might raise the standards of the minor theatres; of his financial success there could be no doubt "if he pursues the same spirited course which was found so beneficial to the treasury of the Olympic."[6] Matters had changed considerably since Elliston took over the Surrey in 1809. The difficulties to be overcome now were less the restrictions of the monopoly laws than those trials all theatrical flesh is heir to.

Elliston took his new theatre quite seriously, and acted there with greater frequency than he had previously at any such theatre. From June to December 1827 he acted as often as six nights a week, at times three roles nightly, going through thirteen of his comic roles, including his Olympic success, Rochester, and four Shakespearean parts, Hamlet, Othello, Mercutio, and Falstaff. He took the precaution of advertising such performances as for 'burlettas founded upon' the originals, but there is no reason to think this meant anything but a shortening to three acts, and the addition of music. That he should still be playing Hamlet and Othello is no doubt surprising, but indicative of his intention of winning the gallery to acceptance of a broad repertorial basis. "His tragic performances are not his best," admitted the *New Monthly* in August, "but they are far better than could be expected from his long devotion to pleasantry and whim; and, if deficient in intensity of passion, have no want of rapidity and life." But his merits are best represented at this time by his incomparable Falstaff.

He first appeared as Falstaff at the Surrey on June 11, in an adaptation of *1 Henry IV* called *The Battle of Shrewsbury*. Clearly, he gave of his best, aware that certain critics, sympathetic to his situation, would be inclined to judge his theatre by his own endeavours. The *New Monthly,* in July, considered that he played Falstaff "with all the discrimination which we observed at Drury-Lane, and with even more richness and ease." The *Weekly Dramatic Register* (June 16) saw the skill that went into the performance:

The smaller size of the Theatre enables us to perceive all the minute and elaborate beauties of his acting; the smile trickles from the mouth and eye perceptibly, however unforced and unexaggerated; the chuckle of laughter is enjoyed from its commencement to its climax. . . . We are delivered from those conventional signs, which the larger theatres force upon the actor. . . . The voice too may be heard in its own key, and avail itself of the richness and depth of the lower tones without the forced expedient of an artificial loudness.

Elliston now, apparently, produced the performance which Macready found so impressive in rehearsal at Drury Lane. "The reading was not only true," went on the *Dramatic Register,* "but most intellectual . . . the true blending of humanity with Comedy . . . the most Shaksperian comic personation we ever beheld." *The Examiner* (June 24) found the interpretation "at once original and felicitious," and it is clear that Elliston put all he knew, all of his own personality into the part. The result was a gentlemanly, rakish Falstaff, good-humoured and well bred to gether. It was undoubtedly the best thing he ever did, the culmination of his acting career. Looking back at the performance a few year later, the *New Monthly Magazine* singled out one scene in particular where Elliston's genius was best displayed:

We shall never forget his look, attitude, and voice when narrating the famous Gadshill fight. As he proceeded, detailing his prowess, like a true liar, he became a convert to his own falsehood, and his frame dilated, and his voice deepened and rolled with his imaginary triumphs, and for the time he stood, in his own conviction, the breathing Hector of his own lie. Nothing could be more exquisite—no expression could more perfectly catch the subtle spirit of Shakspeare than the glance of Elliston —his flushed face, quivering with conquest, and his whole mountain of a body big with the hero, as he cried, 'Thou knowest my old ward; here I lay, and thus I bore my point. Four rogues in buckram let drive at me!' Of a piece with this was his rallying under the exposure of the Prince; and when asked by *Hal,* 'What trick, what device, what starting-hole, canst thou find out to hide thee from this open and apparent shame?'— gathering himself up, fairly melting his face with a smile, and his eye glowing like a carbuncle, Elliston fulmined rather than spoke, 'By the Lord, I knew ye as well as he that made ye!'[7]

But Elliston did not rely solely on his own acting abilities to make his theatre a success. He determined to present a full bill, with change of programme every evening. This meant, for example, no less than seventy productions before the end of 1827, and usually more than that number of fresh productions every year thereafter. He needed a full acting company, obviously, for such a programme. For the most part, he had to make do with second-rate actors, such as Mrs. Egerton, known as the Siddons of melodrama, and Henry Kemble, nephew of the latter, known for the "strongest lungs and weakest judgement" of any actor at the minor theatres.[8] Elliston had one star attraction, however, to complement his own talents. This was the child actor, Joseph Burke, who made his debut at the Surrey on July 23. Since he does not appear to have received notice heretofore, and since his acting abilities show the influence of Elliston himself, his career will be briefly outlined.

Joseph Burke was a phenomenon. Born in Galway, Ireland, in 1818, he showed a taste for music at the age of six months, could sing every song he heard at the age of one year, and could play the violin at three.[9] At five it was noticed that he had acting talent. He made his debut at the Theatre Royal Dublin in May 1824 as Tom Thumb; immediate success led to a provincial tour in England. One year later, on June 4, after a successful provincial tour during which he sang and acted in farces, Master Burke made his London debut at the Haymarket. He next went to Paris, where he was trained in the violin and dancing by one M. Ambroise of the Académie Royale. Elliston then engaged him at the Surrey, entering into an agreement with Dr. Burke, the boy's father, for three years at twenty pounds a week,[10] an extraordinary salary for a minor theatre.

Master Burke made his Surrey debut as Doctor O'Toole in *The Irish Tutor*, a farce by O'Keeffe. The aged playwright, who had seen Burke in this role earlier at Chichester, is reported to have been so delighted with the performance that he presented Burke with a pair of silver shoe buckles worn by himself as a boy, and a lock of his hair to be worn in a ring when O'Keeffe should die.[11] Burke also played the violin, sang a parody of an Italian aria, and led the orchestra in Rossini's overture to *Tancredi*. Two days later he played Sir Callaghan in Macklin's *Love à la Mode*. He continued with this kind of material until August 24, when he was provided with a piece especially written for the display of his varied talents. *The March of Intellect* was a huge success, playing sixty-four times before Christmas. Burke played Socrates Camelion, a youth who, in order to make fun of the pretensions of a bluestockinged guardian, impersonates various people applying to be his tutor. This involved the playing of six widely contrasting roles. There was a critical prejudice against child stars ever since Master Betty had grown up to embarrass former enthusiasts, which made English critics slow to acknowledge this bright particular star, but the testimony of a foreigner, Prince Pückler-Muskau, indicates the scope of Burke's performance. Writing to a friend in December 1827, when *March of Intellect* was still running, the Prince observed: "You have heard of the English Roscius. A new little wonder of this kind has appeared, and the maturity of his early talent is really astonishing. Master Burke . . . acts at the Surrey Theatre. Though only ten years old, he played five or six very different parts, with a humour, apparent familiarity with the stage, 'aplomb,' volubility of utterance, accurate memory, and suppleness and power over his little person, which are perfectly amazing. What struck me most, however, was, that in a little interlude he acted his own natural part,— a boy of ten years old,—with such uncommon truth that the genuine 'naiveté' of childhood he represented, could be nothing but the inspiration of genius,—it is impossible it could be the result of reflection in such a child. He began with the part of an Italian music-master, in which he displayed extraordinary mastery of the violin, and that not only in acquired dexterity, but in the good taste of his playing, and a fulness and beauty of tone seldom equalled. You perceived in his whole performance that he was a born musician. Next followed a learned pedant; then a rough captain of a ship; and so on;—every part admirably filled, and the by play, in which so many fail, peculiarly easy, clever, and appropriate."[12] Among the roles not mentioned here by the Prince was that of Napoleon, which if rather inappropriately forced into the farce, gave Burke an opportunity of trying a deeper kind of impersonation. The abstracted air with which he took snuff in the role, and then shook his wrist, was one of those pieces of "by play" for which he was so admired. After this success, Burke played not only in farces, but also in legitimate fare, usually in excerpt form.

In October, 1827, illness forced Elliston off the stage. He did not appear even on his benefit night, December 20, which was taken by his son, Charles Robert. Luckily, he was able to engage a singer of considerable reputation, Miss Graddon, who enabled him to keep up his production standards. Miss Graddon had made her debut at Drury Lane in 1824, under Elliston's management, at the age of eighteen; a disagreement with the new management it seems now made her available to the Surrey. She introduced opera into the repertory, beginning with the *Siege of Belgrade,* October 4, and going on to include *The Devil's Bridge,* October 13, *The Marriage* of *Figaro,* October 29, *No Song No Supper,* November 5, and *Der Freischütz* (Soane's version), November 10. Her last performance of the season was in *The Slave,* which opened on December 13. The season closed on December 23.

Three days later, however, the Surrey reopened for a winter season. The chief attraction was a new pantomime, *Harlequin and the Astrologer of Stepney,* written by the ever-reliable Moncrieff. A notable feature was the scenery. Elliston had attracted to the Surrey two artists named Phillips and Marshall, capable of the kind of scenery Elliston had promoted at Drury Lane. Marshall, in fact, was a former pupil of Marinari, and had worked at Drury Lane with Stanfield and Roberts. The pantomime included a diorama which presented, in the form of an "allegorical vision," a depiction of the battle of Navarino, between the Turkish, Egyptian and Tunisian fleets, on the one hand, and the English, French and Russian on the other, culminating in the "Total Annihilation" of the former.[13] The following day, Elliston proudly declared in his playbill that the pantomime was the most splendid production ever witnessed *"on this side of the water." The Times* was in agreement, considering it "really a clever production, most splendidly got up. . . . The scenery in general was excellent; some of it was truly splendid, and would have done honour to Covent Garden or Drury."[14] The pantomime was voted a hit and was repeated every evening for forty nights. Even after its run, the diorama was staged on its own, from time to time.

From January 8 Master Burke appeared in a new farce written by Moncrieff, called *Home for the Holidays!* Miss Graddon sang in *Rob Roy, Guy Mannering,* etc., and did a Vestris in *Giovanni in London.* It occurred to Elliston that child opera had not been tried before. He engaged other midgets, expanded his orchestra to thirty-two, and treated his audience to productions of *Die Nachtigal* (May 8), *Swiss Family* (June 27), *Artaxerxes* (September 16), etc. The scenery for these operas was scaled proportionate to the performers, and the music was "adapted" by the resident leader, one Mr. Blewitt. Elliston advertised what he called "Juvenile Nights," on which half price was offered to children under the age of twelve; on other nights these midget operas were placed in the bill so as to allow the midget audience to leave for bed at ten o'clock.

Visiting actors also added a certain novelty to the playbill.

Nobody of great reputation was attracted, but confirmed theatre-goers would be interested in the work of provincial actors such as Lionel Rayner and David Osbaldiston. The latter came to the Surrey to stay, as it happened. On February 27, 1828, he was on his way to rehearsal at the Royal Brunswick Theatre, where he was making his London debut, when news of one of the worst theatrical disasters of the time stopped him in his tracks, and diverted him, so to speak, to the Surrey. The iron roof of the Royal Brunswick had collapsed, dragging the walls with it; thirteen people, including Elliston's erstwhile business associate, Maurice, were killed.[15] Osbaldiston, who had made his name in Manchester, came to the Surrey as leading actor and stage-manager. He was ambitious, energetic, and capable. During his first season he played William Tell, Virginius, the Stranger, and Rolla, as well as such Shakespearean roles as Richard III, King Lear, Jaques, Macbeth, and Othello. The quality of his performances was not great, but he served to keep legitimate drama alive at the Surrey.

It may be wondered whether Elliston was so callous as to engage Osbaldiston and ignore the tragic circumstances which made that actor available. On March 2 Elliston wrote to the newspapers, offering his advice on how relief might be organized. He also issued the letter as a handbill (dated March 4). He suggested the compilation of a list of all people who belonged in any capacity to the Royal Brunswick; these should then be classified as to department, salary, and general circumstances. A register, comprising these lists, should then be presented at a meeting where a local committee should be formed to centralize funds and distribute aid. Provincial theatres should be approached and asked to take on the people rendered unemployed. He himself would hold a benefit performance at the Surrey on March 11. He also organized a local committee along the lines of his own suggestion. The post-script appended to the handbill shows, perhaps, his feelings over this matter:

I have foreborne to touch upon other important points in this distressing case; such as the losses of tradesmen connected with the Establishment, the misfortunes of the [o]pposite neighbours, the miserable chagrin of those who have advanced money—perhaps their little all—upon situation in the Theatres, and the ruinous consequences to the proprietors, but have no doubt the sympathy of the Public will not fail to take them into serious consideration .

When the season closed, on December 20, the scope and quality of Elliston's repertory was a matter of public praise. The *New Monthly Magazine,* which in February had called the Surrey, "the most flourishing theatrical establishment about London," in December reviewed some of the reasons for Elliston's success. The frequent and varied production of "tragedy, comedy, opera, farce, and melodrame . . . bidding high defiance to patent rights," was one factor; his company, with the particular talents of Burke and Osbaldiston, was another. To these *The Examiner* added "the evident good taste exerted, to *lead* rather than *follow* the public taste . . . the handsome manner in which the scenic and subordinate departments are filled up; the liberal complement of orchestral performers . . . [and] resulting from all this praiseworthy ambition and good taste, we have an orderly, silent, and attentive audience, because they are interested in the entertainment set before them."[16]

Elliston returned to the stage himself, as Sheva, on December 23, as the winter season got under way. On December 31 he added Dr. Pangloss, in Colman's *Heir At Law,* to the repertory; it was quite favourably received. Thereafter he continued to add more from his vast stock of comic roles, e.g., Captain Absolute, Charles Surface, Doricourt, etc., as he acted three or four times a week until May 25. On March 10 he played Falstaff again, with Osbaldiston as Hotspur, and repeated it four times before the end of the month. It was once again cited as "an admirable piece of acting," excelling all competitors.[17] A feature of the stock comedies in which Elliston now starred was that they were well cast, an unusual matter at a minor theatre where everything tended to hinge on one or two good actors. Another matter of importance was the fact that Elliston did not scruple any more to present a comedy in its full five acts, as with Vanbrugh's *Provoked Husband* on April 2. On the serious side of the entertainments, Osbaldiston continued his forays into Shakespeare (launching into Shylock and Cardinal Wolsey) and contemporary tragedy. Here too the five-act structure was initiated, beginning with *William Tell* on January 28 and culminating in "Shakespeare's Tragedy of *King Lear*" on March 9.

To have shown once again that a minor theatre could provide a bill that was not necessarily moronic in content, and that the audience of a place like St. George's Fields was not incapable of appreciating 'rational entertainment,' was an achievement in itself. It parallels, of course, his achievement of twenty years earlier, when the repertory was seventy-five per cent classifiably "dramatic." For this reason the point will not be laboured further: it may be taken that after 1829 the patterns of a well-balanced repertory and mischievous novelty were sustained at the Surrey. But there was another area where Elliston's theatre had a contribution to make in the evolution of nineteenth-century stage conditions: the realm of original, rather than adapted, drama.

In former times, when he managed the Surrey and Olympic, original pieces were usually either melodramas of such inferior quality as to preclude first-rate actors (in fact, horses and dogs were infinitely preferable), or farces which indeed provided a vehicle for histrionic display but little scope for the playwright or scenic artist. In recent years, however, this picture had changed. At the Lyceum, the Coburg, and the Adelphi, writers like Fitzball, Buckstone, and Jerrold were supplying melodramas demanding the talents of capable actors and imaginative scenic artists. The significance of this new movement was that at the minor theatres writers, actors, and *metteurs en scène* were opening up a market hitherto unknown. In time this brought more talented writers back into the theatre, and it was the writers who eventually banded together (in the 1830's) for the cause of "dramatic literature" and demanded the freeing of the theatres on which their livelihood depended. Elliston's role in this movement, it is here being emphasized, was not that of an innovator. He had given the impetus by the freedom he gained for the theatres in 1818, but the real development was done between that date and the time of his undertaking the Surrey once more. But in grafting the new movement into the theatrical structure so well established at the Surrey, Elliston lent it powerful prestige; in attracting actors and writers away from these rival theatres to the Surrey, he placed his theatre in the van of the struggle for a fully-freed stage.

Elliston had an excellent eye for good theatre. Fitzball records how he first began to write for the Surrey. Elliston had a melodrama which he felt needed touching up; he sent for Fitzball and asked him to do it. The latter, reluctant to tamper with another man's work, named an extravagant fee, hoping to put Elliston off. To his surprise, Elliston accepted. When he brought back the doctored play next day, he found Elliston seated "like Cardinal Wolsey, in his chair of state," waiting for the script. Fitzball stayed while Elliston read it through. At every page Elliston's eye brightened, and when he came across a piece of claptrap in praise of female innocence he "smiled one of his George-the-Fourth smiles, and exclaimed, rubbing his hands, exultingly, 'That will do, sir, that will do; now we *shall* bring them down!' Then, pointing with kingly dignity towards the mantelpiece, I found lying there, according to royal promise, the gold from the exchequer which was to requite me of my labour."[18] It is not known what the title of this piece was, but some time afterwards, when the Surrey was firmly established, Elliston wooed Fitzball in earnest. Meeting him on the street he asked Fitzball if he had anything "good enough for us, eh?" The latter mentioned a melodrama he had just completed, *The Inchcape Bell,* which he agreed to read to Elliston at a time then appointed. After one scene, Elliston fell asleep. Annoyed, Fitzball skipped on to the end, read the catastrophe, and shut the book with a bang. Elliston, aroused, looked vacantly around, focused on Fitzball, and exclaimed "Good! . . . exellent melodrame for the Cobourg: take it there, sir; they will do it justice."[19] Two weeks later Elliston again encountered Fitzball on the street asked him if he had anything for him. Fitzball allowed he had a nautical drama. "The very thing," declared Elliston, and asked for the title. Thinking to embarrass him Fitzball said blandly, "*The Inchcape Bell.*" Nobody, however, could get the better of Elliston. "Excellent!" he replied, to Fitzball's astonishment, "the very sort of title to make out our bill. Let me have it to read directly, sir— this very evening." Uncertain as to how much of this was at his expense, Fitzball nevertheless complied, and his play was subsequently brought out at the Surrey on May 26, 1828.

The play was well cast, with Osbaldiston as the villainous Hattock, Rayner as Guy Ruthven, the hero, and Miss Scott as the dumb boy, archetypal victim. The scenery was practical and realistic. The last scene represented the deck of the pirate ship, on to which Ruthven makes his way in order to free the boy. When the ship goes aground and begins to sink, there is at least one practicable mast on to which he and the boy hold, while a boat "*is seen leaving the shore in the background, R., and crossing to L., just as Guy Ruthven, the Dumb Boy, and Jupiter are sinking with the mast, which is struck by a thunderbolt.*"[20] This boat then re-enters and the three above mentioned are dragged into it and safety just as the pirate ship sinks. *The Times* of May 28 found this scene "one of the most effective things of the kind we have for a long time witnessed." It is a very clear example of how spectacle was now being made to take an active, not to say moral, part in the stage picture.

The audience that could accept realism when it assisted the total picture of a moral universe was not prepared to raise a cheer for it if it merely reflected the disturbing truth. This was clearly indicated by the reception given a new play by Moncrieff, based on a melodrama currently playing in Paris. *The Pestilence of Marseilles* was first staged at the Surrey on October 20. In the playbill, Moncrieff was at pains to declare that the original was too horrible for the English stage, and that his version relied on primary sources. For the staging, however, he expressed indebtedness to Pixérécourt and to the "Décorateur" of the original, one M. Gué, who had supplied him with sketches. At the Surrey, Marshall looked after the scenery, and a newcomer, Edmund Bradwell, whom Elliston had brought from the Theatre Royal, Dublin, was in charge of properties. The first scene of act two represented Marseilles under plague. According to the published text,[21] nothing short of complete realization was called for. Lighting played an important part in establishing the mood, the stage being in gloom all through the act, and the moon giving off *"a dull blood tint."* The opening action was all dumbshow: death carts were dragged across the stage in one direction, litters with the dying were carried in another. Various characters enter in varying degrees of illness and despair, and collapse. A wife tries to get a passer-by to help her dying husband: *"he flies in terror, and the wife sinks in despair on the body of her husband,"* forming a *"tableau of desolation."* A death knell tolled solemnly at intervals. This was Theatre of Cruelty before its time. It proved too grim for its own time. In spite of Elliston's puff next day in the playbill, *The Pestilence* had to be taken off after only six performances.

It was Easter 1829 before Elliston again attempted an original drama worthy of comment. This was *John Overy, The Miser of the Southwark Ferry!* by Douglas Jerrold. Then twenty-six, Jerrold had been writing for Sadler's Wells and the Coburg for several years, and towards the end of 1828 had been made a salaried author by

Davidge. How Elliston enticed him to the Surrey is not clear, but
on February 13 Jerrold won favour with a melodrama called
Bamfyde Moore Carew. He now had the honour of starting off the
summer season, on April 20, with *John Overy*. This was a three-act
piece, with a strongly written central character. Again the emphasis
was on sordid authenticity, and the setting was used to assert this.[22]
For this reason, perhaps, it too did not prove very attractive, and
on May 18 it was demoted to the position of afterpiece. Elliston,
however, was quite impressed with his new playwright. "I think he
is the most rising Dramatist that we have," he wrote to T. P. Cooke
on May 19.[23] Jerrold's second play for this season, *Law and Lions*
was presented on May 21, but it was the third, *Black-Eyed Susan,*
that made him famous, won a fortune for Elliston and gave T. P.
Cooke a role he was to play almost eight hundred times before the
end of his career. It was about *Black-Eyed Susan* that Elliston
wrote to Cooke on May 19. Cooke was currently engaged as actor
and stage-manager at the Adelphi, and came to the Surrey for a
brief engagement only. The main feature, when he first appeared at
the Surrey (June 8), was not *Susan* at all, in fact, but the play in
which he had made his name at the Adelphi, *The Pilot*. The audience flocked to see Cooke as Long Tom Coffin in Fitzball's nautical
melodrama. *Susan* was intended only as an afterpiece: by the third
night, however, it was being given top billing. Elliston afterwards
said, when accused of clearing many thousands of pounds on the
play while Jerrold merely got sixty, that he had staged it for its first
forty-seven nights at a loss.[24] This may be true in a literal sense,
but the fact remains that Cooke was engaged for only eight nights at
first,[25] and by the last night so great was the popularity of *Susan*
that Elliston re-engaged him, and kept re-engaging him all through
the summer, at twenty-five pounds a week, until November 28, by
which time *Susan* had played a phenomenal one hundred and fifty
times.

Several factors contributed to the effectiveness of this melodrama.[26] Many of these add up to authenticity. The music and songs
adapted from Dibdin the Elder set the marine mood. T. P. Cooke,
as William, was unrivalled as a portrayer of sailor characters, having been a sailor in his youth. Miss Scott, as Susan, was a prototypal
helpless heroine. The language was of the right smack (to excess, of
course), for Jerrold too had served at sea as a boy. Add to this
the realistic costumes and scenery: both the court-martial scene

and the execution scene were set with great attention to detail. The former represented a state cabin, with a long table, centre, displaying a large law book, writing paper and a huge inkstand; at the head, with the Union Jack over his chair, sat the Admiral, and six captains sat on each side of the table. The last scene showed the scaffold, "rigged out between the cat-head and the fore rigging." It was a full set, with a practical gangway on one side, a platform covered in black on the other, a foremast centre, with shrouds from it to the bulwark wings stretching upstage right and left, and a line up which is run a yellow flag and the Union Jack; a mizen-mast and a main-mast were painted on flats, with a deep border drawn to match; there were also arch sky borders and a horizon, to give the illusion of an open deck.[27] This scenery was designed and painted by Marshall, while Bradwell and Hagley were responsible for properties and machinery.

Apart from the authenticity there was a novel feature about the play itself. Heretofore sailors or jolly tars had long been popular on the stage, but always as caricatures rather than characters. Moreover, they were always peripheral, like clowns or servants; more recently, there was the sailor as villain. Now Jerrold had presented the sailor as noble hero, one with whom the lower classes could identify. A formula for a whole new genre had been found, which continued unchallenged until W. S. Gilbert knocked it on the head in *H. M. S. Pinafore.*

The Coburg brought out a melodrama with the same title at the same time as Jerrold's *Black-Eyed Susan.* Elliston soon turned this to good account, by attacking the Coburg in his playbills and attracting greater attention to his theatre. The Coburg was forced to a public apology within a week, which drew from Elliston a Parthian shot, whereby he denied anything like rivalry with such a contemptible place as the Coburg. "He condescends while he castigates," he announced in red type on June 15, "and as this is probably the last time that he will ever be induced to drag that Theatre even into a temporary notice, by his observations, he assures the illustrious Charlatan of that classical and highly talented spot, that he shall leave him in the full and solitary enjoyment of his ingenuous machinations and contrivances for the decadence of the National Drama."[28]

Cooke was engaged only until the opening of the Adelphi. It so happened, however, that this theatre, perhaps as jealous as the

Coburg of Elliston's success, reopened five days before Cooke's term
was up. On asking leave to finish out at the Surrey Cooke was refused. He then considered himself free of the Adelphi and opted to
stay on with Elliston until *Susan* reached its hundredth performance on October 1. Meantime he also assumed that he was free
to act two roles, both nautical, in which he had starred the year
before at the Adelphi and which he had promised to act nowhere
else. These were Fid in *Red Rover* and Vanderdecken in *The Flying
Dutchman*, both spectacular melodramas by Fitzball. With the
production of the latter play, for which Cooke supplied the script
and did the direction, Elliston ran into trouble. The Adelphi took
action and brought an injunction against the production.

Elliston had now the kind of situation in which he revelled.
Susan had sailed past her hundredth with flying colours, the Surrey
being illuminated for the occasion, as if for a naval victory. Now a
controversy prevented an anti-climax and kept the theatre in the
public eye, until the one hundred and fiftieth performance of *Susan*
seemed a not unlikely target. Cooke stayed on.

The subsequent flurry over *The Flying Dutchman* is of absolutely no real consequence. But Elliston dramatized it to the full,
issuing explanatory playbills, deputing Osbaldiston to make long
and serious curtain speeches about Elliston's willingness to suffer
prison for his theatre (were it not that Cooke should be forced to
suffer the same pains), dashing down to Brighton to see the Master
of the Rolls in an effort to have the injunction lifted, and returning
in ill-concealed triumph to announce, with appropriate exclama-
tion points, his success. While all this to-do was going on, Elliston
got Jerrold[29] to come up with another melodrama, identical in every
respect with Fitzball's except that in the subtitle the word
"phantom" was replaced with "spectral." *The Flying Dutchman;
or, The Spectral Ship*, was, accordingly, staged on October 15.
After the quashing of the injunction Elliston had so much to say on
the whole subject of copyright, the Adelphi, Cooke, and himself
that he could not possibly fit it all into a playbill. With merciful
restraint, therefore, he reserved much of his voluminous documentation for a preface to Jerrold's play, published as quickly as
possible,[30] and contented himself with staging Fitzball's version
once again, on October 19, as an exercise of his much-vaunted
rights.

When Jerrold's *Dutchman* was presented, no orders were admitted and the free list was supended, twin auguries of prosperity. The play itself, however, having been written, rehearsed, and staged within five days, is of no importance. Like Fitzball's, it had a good deal of the kind of supernatural spectacle made fashionable by *Der Freischütz* and *Faustus*. But its production made clear that Elliston had successfully stolen the thunder of the Adelphi, as he had already squashed the Coburg. Among the "new wave" minor theatres, Elliston's waves were now higher than anyone else's.

So confident was he of the status his theatre had reached that Elliston began to dabble a little in literary drama. On November 17 he presented on stage the only play of Sir Walter Scott ever to be awarded that honour. It will be remembered that Elliston had several times, to no avail, pressed Scott for an original play. Now, with the publication of one of Scott's six efforts in the dramatic form, Elliston staged him, as he had done Byron, without permission. *The House of Aspen*, a prose tragedy in five acts, was written in 1800.[31] According to Scott's Advertisement, it was once to have been played by Kemble and Mrs. Siddons, but there were too many objections at the time. Written under the influence of *fin de siècle* German romanticism, the play had melodramatic qualities which probably attracted Elliston to it now. Published in the annual *Keepsake*, the play had, if Elliston's playbill is to be believed, "created considerable interest, and much discussion, relative to its probable Dramatic effects if represented." He offered admirers of Scott's work an opportunity of judging for themselves. Elliston had one other apology to make: "It is necessary to state, that considerable liberty has been taken, as to curtailments and transposition of speeches and scenes; some interpolations have also been ventured: but it is humbly presumed that nothing has been attempted that will injure any effect the Poet intended to convey."[32] Only *The Times*, it seems, took any notice of this noble gesture, in a review of November 19. Osbaldiston and Mrs. Egerton were deemed "effective" in the lead, but, all in all, the production won no laurels, and played only three times.

Following Scott, Elliston brought out Jerrold's most ambitious play to date, the first dramatization of the tragedy of Thomas à Becket. Advertised as in preparation since November 3, *Becket* finally appeared on November 30. It was a careful, deliberate production, and should probably rank as forming the high-water mark of Elliston's Surrey management. In his "Remarks" on the play the editor of *Richardson's Minor Theatre* (Moncrieff?) paid tribute to Elliston for producing what was "more a dramatic poem than an acting play." Elliston showed thereby "a real feeling for his art, and displayed a taste as commendable in managers as it is unusual."[33]

Jerrold's tragedy is also remarkable in that it was written in five acts of prose, without songs, the first such full-length original play to be staged at a minor theatre. Jerrold, in his prologue, made much of the fact that his subject-matter was English. This was another important aspect of the play, as it was of Jerrold's work in general. He was determined to counteract the craze for French melodrama by cultivating native themes and aiming at a "national" drama. With this aim, it may be assumed, Elliston was also in agreement.

It has to be admitted that Jerrold does not really rise above melodrama. Becket's division with Henry is made to arise over the refusal of Breakspear to give up the love of Lucia, an erstwhile nun. At the Council of Clarendon Becket appears as a rather humourless and extremely autocratic spoilsport. Even the King cannot get him to stop seeing red. Whether or not reflecting sectarian opinion at the time of the passage of the Catholic Emancipation Bill, Jerrold paints Becket and the clergy in general as over-powerful, arrogant, and corrupt. This is the play's weakness, finally, for it makes the ending ambivalent: Breakspear, like Crosstree in *Black-Eyed Susan,* bursts into Canterbury Cathedral crying "hold," only to find he is too late, the assassins have done their turbulent task. In the light of Becket's character and unpopularity as seen earlier, the final picture of him with "*the silver cross lying between his arms upon his breast,*" could be viewed as ironic.

Though the critics faulted the play on many counts, it is notable that all took it as a serious attempt at tragedy: there is no hint of condescension towards author or theatre. The play itself was found, as no doubt would have been the case even at Drury Lane, excessively prolix. (It took three hours to perform.) Rumball, the latest of Elliston's acquisitions for his legitimate fare, played Becket well, if unevenly, while such seasoned melodramatic performers as Dibdin Pitt, Rayner, Almar, Gough, Vale, and Mrs. Egerton ensured the play of "every justice in the acting." Marshall's scenery was declared to be effective also. The audience, surprisingly, sat through the play with interest, but did not, of course, vote it a hit. On December 2 Elliston announced that he had received so many enquiries about T. P. Cooke and *Black-Eyed Susan* that he had re-engaged Cooke; on December 7, accordingly, *Becket* was dropped after a mere six performances.

The season closed on December 21, with an address of thanks by Elliston himself. It goes without saying he had much to be thankful for. In the twelve-month period he had staged roughly one hundred and ten productions, of which over twenty-five per cent were of legitimate plays, including ten Shapespearean;[34] he had the best melodrama of the year, if not of the decade, in *Black-Eyed Susan,* which had played a total of one hundred and sixty-seven nights, including half a dozen (by special desire) at Covent Garden, and was reported to have netted six thousand pounds for Elliston.[35]

The remainder of Elliston's term of management may be chronicled without too much detail. With the pantomime on December 26, the winter season began, running, as usual, until the end of March; the summer season opened on Easter Monday, April 12, and ran uninterrupted until December 15. It was an uneventful season in comparison with 1829. T. P. Cooke and Master Burke divided the attention between them. Cooke played William for eleven nights in January; Burke made his return on April 12, and after proving that his popularity and talents were as great as ever, was re-engaged, several times, until May 29; Cooke returned on May 31 and played until August 28, by which time *Black-Eyed Susan* had run up two hundred and eight performances; Burke returned on August 30 and played until September 28, when he made his farewell appearance prior to leaving for the United States for good.[36] Elliston himself made his first appearance in almost a year on April 23, when he played for a month in a Shakespeare pageant; he did not return until December 10, when he played Sheva four times before the theatre closed. Osbaldiston, for his part, continued to appear in Shakespeare and other legitimate fare through the year.

Jerrold came up with another nautical melodrama for T. P. Cooke, entitled *Press Gang,* which first played on July 5. *The Examiner* voted it well worth seeing, through not as good a play as *Susan,* admiring not only the effective acting of Cooke ("every inch a sailor, even to the mode of holding his hands") and Miss Scott, but also the liberal sentiments of the play itself. The subject, apparently, was treated ironically; in a key scene a pressed man is saved from a flogging only when it is discovered he is a peer. Moncrieff tossed off a couple of farces in which the virtuosity of the twelve-year old Burke was allowed its accustomed scope: *Barney Brallaghan,* produced on April 19, and *Old Heads on Young Shoulders* on May 7.

Vehicles of another kind, however, are of more interest. On February 11 Elliston presented *Van Diemen's Land,* an operatic extravaganza written by Moncrieff at Elliston's request. In September 1829 two of Elliston's sons, the eldest, William Gore (for whom the theatre obviously held no future) and the youngest, Edmund, aged thirty-one and sixteen respectively, had left England to seek their fortune in Tasmania. Before they left, Elliston held a magnificent party in their honour at his new home at 84 Great Surrey Street, just across from the theatre. Without question, the spectacle now written by Moncrieff was also produced in their honour. Its main attraction was a diorama by Marshall which took the spectator on a guided tour of the island as the settlers journeyed in search of their specific Eden. Occasionally, the diorama would stop for a scene or two in a fixed place. There would be songs (often nostalgic), some illustration of local customs, some adventure, and then it would move on once more.[37] The costumes, it might be added, provided another bit of exotic appeal, with the introduction of natives, bushrangers, etc.

Van Diemen's Land proved popular, and was adjudged by *The Age* on February 21 to be "carrying all before it." The blending of music, scenic spectacle, and plot was found attractive, and only the play's slightly liberal attitude towards the "mistakes" of the "colonists," i.e., transported convicts, was frowned on. Once again, however, this only goes to show that the Surrey was beginning to express ideas on stage instead of being content with mindless spectacle.

Moncrieff followed up with a piece called *Shakespeare's Festival; or, A New Comedy of Errors,* which was presented on April 23, and which ran for a month. This was in two acts, the second being Garrick's pageant new dressed. Scenes from fourteen plays were presented in tableaux: Master Burke appearing as Shylock and Richard III, Osbaldiston as Coriolanus, and Elliston as Falstaff in *The Merry Wives*. This latter tableau was entitled, "Hail, Kissing Comforts," and included Bardolph, Pistol, Mrs. Ford, and Mrs. Page. It was not altogether mute, Elliston's "unctuous tones" as well as his "looks" and "gestures" receiving high praise.[38] Songs from various plays, arranged by Blewitt, accompanied the pageant. It was also quite richly costumed. The first act, the farce proper, undercuts the tone of conventional Bardolatry suggested by the pageant, indicating, indeed, Elliston's ambivalent attitude towards Shakespeare as much as Moncrieff's. Elliston was Chairman of the Surrey branch of the Shakespeare Club, and walked in the annual procession. At the same time, he was alive to the element of the ludicrous inherent in such celebrations. He once turned a celebration dinner into a testimonial for his own endeavours, treating the assembly to "one of his characteristic rhodomontades about the thousands he has lost and won for the drama, and that he is ready to lose again if he had them."[39]

During December 1830 the theatre was altered, in boxes, pit, and gallery, according to designs by Charles Robert Elliston. Family boxes were made available, along the lines of the major theatres. The winter season then began on January 2, 1831. It was uneventful, dominated by Osbaldiston's ambitions in stock tragic roles, a pantomime with a diorama, and an occasional new melodrama. On April 20, two weeks after the summer season opened, Elliston appeared as Young Meadows (in *The Deaf Lover*), following up with Sheva on April 21, which he repeated on succeeding nights. He had been ill just after Christmas but was in top form once again. "It is almost worth being able to remember him twenty years ago," remarked an admirer, "in order to compare him with what he was at that period, and infer thence that youth is not a thing of the body, but of the mind, and that years are not at the mercy of the human imagination."[40] Cumberland's *The Jew* might be "a false and foolish affair," but "early associations will preserve [it] from contemptuous oblivion so long as Elliston pleases; and no longer. His acting, we are gratified to report, attracts full and respectable audiences." On April 23 *Shakespeare's Festival* was staged once more, in which Elliston again appeared as Falstaff, having played Sheva earlier in the evening; it was repeated every evening until

April 30. Elliston did not re-appear until May 13, when he played Dr. Pangloss in Colman's *Heir At Law*; this was repeated on May 18, yielding to a new melodrama entitled *Napoleon, the Victim of Ambition* on May 21. Osbaldiston played the victim, and Marshall supplied two dioramas, one showing the invasion of Russia, with Moscow in flames, the other showing the battle of Waterloo, with Napoleon in flight. The play, which followed Napoleon to his death-chamber in St. Helena, ended with an "allegorical device," showing the rise and fall of Napoleon, with a view of his tomb. *Napoleon* was not popular and by June 6 the playbills were offering "Napoleon at Half Price!" On June 7 T. P. Cooke made his only appearance of the season, not as William, now being played by C. Hill, but in a nautical sketch. On June 24, "By Special Desire," Elliston returned as Sheva. It was his last performance. He was advertised to reappear on June 28 as Megrim, but it was announced in the playbill of that day that "a severe cold and hoarseness" prevented his acting.

Time was quickly running out for Elliston. He had found a haven at the Surrey, his "last retreat and recess," in Lamb's phrase. He was accustomed now to say it was *the* theatre after all, "and he would not leave it to be the king of the first playhouse in London." It had been kind to him. It had enabled him to raise himself to a certain degree of sobriety and steadiness once again, after the reckless years of the early 1820's. It had spared him the kind of deterioration daily haunting Kean, and the miserable anxiety dogging Charles Kemble at Covent Garden. At one time he even considered remarriage, to a gentle spinster of earlier acquaintance at Bath; but the fact that she had two sisters equally confirmed with herself to inseparability, apparently melted Elliston's resolve.

The repeated shocks of earlier illness, however, left their mark, and he was often forced to abandon the stage for the bed: he suffered moreover, from chronic gout. The passing of George IV, in June 1830, brought an era to an end. Elliston, who had identified with George in many ways, and who had tried, in his way, to supply the kind of munificent patronage which George denied the theatre, made his will within two weeks of his monarch's death. Towards the end of the year, his youngest daughter but one, Lucy Ann, nineteen years old, became gravely ill. She died on January 28, 1831. Elliston was shattered. But his courage did not fail him, as he wrote to cheer up two other children. "We must do our duty," he said, with no trace of pomposity, "while there is any spark of animation remaining."[41] Thus, he took to the stage again on April 23. In June he was ill again. As soon as he was well enough, on July 5, he visited his married daughter, Frances Maria, driving out in the early morning to Norwood so as to be back in time for a full day's work. On July 6, during another such visit, he fell ill on the road, suffered what Raymond calls an "apoplectic fit," and, on being taken home, lingered a day and died on July 8.

The Surrey theatre was left in the hands of Charles Robert, who retained it only until December 1831 and then sold his interest to Osbaldiston for three thousand pounds.[42] Perhaps it was because he recognized, for all his regal pretensions, that he had founded no theatrical dynasty, that Elliston had commanded a Latin plaque for his coffin. He who had begun his career at classical St. Paul's, and had hungered all his life for popular applause, was reluctant to leave not a rack behind. And yet he left, if not a monument more lasting than bronze, at least a signpost, showing the way in which nineteenth-century theatre might carry on his efforts. But this is matter for a final chapter.

SEVEN

Elliston as Manager

'Grand, grand; you should folly that up,
you should folly that up.'
O'Casey, *Juno and the Paycock*

IN REGENCY times, a theatre manager's duties covered all aspects of administration. In 1813 a case was heard in Chancery which throws some light on the nature and scope of these duties. In that year George Colman the Younger was charged with managerial incompetence by David Morris, his fellow proprietor at the Haymarket. In order to rule on the matter, the Lord Chancellor required some guidelines as to what it was a competent manager should do. Among the affidavits supplied in Colman's defence was one outlining the duties of a manager. Since this was accepted by his Lordship it is not without a certain interest. More importantly, in the present context, Elliston was among the friends of Colman who supplied affidavits: considering his experience as Colman's acting manager it is not extravagant to imagine that the affidavit in question reflected his ideas on management. According to the affidavit, it was the duty of a manager: (1) To attend the theatre every morning for four or five hours while rehearsals of new and revived plays were being held; otherwise rehearsals became "a scene of rude mirth and jollity." (2) To read new plays to performers, and cast the parts. (3) To attend to costumes, set a limit on expenses for them, and resist the importunities of those actors who thought that they should have better costumes than others. (4) To examine new plays sent in, and get rid of authors whose plays had been rejected. (5) To supervise doorkeepers, musicians, singers, dancers, and other personnel.[1] In addition, one other point was made: although a manager could delegate much of this work to a good acting or stage manager, he himself remained responsible. Mundane as these factors may be, they offer a means of considering and of assessing Elliston's managerial abilities. They say nothing of greatness, which, of course, is in a category above competence, and which in the theatre seems to be characterized by visionary imagination and technical inventiveness.

Elliston's policy in regard to delegation was to have as good an acting manager or stage manager as possible. Thus he had, at various times throughout his career, Thomas Dibdin, James Winston, James Wallack, and David Osbaldiston. But Elliston never let go the reins himself. Even when he was away from his theatre, whichever one it might be, he kept in touch daily with his deputy manager. His letters to Winston at the Olympic bear ample testimony to his keeping complete control himself. Besides instructions on matters of general import, such as the redecoration of the theatre, Elliston supplied the answers to a host of questions. If an actor wanted an increase in salary he knew whether he was worth it; if a composer or playwright claimed copyright of a piece written for the Olympic Elliston was in no doubt as to his own rights in the matter. If an agreement was made with anybody, or a contract terminated, it would have to be in writing and duly witnessed. Once, when Reeve the composer's status at the Olympic was unclear, Elliston warned Winston to make it "distinctly understood," before a witness, "that he is a [vo]lunteer in the cause," since otherwise "there will be after demands of a disagreable [sic] nature."[2] No actor was to be allowed to appear at the Sans Pareil, a nearby rival theatre; no theatre was to be allowed to stage an Olympic piece: Winston was to ascertain whether this was going on, and, if it was, to put a stop to it.[3] The letters of Brunton and Ashley from Birmingham indicate a similar control over that theatre's affairs; the letters from Winston, Reynolds, etc., during the Drury Lane management indicate the same regarding that theatre, while Elliston's own letters, whenever he was in the provinces, continue to show that he alone made out the daily bill, cast plays, and made final decisions. During his months at Ramsgate, when he was recuperating from his stroke, in 1825, the constant stream of letters to Winston on all aspects of the theatre indicate that the control, which had faltered somewhat from 1823 as Elliston sought to divide his authority between too many deputies, was restored. At that time, of course, he also had his son, William Gore, installed at Drury Lane *in loco parentis*. At the Surrey, from 1827, he was mainly on hand himself, while he had Charles Robert to supervise in his absence. Elliston's relationship with Osbaldiston is undocumented, but the favourable reputation the Surrey achieved at this time would indicate a continuance of Elliston's practice of total control.

The quality of this control was almost proverbial. His obituary, fulsome as it was in its praise of his acting style, had this to say of Elliston's managerial approach: "Behind the curtain he was rigid, and perhaps dictatorial; but he always carried himself with the politeness of a courtier—except when an occasional flash of temper suffered him to forget his interests and his station."[4] From his first undertaking management in 1809, Elliston ensured that every actor hired signed a lengthy agreement binding him under all sorts of regulations. For the Royal Circus, even, this agreement ran to three pages of print. It was heavily loaded in Elliston's favour. The actor bound himself, under pain of a sizeable sum of money, to act at Elliston's theatre only, to act any and every role handed him, whether singing, dancing, or whatever, and to "diligently and duly attend all and every Rehearsals or Practices of all Pieces or Performances Wherein [he] shall be directed or required to act, sing, dance, and perform."[5] Each actor also agreed to pay fines *"for neglect or refusal to attend, accept of, study, practice, rehearse, or publicly perform any Part or Parts, Character or Characters."* These fines, according to the Royal Circus agreement, were laid in relation to a Table of Forfeits, *"affixed up in the Treasurer's Office of the said Theatre."* By the time he undertook management of the Olympic, however, Elliston had incorporated this Table of Forfeits into the agreement signed by each performer. It comprised twenty clauses,[6] which can be combined under various headings (one should bear in mind that the average weekly salary would be about thirty to forty shillings):

Rehearsal: Attendance was mandatory; grace of fifteen minutes was allowed, after which time a fine of one shilling was imposed. For non-appearance, if through illness, a fine of five shillings; if through wilful neglect, a full night's salary. For "inattention or neglect" during rehearsal, one shilling.

Performance: Refusal to play a part assigned meant forfeit of one week's salary. Every actor was required to attend one half hour before curtain time, under fine of two and sixpence. Absence for any reason, "real illness excepted," meant either a fine or dismissal, at Elliston's option. Any actor imperfect in his part, making a wrong entrance, or making the "stage business stand," was fined five shillings. Any actor who introduced improper jokes, or indulged in improper behaviour on stage, was fined one guinea; if a quarrel between actors interfered with an act, both were fined one guinea, or, in the case of a blow being struck, one week's salary; if an actor was drunk on stage, he was fined one week's salary, and was subject to dismissal on his second offence. Any actor stealing the "business" of another led to the fining, strangely, of both actors involved, at the rate of one week's salary. Offstage also standards were enforced: standing in the wings in sight of the audience meant a fine of two and sixpence, as did looking through the green curtain at the audience or climbing (for reasons unspecified) up to a balcony box.

Costume: Refusal to wear, or alteration of, dresses regulated and approved by the acting manager meant a fine of one guinea. If the actor was not neat and clean in his costume, or if he sneaked off with part of it under his own clothes, he was fined one shilling.

Properties: Any actor fooling with or neglecting to hand in a prop was fined five shillings; if he wilfully destroyed it he had to make restitution in full.

Benefit Nights: The actor had to stand a charge of five guineas for advertising [exclusive of the standard "charges" which went to Elliston first before the actor got a penny; these charges amounted to around one hundred pounds maximum at the minor theatres, and twice that at the majors]. Any actor who abused the benefit privilege, by disposing of it "in part or parts," or by issuing tickets in the name of another, was fined fifty pounds.

Prompter: He it was who had to enforce the above fines. Failure to do so meant subjection to fine himself, from one shilling to one guinea for each incident.

There were also regulations to be observed, under comparable penalties, by the orchestra, the money-takers, and even the "Dressers, Sweepers and Other Servants of the Theatre." All personnel, in short, were under the same strict discipline. These regulations, it need hardly be said, were retained and refined upon during Elliston's management of Birmingham and Drury Lane, and presumably (for want of documentary evidence) existed also during his second period at the Surrey. They tended to get stiffer with the years. The Drury Lane regulations placed much more emphasis on rehearsal and the actor's being perfect in his part; from this and from the foregoing it may be concluded that rehearsal was something by which Elliston set considerable store. At the Surrey in 1812, indeed, he went so far as to fight a duel with one of his actors on this account. There were some who whispered that the real reason for the duel was De Camp's appearing (successfully) in Elliston's role of the three Singles; but the *Morning Chronicle* (September 15, 1812) put the loftier construction on the affair. Elliston did not shoot all his actors who neglected rehearsals, but it seems that he himself made a practice of attending. A letter to Winston in 1825 indicates that he supervised even interludes and afterpieces.[7] Stock plays, e.g., *Othello* (mentioned in this letter), were given rehearsal also, although it is doubtful if the star actors, such as Kean or Macready, attended. For new plays, however, even the stars were obliged to attend. In May 1825, for example, Macready, himself in later years a strict enforcer of rehearsal discipline, was taken to task for neglecting rehearsal of *William Tell*.[8]

The best kind of evidence of enforcement of these regulations would be entries in the Treasurer's books of the penalties involved. These are available for Drury Lane only, but the fines appear with such regularity in them that it may be assumed that the books of Elliston's other theatres would reflect the same tale. Sometimes the fines reached as high as three-quarters of the weekly salary of an actor. Minor fines of one shilling and two and sixpence were strictly enforced at the outset, i.e., after the date upon which Elliston first began to use his printed agreements and regulations at Drury Lane, October 28, 1820; the fact that these tapered off after a time would indicate that the performers learned to respect Elliston's insistence on discipline. He was hardest on members of the orchestra, who, it seems, tended to drift nightly from theatre to theatre if they were not tightly controlled. A clause in their regulations said that any member absent from Drury Lane for one night would be fined a full week's salary. The enforcement of this clause caused trouble. In January 1821 the whole orchestra walked out after one man was so fined. Elliston took legal action and charged a conspiracy on the grounds that the musicians had entered into a "combination" for an illegal purpose. Since this was a legitimate charge under the Combination Act, the magistrate had no option but to find in Elliston's favour. Satisfied at having made his point, Elliston did not press charges. Thereafter, however, members of the orchestra applied formally for leave of absence.[9]

Over this iron hand was a famous velvet glove. Examples of Elliston's ability to win over even the most temperamental performers are widely available. Kean was anything but happy about the idea of serving under Elliston in 1819, and made little secret of his resolution of throwing his agreement in Elliston's face and departing for America. No sooner had Elliston, using all the charm at his disposal, persuaded Kean to change his mind then he was perplexed by another source of discomfiture to the great actor: a fellow-actor's name was in larger letters on the playbill than Kean's! This seemingly insoluble dilemma (for both Dowton and Kean had a clause in their agreements guaranteeing 'literal' supremacy to each) was settled once again in Kean's favour by Elliston's diplomatic handling of Dowton. Through all his vicissitudes, Kean found in Elliston a man whom he could not ruffle, a man always ready to accommodate his wishes, but at the same time a man quite firm in making him fulfil his engagements to the full. It is indicative of Elliston's skill in this kind of personal relations that when Kean made a farewell speech in 1825, after his notorious adultery case, he paid tribute to his old enemy as follows: "The Manager has acted towards me in the hour of adversity with the affectionate kindness of a father, a brother, and a friend."[10]

The honeyed approach was Elliston's forté. It is a treat to read some of the letters in which he sought to attract actors to his theatre under terms favourable to himself. When trying to entice John Cooper to Drury in 1820, for example, he first patronized him, then deflated his provincial reputation, and finally attacked, in his best curmudgeonly style, the evil of high salaries. If Cooper would moderate his ambitions for the good of the theatre, as any self-respecting actor worthy an offer from Elliston might be expected to do, Elliston would be happy to offer him a position. "I take the liberty of an old friend, to speak openly at once," he says, this being, somehow, "the shortest road to a steady acquaintance, if any be made"; should Cooper decide to do the right thing, "I trust, it would be with an understanding, that would make your stay on those boards pleasant."[11] Cooper, however, was one of those rare people able to resist Elliston's approach, and he declined to appear at Drury Lane until he got his own terms.

One final example of Elliston's gift of handling actors must suffice, and, happily, this story illustrates both the iron hand and the velvet glove. Joseph Cowell relates that shortly after Elliston graduated to the heights of Drury Lane he sent to the Adelphi for him, and "in his bland and most insinuating manner . . . 'regretted *with all his heart and soul, that such enormous talent* should be wasted at a *petty minor theatre.*' "[12] He then persuaded Cowell to come to Drury Lane at the same salary he was receiving at the Adelphi. Since there was no immediate prospect of Cowell's getting a role at Drury, Elliston consented to his being free to take a brief engagement in the provinces, should an opportunity arise. When Cowell got such an offer from Worcester he applied to Elliston, more or less as a matter of form, for permission to accept. " 'You can't go, sir,' said the barefaced cajoler. 'Why, sir,' I replied, 'you yourself pointed out the advantage to the treasury my occupying as much of my time elsewhere as possible. . . .' 'Why, so I did,' said he: 'that's all true enough; but if you refer to your articles, you will find that permission for your absence must be first had and obtained in *writing,* and I don't think proper to write; for,' continued he, in a very important tone, 'I find the interests of the theatre demand that I should immediately bring you before the public, and I intend to produce *Blue Devils* on Thursday next, with a *powerful cast,* and you must make your first essay this season in the part of James.' " This was delivered while Elliston sat in his manager's room in the throes of revising *King Lear,* a pen behind his ear, another just removed from his mouth, his hair thrust up from his forehead "and standing in all directions, after the manner of a mad poet," his bulky frame enveloped in an impressive morning-gown. Cowell was speechless. "The man's style was so bombastically comic," he concludes, for remonstrance was, of course, in vain, "that to be angry, or even refrain from laughing, was impossible." He adds, significantly, that he "never asked for leave of absence afterward."

There was a another side to Elliston's relationship towards

actors, however, that is less often commented upon. He was strict, he was self-willed, he was even mean as regards remuneration except where star-appeal promised a good return for high salaries; but he was also, by and large, fair. Writing to an actor in 1813 he was more frank than was customary: the salary was small, he admits, but the offer was a sure one. "By experience," he adds, "you know the difference between Managers who will & can pay, & those who promise any thing meaning perhaps never to acknowledge their obligations."[13] In the constant disagreements between actors regarding the roles they did or did not want to play, Elliston never gave in if other actors would thereby be injured. In Birmingham, once, Lee's being cast as Sir Peter Teazle raised objection among the jealous company, including T. P. Cooke, whom Elliston rebuked in terms of far-reaching significance: "Is not this a little like Child's play, & are you one of those who ought to join in the game?—Reflect a little; I wish to treat all my performers as Gentlemen & brothers, but they mar my intentions."[14] To alter the cast within a matter of days, he continues, would be unreasonable; he would, however, yield "very readily" to any "fair representation" of Cooke's wishes for the rest of the season. At Drury Lane, as has just been pointed out, Elliston had constantly to deal with friction of this kind, especially where Kean was involved; in this case, however, Kean often got his own way, in particular marring Elliston's intentions of matching him with Macready.[15] In general, however, Elliston did not allow actors to take advantage of their position as did Kean. When Cooke left Birmingham on one occasion without waiting until the benefit nights were finished, Elliston took him to task, "not for myself, for I shall save a salary by your departure, but I think it hard they [the other actors] should be deprived of your services."[16]

Apart altogether from the question of agreements, regulations and penalties, Elliston was a noted disciplinarian over stage management. If a production flopped, there was sure to be a noisy post-mortem. James Robinson Planché records the style in which this took place. After the failure on opening night of his *Rodolph the Wolf*, all carpenters, scene-shifters, property-men, machinists, etc., were ordered to assemble on the Olympic stage. Elliston led Planché forward, and standing centre stage himself, back to the footlights, he faced his employees and "harangued them in the most grandiloquent language—expatiated on the enormity of their offence, their ingratitude to the man whose bread they were eating, the disgrace they had brought upon the theatre, the cruel injury they had inflicted on the young and promising author by his side; then pointing in the most tragical attitude to his wife and daughters, who remained in the box, bade them look upon the family they had ruined, and burying his face in his handkerchief to stifle his sobs, passed slowly through the door in the scene, leaving his auditors silent, abashed, and somewhat affected, yet rather relieved by being let off with a lecture. The next minute the casement in the other flat was thrown violently open, and thrusting in his head, his face scarlet with fury, he roared out, 'I discharge you all!' "[17]

Even the audience, courted as it was, for the most part, with curtain speeches which were an entertainment in themselves, occasionally was made to recognize that Elliston's authority stretched across the footlights too. This was the case, mainly, at the minor theatres, where the audience was very much under the spell of his imperious personality. Even here, Elliston's flair for self-mockery tended either to undercut his imperiousness or enlarge it into the ridiculous. Stories illustrating this subject are legion and rather fun, but only one can be recounted here. During the successful run of *Rochester,* in 1818–19, the little pit of the Olympic tended to become very crowded. One night, after second price, it became so crowded that the audience took fright and began to climb into the boxes, to the confusion of those therein ensconced. The tumult came to a head just as Elliston, as Rochester, was placating a chambermaid's jealous tantrum with a song which began, "A fig for nonsensical speeches,/For sighing and dying and stuff,/ Dear girl 'tis a man that beseeches,/I love you, and that is enough."[18] As the noise reached pandemonium proportions, Elliston broke off in the middle of line four, dropped Mrs. Edwin's pearly hand, advanced to the footlights and demanded the reason for the disgraceful disturbance. Underlying the garbled replies was an unmistakable unanimity. " 'Do I understand aright that you complain of the house being too full? Who dare assert it?' he replied, and drew himself up as if he felt it was impossible that anyone could or would challenge him. 'I do,' said a brave one in the pit, maintaining that there were more in the pit now than it was ever intended to hold, while the doorkeepers still admitted others. 'How dare you, sir, contradict me in my own house? I say the pit is not too full; and to your confusion I say it, that I have had £100 more in that pit than there is at the present moment.' " With the audience stunned into silence, he turned abruptly, picked up Mrs. Edwin's hand again, turned on his blandest and most insinuating smile, and resumed the refrain, "E-e-e-enough—e-e-e-enough—and that—and that is enough." The transition was so abrupt and the words so ridiculously appropriate that the audience forgot its discomfort in a roar of appreciative laughter.[19]

At Drury Lane, however, Elliston soon found that to question the audience's loudly attested right to capriciousness could be dangerous, e.g., on the occasion of his trying to save *Gallantry* from a first-night death by insinuating that his own experience was a truer guide to the play's merit than the audience's critical incompetence: incompetent or not, the audience had power, and to this power Elliston was forced to yield.

Elliston's managerial policy or "philosophy," if such is not too incongruous a word to use regarding the least contemplative of men, is easily summarized. Of primary importance, because representative of a whole approach, was his attitude towards the theatrical structure itself. In an age when a theatre was far more of a social and cultural centre than it is today, and an age, moreover, with a fine appreciation of luxury and elegance, it made good sense to translate such a structure into an environment of fashionable rendezvous. We may recall Elliston's comment to Winston regarding the renovation of the Olympic: "You shall have a good Company, if you astonish the town with the Theatre." An attractive theatre, where no expense had been spared to provide areas of social encounter other than the merely theatrical, i.e., lobbies, saloons, refreshment stalls, coffee-rooms, etc., would set up a chain reaction: it would inevitably draw crowds of interested, or bored, people, and in turn this would attract performers, playwrights, scenic artists, etc., anxious to get a foot into a going concern. This was particularly true in regard to the minor theatres, which had a long way to go, before Elliston came on the scene, towards anything like social acceptance. Rebuilding and redecorating the Royal Circus and the Olympic, and also Birmingham Theatre Royal, was the first step towards breaking down social prejudice, and opening up such theatres to the possibility of attaining standards by no means inferior to those obtaining at Covent Garden or the Haymarket or Drury Lane. Because of the tendency of the upper middle class to stay away from the theatre during this time, Elliston found it necessary to lure a new audience to the legitimate theatre by completely rebuilding and transforming Drury Lane in 1822. The crowds that thronged the major theatres were only indirectly interested in drama. Tom Dashall's friend, Sparkle, probably spoke for many when he described the theatre, in *Real Life in London* (I, 209), as "a sort of enchanted island, where nothing appears as it really is, nor what it should be. In London, it is a sort of time-killer, or exchange of looks and smiles." The most a manager could do was to see to it that the bucks and blades and their easy female quarries were provided with an environment spectacular enough to sustain a romantic atmosphere.

The practice of 'making a splash' with the theatre decor was coupled invariably with Elliston's flair for advertisement. He was one of the first men of the theatre to realise the power of advertising. Hazlitt said of him that in the abuse of "puffing" he left all competition behind. Through speeches from the stage, notices in the newspapers, and above all through playbills which at times ran to two pages, Elliston unashamedly sought publicity for his theatre.

If his attitude towards his actors was to treat them as "Gentlemen & brothers," Elliston followed the same practice with the audience, whether at minor or major theatres. Miscreants in the pit of the Surrey or Olympic were astonished to find themselves addressed as if they were in full dress in the boxes of Drury Lane, and the playbills and other managerial pronouncements never talked down as to an uncomprehending clientele. Conversely, Elliston was on familiar terms with London's nobility, the members of which were courted for their patronage, but were given no preferential treatment. The dress circle, initiated by Elliston at Drury Lane, was open to anyone who could afford it. There was just one audience in London, as far as Elliston was concerned, a conviction borne out by his experience at Drury Lane. This concept, of course, guided his approach to repertoire, and is one of the chief factors that contributed to his equating minor and major theatre entertainment.

Regarding the company, Elliston invariably sought to attract the

best talent possible. Up to the year 1822 this was done without payment of exorbitant salaries. At the Surrey, indeed, he paid Dibdin,
as acting manager, three times what he had got at Covent Garden,
and he offered Charles Mathews fifty pounds a week if he would be
leading actor in 1811; but with the hard times that arrived as the
decade advanced this practice was abandoned for the penny-saving
method. The year of his rebuilding Drury, however, was a water-
shed. Thereafter he disrupted the harmonious and traditional
practice which kept salaries at Drury Lane and Covent Garden
more or less on a par. By paying twice or three times the salary
obtaining at Covent Garden, Elliston attracted the best talent to
his theatre and thus declared open war on salary control. By 1825
Elliston had a first-rate company, but he was paying incredible
salaries, with Kean, at the top, drawing fifty pounds a night, singers
like Miss Stephens and Sapio getting eighty and a hundred and
thirty pounds a week respectively. Elliston carried this practice into
the Surrey in 1827, where Burke and T. P. Cooke received sums
unprecedented at the minor theatres; it was even rumoured, at one
time, that Elliston had persuaded Kean to play at the Surrey for one
month in return for a phenomenal salary.[20] For the major theatres,
this policy, successful in the short run, was ruinous in the long
run. By dividing the theatres with cut-throat competition, it defeated them economically. By the 1830's expenses had spiralled so
dangerously that the only visible solution was a merger of Covent
Garden and Drury Lane, which was tried under Alfred Bunn;
other factors, administrative and otherwise, made such a venture
hopeless. On the other hand, free and open competition lent unity
and solidarity to the minor theatre cause. Higher salaries ensured a
continual rise in standards, as more and more better-equipped
actors exchanged lesser-paid provincial or non-starring positions at
Drury and Covent Garden for the enticing rates offered by Elliston
and his successors.

Elliston's policy regarding the bill of entertainment was to present novelty and variety, as the times demanded, but to maintain
respectability and standards of 'rationality' at the same time. This
policy was most innovative at the minor theatres and led to the
establishment of a repertory, which, if anything, was probably more
'legitimate' than that tolerated by audiences at Drury Lane. Because of this fact, Elliston may be credited with shaping the taste

at the minor theatres,[21] while succumbing to it at the majors, i.e., both at Birmingham and at Drury Lane. He achieved the former through the stratagem of the burletta, disguising Shakespeare and his successors in the only form permissible at the minor theatres. In succumbing to public taste at the majors, however, Elliston admitted the importance and viability of non-literary forms like pantomime and melodrama, and cultivated what might be termed an aesthetic of imaginative spectacle to fill the vacuum left by the failure of the representatives of literary tradition to produce a living drama. Using minor-theatre methods, whether of Paris or London, Elliston came up with a substitute for the stale rhetoric and Shakespearean pastiche of the dramatic poets: a theatrics of music, pageantry, scenic and lighting effects. This was to reverse the direction in which he had moved at the Surrey and the Olympic, where the fight was to have language established in place of dumb-show and recitative. Elliston's final period of management at the Surrey saw a synthesis of these antithetical kinds of theatre, revealing the potential of the minor theatres to present popular entertainment of varying forms in terms responsive to a unified public taste.

The success of Elliston's methods has been lost sight of. His biographer, Raymond, laid such stress on Elliston's personality and on the variety of his activities that the prevailing image history has received is of one who was everything by starts and nothing long. This was not the view which his contemporaries had of Elliston. Were there any basis for the image, William Oxberry would not have hesitated to provide it in his undisguisedly hostile Memoir of Elliston, in his *Dramatic Biography*; but Oxberry's criticisms are chiefly moral. Macready spoke for many when in his *Reminiscences* (I, 276) he praised Elliston's "enterprise and tact" as manager. It is true that for a couple of years at Drury Lane he let matters slide. He was inept during those years, but he was a sick man. Moreover, he was faced with an impossible task; Charles Kemble, it should not be forgotten, could do no better at Covent Garden. The major theatres were, in fact, unmanageable. The fact that Elliston, whose administrative skills had been demonstrated at the Surrey, the Olympic, and Birmingham theatres, failed to show an overall profit at Drury Lane is evidence of this. The fact that, in the years after Elliston's term, Drury Lane continued to fail financially, even when the rent was reduced by thousands of pounds *per annum*, is further corroboration. *The Atlas*, at least, appreciated what Elliston had achieved, mourning only how his imaginative flights won little support: "ELLISTON was the only man to manage a *national* theatre, such as our national theatres are, and had he not been hampered by duns, and driven to drink by involvements, and deafened by cries of SHAKSPEARE and legitimacy, *he* would have been the genuine restorer of the *national* drama," said the theatre critic (September 24, 1826). "It was a noble idea that of engaging the entire stud of DUCROW," he muses, thinking of the *Enchanted Courser* production in 1824, when Elliston had not feared to throw to the winds the principles he had so eloquently upheld in his Defence of the Olympic Theatre in 1818.

It should also be recalled that for every year before 1825 Elliston's receipts were greater than his expenses; and that he reduced to negligible proportions the debt with which the theatre was crippled on his assuming management. He was a businessman and a lawyer as much as an actor. If he was not a director in the same sense as were Garrick and John Philip Kemble, this left him all the more time for administration. Though he tended to overuse this time by handling many theatres simultaneously, his touch faltered only once. His subsequent success at the Surrey, which he redeemed for the second time, as one critic put it, from "being nearly the worst, to be among the best" of theatres, was a final vindication of his abilities.

At the same time 'greatness' or 'genius' are concepts scarcely to be invoked in description of Elliston's managerial abilities. His raptures were not fire and air, but brandy and water. In a word, he was a showman. Moreover, he was active during a period of transition, which failed to find a balance between romantic impulse and the intellectual discipline necessary for dramatic art; it was an age of dissipation. At his death a whole new era began, symbolized by the arrival of the railway and the passing of the first Reform Bill. The gap between Regency and Victorian thought is wide, as is well known. To Thackeray, it may be recalled, George IV, the quintessence of the Regency spirit, was but suit upon suit of elegant clothing with nothing inside. It is possible to see Elliston in the same light. Certainly, he did not possess the kind of high seriousness likely to have earned him a knighthood from Victoria. He was more likely to have been told to fall to his prayers. For all that, Elliston left his mark upon the development of the nineteenth-century theatre.

In 1832, one year after Elliston's death, certain young dramatists, headed by Edward Bulwer, were successful in persuading the government to set up a Parliamentary committee to consider the whole question of monopoly and theatrical conditions.[22] Popular opinion was by this time very strongly against monopoly, and the winds of reform were blowing loudly around the portals of Drury Lane and Covent Garden. The investigating committee, which examined thirty-nine witnesses from all walks of theatrical life, including many former associates of Elliston, e.g., Winston, Osbaldiston, Moncrieff, etc., was left in no doubt as to the opinion within the theatre itself. As a result of its investigations, the committee sponsored the Dramatic Performance Bill recommending the freeing of the theatres. This was presented by Bulwer in 1833. As was expected, it passed the House of Commons; then, in August of that year, the House of Lords threw it out, fearing its implications that royal prerogatives were subject to Parliamentary annulment. But this defeat could not turn back the clock. Monopoly was a thing of the past. Though ten years passed, during which the major theatres frantically maintained a last-ditch attempt to enforce the law against the minor theatres, the tide had turned with Bulwer's bill in 1833, and the major theatres were really fighting the waves. Elliston did not live to see the passing of the Theatre Regulations Bill, which, on July 26, 1843, finally revoked the Licensing laws and freed the theatres; he did not even live to testify before Bulwer's committee. Yet his contribution to the movement that led to the formal act of revoking the monopoly laws was perhaps greater than that of anyone who lived to see the day. He it was who had initiated the establishment of the minor theatres as places where self-respecting actors and authors might find an outlet for their talents. He it was who had proved that these places could achieve and maintain artistic standards. By so doing he had given the playwrights and actors a stake in the minor theatres, and the question of monopoly came to be regarded as central to the future of English dramatic literature. Once it reached this level success was inevitable. Elliston had achieved such standards, not by breaking the law but by driving a coach-and-four through it. There are signs, however, that as he reached the end of his days he was in favour of changing the law itself, and that he would have championed Bulwer's cause had he lived to see its launching. After the dispute over the copyright of *The Flying Dutchman*, Elliston wrote in a preface to Jerrold's version of the play: "No one can wish more ardently than I do, that the whole state of the drama should be revised by the legislature; by such a review must the stage be benefited—authors would be better paid—actors would have greater excitement for their ambition—more men of real literary reputation would then turn their thoughts to what would be deemed a worthy arena for their talent,—pretenders of every sort would sink to their proper level, while merit, which is now often obscured either by intrigue, ignorance, or pseudo patronage, would then find a proper haven to shelter in."[23] Since this was precisely the spirit in which the monopoly laws were finally overturned, Elliston may well be called the author of the Theatre Regulations Bill.

Apart from the monopoly question, or perhaps associated with it, Elliston's imprint on the development of the nineteenth-century theatre can be seen in other respects. Alfred Bunn, successor to Elliston at Birmingham, assistant manager to him at Drury Lane in 1823, was the leading figure at Covent Garden and Drury Lane, which he managed simultaneously, in the 1830's. His admiration for Elliston was undisguised, a man, he said, who knew as much of the stage, "its capabilities, and its necessities, as any man that ever crossed it. . . . His fertile mind was ever on the rack of invention."[24] Bunn was proud to admit his imitation of Elliston's techniques, and managed the two major theatres in the spirit of a true disciple. Though despised by the purists, notoriously by Macready (who once floored him in the name of legitimate drama), Bunn saw that the future of the major theatres lay with opera and spectacle. The failure of Macready himself at both theatres during four years of management before 1843, proved Bunn right. After that date, once the theatres were free to follow the paths for which they were best suited, Drury Lane became the centre of pantomime, spectacular melodrama and musical comedy; Covent Garden converted to opera and ballet.

On the other hand, the Surrey and the Olympic lived on to flourish as centres of melodrama and legitimate drama rendered popular through attractive staging techniques and good acting. The

Surrey became the home of nautical dramas of the *Black-Eyed Susan* genre, known simply as "Surrey pieces." The Olympic was taken by Madame Vestris, who, with the aid of Planché, raised it to new heights after Elliston's death. The future plainly lay with the minor theatres. After 1843 Sadler's Wells was taken over by Samuel Phelps, the Princess' Theatre by Charles Kean. The success of both in staging Shakespearean productions of unrivalled scope and number is perhaps one of the most satisfying vindications of the whole struggle for a free stage. It is not without significance also that both men did not scruple to make use of the pantomimic scenic devices, the diorama and other techniques, first introduced into legitimate drama by Elliston. The aesthetic of imaginative spectacle, in fact, came home to roost in the minor theatres, where it was put to work as part of a general movement to bring Shakespeare to the people. Thus did Shakespeare and Harlequin make their peace at last.

Selected Bibliography

Account of the Proceedings before His Majesty's Most Honourable Privy Council upon a Petition for a Third Theatre. London, 1810.

Archer, William, "Robert William Elliston," in *Actors and Actresses of Great Britain and the United States,* ed. J. Brander Matthews and Laurence Hutton. Vol. II. New York, 1886.

Arnold, Samuel J. *A Letter to All the Proprietors of Drury-Lane Theatre.* London, 1818.

Ashton, John. *Social England under the Regency.* London, 1899.

Bagster-Collins, Jeremy F. *George Colman the Younger 1762–1836.* New York, 1946.

Baker, David E. *Biographia Dramatica.* 2 vols. London, 1812.

Baker, H. B. *Our Old Actors.* London, 1878.

Barbeau, Alfred. *Life and Letters at Bath in the XVIIIth Century.* London & New York, 1904.

Barker, Kathleen M.D. *The Theatre Royal Bristol: The First Seventy Years.* Second ed., Bristol, 1963.

Bernard, John. *Retrospections of the Stage.* 2 vols. London, 1830.

[Birmingham]. "Minute Book of the Proprietors of the Theatre Royal, 1773–1821." Reference Library, Birmingham Public Libraries.

Boaden, James. *The Life of Mrs. Jordan.* 2 vols. London, 1831.

————. *Memoirs of the Life of John Philip Kemble.* 2 vols. London, 1825.

Booth, Michael. *English Melodrama.* London, 1965.

Brayley, Edward W. *Historical and Descriptive Accounts of the Theatres of London.* London, 1826.

British Museum, Department of MSS. *Catalogue of Plays Submitted to the Lord Chamberlain 1824–1851.* London, 1964.

Britton, John, and A. Pugin. *Illustrations of the Public Buildings of London.* 2 vols. London, 1825–28.

Broadbent, R. J. *A History of Pantomime.* London, 1901.

Bull, John [*pseud.*]. *Master Burke.* Newcastle, 1829.

Bunn, Alfred. *The Stage.* 3 vols. London, 1840.

[Burke, Joseph]. *Biography of Master Burke, the Irish Roscius.* 7th ed., Philadelphia, n.d.

[Carlisle, Frederick H.]. *Thoughts upon the Present Condition of the Stage*. London, 1809.

Chancellor, E. Beresford. *Life in Regency and Early Victorian Times*. New York & London, 1926.

Colman, George the Younger. *Random Records*. 2 vols. London, 1830.

Considerations on the Past and Present State of the Stage. London, 1809.

Cooke, James. *The Stage Its Present State, and Prospects for the Future*. London, n.d.

The Covent Garden Journal. 2 vols. London, 1810.

Cowell, Joe. *Thirty Years Passed among the Players*. New York, 1845.

Cross, John C. *Circusiana*. 2 vols. London, 1809.

—————. *The History, Murders, Life and Death of Macbeth*: and a Full Description of the Scenery, Action, Choruses, and Characters of the Ballet of Music and Action of that Name . . . London, n.d. [1809] Copies in the Harvard Theatre Collection, New York PL, and the Folger. Cf. Sprague below.

—————. *Recitatives, Songs, Duets, Chorusses, &c. &c. &c. in the New Burletta, Melo Drama, in Three Parts, Founded on . . . The Beggar's Opera*, London, n.d. [1809] A copy in the Houghton Library, Harvard University.

Cunningham, John E. *Theatre Royal*. Birmingham, 1950.

Daniel, George, ed. *Cumberland's British Theatre*. 44 vols. London 1826–61.

—————.*Cumberland's Minor Theatre*. 16 vols. London, n.d. [1829–43].

Decastro, Jacob. *Memoirs of J. Decastro Comedian*. London, 1824.

Dent, Robert K. *The Making of Birmingham*. Birmingham, 1894.

—————. *Old and New Birmingham*. Birmingham, 1880.

Dibdin, Charles I. *History and Illustrations of the London Theatres*. London, 1826.

Dibdin, Thomas J. *Reminiscences*. 2 vols. London, 1837.

Donohue, Joseph W., Jr., ed. *The Theatrical Manager in England and America*. Princeton, 1971.

Doran, John. *Annals of the English Stage*. 3 vols. London, 1888.

Downer, Alan S. *The Eminent Tragedian William Charles Macready*. Cambridge, Mass., 1966.

—————. *Oxberry's 1822 Edition of King Richard III*. London, 1959.

[Drury Lane]. *Authentic Account of the Fire which Reduced that Extensive Building to a Pile of Ruins*. London, 1809.

—————. *An Authentic Statement of Facts connected with the Interior Management of Drury-Lane*, for the Last Three Seasons. London, 1818.

—————. A Collection of Memoranda, Documents, Playbills, Newspaper Cuttings, etc., from 1616 to 1830. Chronologically arranged by James Winston. Vols. XXI (1820–22), XXII (1823–25), XXIII (1826–30). British Museum, C.120. h.l.

————. A Collection of Newspaper Cuttings 1805–33. British Museum, 11795. k. 22.

————. A Collection of Newspaper Cuttings, MS Notes, etc., 1777–1834. British Museum, Th. Cts. 40.

————. *Facts Are Stubborn Things!* Being a Brief Review of the Season 1817–18. London, 1818. Attributed by James Arnold to Peter Moore.

————. *Impartial Observations on the Proceedings Instituted by the Proprietors* . . . against the Minor Establishments. London, 1820.

————. MS Inventory of Furniture and Fixtures, 1819. Folger Shakespeare Library, W. b. 383.

————. MS Inventory of Furniture and Fixtures, 1826. Folger, W. b. 384.

————. MS Pay Books, 1818–26. 7 vols. Folger, W. b. 367, 369–70, 372–75.

————. MS Receipt Books, 1819–21, 1826. 3 vols. Folger, W. b. 336–8. The gap from 1822–25 is filled by the following entry.

————. Receipts of Performances. Vol. VIII (1812–1826). British Museum, Add. MSS. 29,711.

Drury's Resurrection: or, The Drama versus the Menagerie. London, 1812.

Duncombe's Edition [of the British Theatre]. London, 1828–52.

Egan, Pierce. *Real Life in London.* 2 vols. London, 1831. Authorship not certain.

Elliston, Robert William. *Copy of a Memorial Presented to the Lord Chamberlain* by the Committee of Management of . . . Drury-Lane and by . . . Covent-Garden, with Copies of Two Letters in Reply. London, 1818.

————. Correspondence, Papers and Clippings Chronologically Arranged with MS Notes by James Winston, covering the Years 1791–1826. 5 vols. Harvard Theatre Collection, TS 1091. 192. Referred to in text as Elliston Papers.

————. *A Dramatic Sketch, Called The Love of Fame.* Bath, 1794.

————. *A Letter to R. W. Elliston, Esq.* . . . on the Injustice and Illegality of . . . Representing Lord Byron's . . . Marino Faliero. London, n.d.

————. *Elliston's Whim,* Being a Choice Collection of Popular New Songs, Now Singing with Unbounded Applause at Surry Theatre. London, 1810.

————. *The Venetian Outlaw.* London, 1805.

Elmes, James. *Metropolitan Improvements.* London, 1829.

Evans, Bertrand. *Gothic Drama from Walpole to Shelley.* Berkeley & Los Angeles, 1947.

Fahrner, Robert A. "The Very Ingenious Mr. Dibdin : A History of the Theatrical Career of Charles Dibdin the Elder (1745–1814)." Diss., Yale University, 1969.

Fitzball, Edward. *Thirty-Five Years of a Dramatic Author's Life.* London, 1859.

Foote, Horace. *A Companion to the Theatres.* London, 1829.

Francis, Basil. *Fanny Kelly of Drury Lane.* London, 1950.

Ganzel, Dewey. "Patent Wrongs and Patent Theatres : Drama and the Law in the Early Nineteenth Century." *PMLA,* LXXVI (1961), 384–96.

Genest, John. *Some Account of the English Stage.* 10 vols. Bath, 1832.

Grimsted, David. *Melodrama Unveiled.* Chicago, 1968.

Halliday, Andrew. *Comical Fellows: or, The History and Mystery of the Pantomime.* London, 1863.

Hanson, Frank B. "London Theatre Audiences of the Nineteenth Century." Diss., Yale University, 1953.

Hazlitt, William. *Criticisms and Dramatic Essays of the English Stage.* London, 1851.

Hillebrand, Harold N. *Edmund Kean.* New York, 1933.

House of Commons, Proceedings of. *Reports from Committees,* vol. VII (1831–32), On Dramatic Literature. London, 1832.

Howard, Frederick. *Thoughts upon the Present Condition of the Stage* and upon the Construction of a New Theatre. London, 1809.

Hunt, Leigh. *Critical Essays on the Performers of the London Theatres.* London, 1807.

————. *Leigh Hunt's Dramatic Criticism, 1808–1831,* ed. L.C. & C.W. Houtschens. New York, 1949.

Hutton, William. *The History of Birmingham.* London, 1819.

Jerrold, Walter. *Douglas Jerrold Dramatist and Wit.* 2 vols. London, 1914.

Kelly, Michael. *Reminiscences.* 2 vols. London, 1826.

Lacey, Alexander. *Pixérécourt and the French Romantic Drama.* Toronto, 1928.

Lacy's Acting Edition of Plays. London, c. 1849–55.

Lamb, Charles. *The Last Essays of Elia,* ed. Edmund Blunden. London, 1929.

Langford, John. *A Century of Birmingham Life.* 2 vols. Birmingham, 1871.

Lawrence, James H. *Dramatic Emancipation.* London, 1813.

Lawrence, W. J. "A Century of Scene-Painting." *Gentleman's Magazine,* CCLXIV (Jan–June 1888), 282–94.

————. "Some Stage Effects: Their Growth and History." *Gentleman's Magazine,* CCLXV (July–Dec 1888), 83–95.

Lennox, Lord William Pitt. *Plays, Players and Playhouses.* 2 vols. London, 1881.

Londina Illustrata, ed. Robert Wilkinson. 2 vols. London, 1819, 1825.

McMillan, Dougald. *Catalogue of the Larpent Plays in the Huntington Library.* San Marino, 1939.

Macqueen-Pope, Walter J. *Theatre Royal, Drury Lane.* London, 1945.

Macready, William Charles. *Macready's Reminiscences,* ed. Sir Frederick Pollock. 2 vols. London, 1875.

Management, a Dramatic Satire, by Humphrey Hum, Esq. Dedicated ... to a Mighty Lessee. London, n.d. [1822]

Mander, Raymond, & Joe Mitchenson. *The Artist and the Theatre.* London, 1955.

—————. *The Lost Theatres of London.* New York ,1968.

[Mathews, Charles]. *Memoirs of Charles Mathews,* by Mrs. Mathews. 4 vols., London, 1838.

Mayer, David III. *Harlequin in His Element The English Pantomime, 1806–1836.* Cambridge, Mass., 1969.

The Microcosm of London. Founded on the original edition published by Rudolph Ackermann (London, 1808–11), ill. by A. C. Pugin and T. Rowlandson. 3 vols. London, 1904.

Moncrieff, William Thomas, ed. *Richardson's New Minor Drama.* 4 vols. London, 1828–30.

—————. *Rochester; or, King Charles the Second's Merry Days :* A Burletta in Three Acts. London, 1819.

—————. *Songs, Duets, Trios, &c. &c. in Giovanni in Ireland.* London, 1821.

—————. *Songs, Duets, Chorusses, &c. Serious and Comick as sung in ... Giovanni in London; or, The Libertine Reclaimed!* London, 1818.

Morazé, Charles. *The Triumph of the Middle Classes.* London, 1966.

Munden, Thomas S. *Memoirs of Joseph Shepherd Munden, Comedian.* London, 1846.

Nagler, Alois M. *A Source Book in Theatrical History.* New York, 1952.

Nelson, Alfred L. "James Winston's Theatric Tourist : A Critical Edition, with a Biography and a Census of Winston Material." Diss., The George Washington University, 1968.

—————, and B. Gilbert Cross, eds. *Drury Lane Journal Selections from James Winston's Diaries 1819–1827.* London, 1974.

Nicholson, Watson. *The Struggle for a Free Stage in London.* Boston & New York, 1906.

Nicoll, Allardyce. *A History of English Drama 1660–1900.* 6 vols. Cambridge, 1952–1965.

Odell, George C. *Shakespeare from Betterton to Irving.* 2 vols. New York, 1920.

[Olympic Theatre]. A Collection of Newspaper Cuttings, MS Notes, etc., 1805–41. 2 vols. British Museum Th. Cts. 47, 48.

Oulton, W. C. *A History of the Theatres of London.* 3 vols. London, 1818.

Oxberry, William. *Dramatic Biography.* 5 vols. London, 1825–26.

—————. *Memoirs of Celebrated Performers.* New York, n.d.

Peake, R. B. *Memoirs of the Colman Family.* 2 vols. London, 1841.

Pearce, Charles E. *Madame Vestris and Her Times.* London, n.d.

Pemberton, T. Edgar, *The Theatre Royal, Birmingham 1774–1901.* Birmingham, 1901.

Penley, Belville S. *The Bath Stage.* London, 1892.

Pilcher, Donald. *The Regency Style, 1800 to 1830.* London, 1947.

Planché, James Robinson. "The Progress of Theatrical Pageantry." *The Era Almanack,* 1874, pp. 65–7.

————. *Recollections and Reflections.* 2 vols. London, 1872.

Poole, John. *Married and Single, a Comedy . . .* To which is Prefixed an Exposure of a Recent Little Proceeding of [Elliston]. London, 1824.

Pückler-Muskau, Hermann. *Tour in England, Ireland, and France, in the Years 1826, 1827, 1828, and 1829,* trans. [Sarah Austin?] Philadelphia, 1833.

Rahill, Frank. *The World of Melodrama.* University Park (Penn.) & London, 1967.

Raymond, George. "The Elliston Papers." *Ainsworth Magazine,* vols. II–V. London, 1842–44.

————. *The Life and Enterprises of Robert William Elliston, Comedian.* London, 1857.

————. *Memoirs of Robert William Elliston Comedian.* 2 vols. London, 1844–5. Extra-illustrated editions in the Library of Congress, Wellesley College Library, Hoblitzelle Theatre Arts Library, and Pierpont Morgan Library.

Read, Thomas. *The History of the Royal Circus.* London, 1791.

Reynolds, Frederick. *Life and Times.* 2 vols. London, 1826.

Richardson, Joanna. *George IV: A Portrait.* London, 1966.

Robinson, Henry Crabb. *The London Theatre 1811–1866,* ed. Eluned Brown. London, 1966.

Rosenfeld, Sybil. "The Grieves' Shakespearian Scene Designs." *Shakespeare Survey,* XX (1967), 107–11.

————. "Scene Designs of William Capon." *Theatre Notebook,* X (Oct. 1955–July 1956), 118–22.

[Royal Circus and Surrey Theatre]. *Hughes' Royal Circus.* 3 vols. of clippings, playbills, and MS notes in the hand of James Winston, from c. 1782–1832. New York Public Library, MWEZ/n.c. 508–10.

————. "Inventory/Surry Theatre No 1 1827." MS Inventory of Wardrobe, Scenery and Properties. Folger Shakespeare Library, W. a. 215.

————. "Inventory Surry Theatre No. 2 1827." MS Inventory of Wardrobe, Scenery and Properties, predating the above. Uncatalogued, Harvard Theatre Collection.

————. *The Two 'Circuses' and the Two 'Surrey Theatres,'* by H.D.M. London, 1866. Copy in the Enthoven Collection, Victoria & Albert Mus.

Russell, W. Clark. *Representative Actors.* London & New York, 1888.

Sandoe, James. "Some Notes on the Plays of T. J. Dibdin." *University of Colorado Studies,* I (No. 2, June 1940), 205–20.

Sawyer, Paul. "Processions and Coronations on the London Stage, 1727–1761." *Theatre Notebook*, XIV (Autumn 1959), 7–12.

Saxon, Arthur H. *Enter Foot and Horse*. New Haven, 1968.

Shepherd, Thomas. *London and its Environs in the Nineteenth Century*. London, 1829.

Sheridan, Richard Brinsley. *Memoirs of the Life of*, ed. Thomas Moore. 2 vols. Philadelphia, 1826.

Sherson, Errol. *London's Lost Theatres of the Nineteenth Century*. London, 1925.

Southern, Richard. *Changeable Scenery*. London, 1951.

————. *The Georgian Playhouse*. London, 1948.

Speaight, George. *The History of the English Toy Theatre*. Boston, 1969.

————, ed. *Professional and Literary Memoirs of Charles Dibdin the Younger (1768–1833)*. London, 1956.

Sprague, Arthur C., and B. Shuttleworth, eds. *The London Theatre in the Eighteen-Thirties*. London, 1950.

Sprague, Arthur C. "A Macbeth of Few Words," in *All These to Teach : Essays in Honor of C. A. Robertson*, ed. Robert Bryan, et al. Gainesville, 1965.

————. "Shakespeare and Melodrama." *Essays and Studies*, N.S. XVIII (1965), 1–12.

Survey of London, gen. ed. F. H. W. Sheppard. Vol. XXV, *St. George's Fields*. London, 1955.

————. Vol. XXXV, *The Theatre Royal Drury Lane and the Royal Opera House Covent Garden*. London, 1970.

Thackeray, Thomas James. *On Theatrical Emancipation*. London, 1832.

Thackeray, William Makepeace. "The Four Georges." No. IV, George IV, *Cornhill Magazine*, II (July–Dec 1860), 385–406.

Thomas, Russell. "Contemporary Taste in the Stage Decorations of London Theatre, 1770–1800." *Modern Philology*, XLII (1944), 65–78.

Thompson, Peter. "Thomas Holcroft, George Colman the Younger and the Rivalry of the Patent Theatres." *Theatre Notebook*, XXII (Summer 1968), 162–68.

Thornbury, Walter. "London Theatres and London Actors." *Belgravia*, VIII (1869), 394–404.

Tomlins, Frederick G. *A Brief View of the English Drama*. London, 1840.

Troubridge, Sir St. Vincent. *The Benefit System in the British Theatre*. London, 1967.

————. "Fitzball and Elliston; or, How to Submit a Play in 1820." *Theatre Notebook*, VII, 3 (April–June 1953), 64–5.

Urwin, C. G. "Alfred Bunn 1796–1860: A Revaluation." *Theatre Notebook*, XI (Oct. 1956–July 1957), 96–102.

Watson, Ernest B. *Sheridan to Robertson*. Cambridge, Mass., 1926.

Wells, Mitchell. "Spectacular Scenic Effects of the Eighteenth-Century Pantomime." *Philological Quarterly*, XVII (1938), 67–81.

Wellwarth, George E. "The Disappearance of the New Royal Brunswick Theatre: or The Mystery of the Iron Roof." *Theatre Notebook*, XXII (Winter 1967–8), 56–63.

Wemyss, Francis. *Twenty-Six Years of the Life of an Actor and Manager.* 2 vols. New York, 1847.

White, Eric W. *The Rise of English Opera.* London, 1951.

White, Henry A. *Sir Walter Scott's Novels on the Stage.* New Haven, 1927.

Wickman, Richard Carl. "An Evaluation of the Employment of Panoramic Scenery in the Nineteenth Century Theatre." Diss., Ohio State Univ., 1961.

Wilkinson, Tate. *The Wandering Patentee.* 4 vols. York, 1795.

Williams, Clifford John. *Madame Vestris, A Theatrical Biography.* London, 1973.

Williamson, Jane Louise. "Charles Kemble, Man of the Theatre." Diss., University of Bryn Mawr, 1963.

[Winston, James]. *Bibliotheca dramatica et histrionica.* Catalogue of the Curious and Valuable Library, Printed and Manuscript . . . of the late Mr. James Winston. London, n.d. [1849]

————. Collection of Miscellaneous Theatrical Papers 1660–1845, compiled by Winston, George Colman, and others, c. 1800–1845. Folger, Y.d.23.

————. *Theatric Tourist.* London, 1805.

Wyatt, Benjamin D. *Observations on the Design for the Theatre Royal Drury Lane as Executed in the Year 1812.* London, 1813.

Wyndham, H. Saxe. *The Annals of Covent Garden Theatre.* 2 vols. London, 1906.

NEWSPAPERS AND PERIODICALS

The Age
The Atlas
Bell's Weekly Messenger
Biography of the British Stage
Bonner and Middleton's Bristol Journal
The Bristol Gazette and Public Advertiser
The British Monitor
The British Stage and Literary Cabinet
The Champion
The Courier
The Drama, or Theatrical Pocket Magazine
The Drama
The Dramatic Censor; or Weekly Theatrical Report
The Dramatic Censor for the Year 1811
The Dramatic Magazine
The Dramatic Mirror
Era Almanack

European Magazine
The Examiner
Felix Farley's Bristol Journal
Gentleman's Magazine
John Bull
Lady's Magazine
The London Chronicle
The London Magazine
The Mirror of Taste
The Monthly Mirror
The Monthly Theatrical Reporter
The Morning Chronicle
The Morning Herald
The Morning Post
The New Monthly Magazine
The New Times
Oxberry's Biography and Green Room Spy
Oxberry's Dramatic Biography
Shakespeare Survey
The Tatler
Theatre Notebook
Theatre Research/Recherches Theatrales
The Theatrical Inquisitor
The Theatrical Observer and Daily Bills of the Play
The Theatrical Reporter
The Times
The Weekly Dramatic Register, compiled from *The Theatrical Observer*

Notes

Chapter One

[1] Charles Lamb, "Ellistoniana," *The Last Essays of Elia,* ed. Edmund Blunden (London, 1929), p. 23.

[2] *Critical Essays on the Performers of the London Theatres* (London, 1807), p. 200. See the full account pp. 180–203.

[3] William Hazlitt, in *The London Magazine,* No. 1 (January 1820). See *Collected Works,* ed. A. R. Waller & Arnold Glover, (12 vols. London, 1902–6), VIII, 392.

[4] "R. W. Elliston, Esq.," *Gentleman's Magazine,* CI, Part II (1831), 184. Even William Oxberry, in an otherwise unflattering portrait, conceded this, in "Memoir of Robert William Elliston," *Oxberry's Dramatic Biography* (5 vols., London, 1825–6), III, 88.

[5] R. W. Elliston, *A Dramatick Sketch Called the Love of Fame* (Bath, 1794), p. 13.

[6] The most thorough study of the monopoly question is that of Watson Nicholson, *The Struggle for a Free Stage in London* (Boston & New York, 1906). See also Dewey Ganzel, "Patent Wrongs and Patent Theatres: Drama and the Law in the Early Nineteenth Century," *PMLA,* LXXVI (1961), 384–96; James H. Lawrence, *Dramatic Emancipation* (London, 1813); Allardyce Nicoll, *English Drama 1660–1900,* I (Cambridge, 1952), 293–301, III, 194, IV (Cambridge, 1955), 137–9; Peter Thompson, "Thomas Holcroft, George Colman the Younger and the Rivalry of the Patent Theatres," *Theatre Notebook,* XXII (Summer 1968), 162–8; F. G. Tomlins, *A Brief View of the English Drama* (London, 1840), pp. 57ff; E. B. Watson, *Sheridan to Robertson* (Cambridge, Mass., 1926), pp. 20–57.

[7] *Op. cit.,* p. 185.

[8] *Ibid.,* pp. 197–8. Hunt places Elliston above Charles Kemble on this criterion. He elaborates on the quality, Appendix, p. 44.

[9] William Oxberry, *op. cit.,* p. 89.

[10] William Archer, "Robert William Elliston," in *Actors and Actresses of Great Britain and the United States,* ed. J. Brander Matthews & Laurence Hutton (5 vols., New York, 1886), II, 160–73.

[11] *Op. cit.,* pp. 167–75.

[12] *Loc. cit.*

[13] George Raymond, "Elliston Papers," *Ainsworth Magazine,* II (1842), 426.

[14] List compiled from playbills, courtesy of City Librarian, York City Library.

15 *The Wandering Patentee* (4 vols., York, 1795), III, 233. Elliston made his debut with Wilkinson at Leeds, acting Eumenes in *Merope*, May 30, 1791. Raymond, *Memoirs*, I, 40, mistakenly follows Wilkinson in citing the part as Dorilas.

16 Figure based on John Genest, *Some Account of the English Stage* (10 vols., Bath, 1832), VII, 175–8, supplemented by lists kindly supplied by Mr. Arnold Hare for the Bath stage and by Miss Kathleen Barker for the Bristol stage.

17 Raymond, *Life and Enterprises*, p. 19. Negotiations broke down between Elliston and Kemble over a position at Drury Lane. Raymond does not notice that these two had met prior to 1793, i.e., when they played together in *Revenge*, at York, on August 20, 1791: playbill, York City Library. Cf. Wilkinson, *op. cit.*, III, 248ff.

18 *Sarah Farley's Bristol Journal*, September 28, 1793.

19 Clipping, Elliston Papers, Harvard Theatre Collection, TS 1091.192. Hereafter cited as EP. Quotations bp permission of the Harvard College Library.

20 James Winston, *Theatric Tourist* (London, 1805), p. 5.

21 Genest, *op. cit.*, VIII, 176. Cf. Belville S. Penley, *The Bath Stage* (London, 1892), p. 76.

22 *Loc. cit.*

23 *Op. cit.*, p. 233, n.

24 *Felix Farley's Bristol Journal*, July 16, 1796.

25 Playbill, Bristol Theatre Royal, Mon. July 11, 1796. Transcript courtesy of Miss Barker.

26 Genest, *op. cit.*, VII, 579. Interestingly, Henry Harris, writing to Reynolds from Paris in 1802, defines melodrama as a "mixing, as the name implies (*mêler drame*) the drama and *bâllet* of action; which latter, it will probably supercede." See Frederick Reynolds, *Life and Times* (2 vols., London, 1826), II, 346.

27 *The Life of the Drama* (New York, Atheneum, 1967), p. 216.

28 At what exact date it is hard to say. Mrs. Elliston to Dr. Elliston, dated August 20, 1797, in the Enthoven Collection, Victoria & Albert Museum, indicates patronage; Elliston to Dr. Elliston, August 15, 1797, refers to "the progress I have made towards a footing in the Bath Theatre, as a proprietor." Raymond, *Memoirs*, I, 101, testifies to Dr. Elliston's financial backing.

29 Penley, *op. cit.*, p. 82.

30 *Felix Farley's Bristol Journal*, July 19, 1800.

31 Elliston to Dr. Elliston, February 23, 1800, EP. Cf. Elliston to William Wyatt Dimond, undated, EP.

32 Elliston to Dr. Elliston, March 27, 1800, EP.

33 Kathleen Barker, *The Theatre Royal Bristol: The First Seventy Years* (Bristol, 1963), p. 12.

34 Raymond, *Memoirs*, I, 101.

35 Kathleen Barker, *op. cit.*, p. 13.

36 See Alfred Barbeau, *Life and Letters at Bath in the XVIIIth Century* (London & New York, 1904), pp. 298ff.

37 *Retrospections of the Stage* (2 vols., London, 1830), I, 184–5.

38 Barker, *op. cit.*, pp. 8–11.

39 *London Chronicle*, August 4, 1801.

40 Raymond, *Memoirs*, I, 151.

41 Raymond, *Life and Enterprises*, p. 60.

⁴² *Bonner and Middleton's Bristol Journal,* June 19, 1802, said that Elliston had "commenced Manager, having taken the theatres at Wells and Shepton-Mallet." Since Elliston was at Bristol until June 30, it was probably after this date that he himself appeared at his theatres. Egan, from Bath, was his assistant manager.

⁴³ Raymond, *Life and Enterprises,* p. 75.

⁴⁴ *Ibid.,* p. 84.

⁴⁵ The idea was to open in strict accordance with the patent rights, in mid-May, and to combat encroachments by the major theatres. See Watson Nicholson, *op. cit.,* pp. 150–58. Cf. Raymond, *Memoirs,* I, 195. Jeremy F. Bagster-Collins, *George Colman the Younger 1762–1836* (New York, 1946), pp. 161–2.

⁴⁶ MS, dated May 12, 1803, Larpent Collection, HM, LA 1383, Henry E. Huntington Library. Reproduced by permission of the Huntington Library.

⁴⁷ *Morning Chronicle,* May 18, 1803.

⁴⁸ R. B. Peake, *Memoirs of the Colman Family* (2 vols., London, 1841), II, 304.

⁴⁹ William Dunlap, *The Life of George Frederick Cooke* (2 vols., London, 1815), I, 163. In accepting the Drury Lane offer, Elliston had hopes of a share in proprietorship: Elliston to Dr. Elliston, April 1, 1804, EP.

⁵⁰ Elliston to Dr. Elliston, October 25, 1804, EP.

⁵¹ *London Chronicle,* February 1, 1805. This paper had been among the severest on Elliston in preceding months.

⁵² *Op. cit.,* pp. 198–9.

⁵³ Genest, *op. cit.,* VII, 640–53. Similar details below from the same source, VII, 698ff.; VIII, 29–42, 62–74, 115–21.

⁵⁴ On September 10, 1804, Elliston held his benefit by special permission at the Opera House. So great was the crush that many were seated on the stage, and very many broke in without paying. Through well delivered speeches, nimble collectors with pewter plates, and pointed advertisement of his home address, Elliston still cleared £600. See W. C. Oulton, *A History of the Theatres of London* (3 vols., London, 1818), III, 55–7; Raymond, *Life and Enterprises,* pp. 105–6; H. B. Baker, *Our Old Actors* (London, 1878), pp. 258–9; Penley, *op. cit.,* p. 78, n.

⁵⁵ George Colman the Younger to Elliston, April 19, 1803, Henry E. Huntington Library, states that Elliston had "full power to proceed in, & to close the treaty" with an actress of his choice for the Haymarket.

⁵⁶ Colman to Elliston, undated, Huntington Library.

⁵⁷ Raymond, *Life and Enterprises,* pp. 98–9.

⁵⁸ *Ibid.,* p. 112.

⁵⁹ *Op. cit.,* VII, 674.

⁶⁰ James Boaden, *Memoirs of the Life of John Philip Kemble* (2 vols., London, 1825), II, 491. Cf. Charles Mathews, *Memoirs* (4 vols., London, 1838), II, 27–37.

⁶¹ Genest, *op. cit.,* VII, 673.

⁶² Raymond, *Memoirs,* I, 270.

⁶³ *Op. cit.,* p. 185.

⁶⁴ *Life and Enterprises,* p. 112.

⁶⁵ *Ibid.,* p. 118.

⁶⁶ Two years earlier he toyed with the idea of buying the Royal Circus outright. His uncle apparently dissuaded him. Elliston to Dr. Elliston, December 8, 1804, Pierpont Morgan Library.

67 Raymond, *Memoirs*, I, 296.

68 Raymond, *Life and Enterprises*, p. 125.

69 Elliston to Dr. Elliston, December 25, 1792, EP.

70 Quoted in *Representative Actors*, ed. W. Clark Russell (London & New York. 1888), p. 297.

71 Raymond, *Life and Enterprises*, p. 139.

72 *Ibid.*

73 Elliston to Trustees of the Royal Circus, February 23, 1809, EP. He also recognised the claim of George Jones, the equestrian, to two benefits annually, with six free admissions nightly, a claim dating from 1798. See "Extract from the Deed Executed by James Jones, John Tanner, Sir Charles Price (?) and Richard James to Mr. George Jones. For R. W. Elliston Esqr," MS, Hoblitzelle Theatre Arts Library, University of Texas at Austin.

74 Elliston to Trustees, *loc. cit.*

75 *London Magazine*, IX (September 1820). See *Works, op. cit.*, p. 472.

76 *The Times*, February 25, 1809. Cf. *Authentic Account of the Fire* which reduced that extensive building of the Theatre-Royal, Drury-Lane, to a Pile of Ruins, on the evening of the 24th of February, 1809. (London, 1809).

77 Raymond, *Life and Enterprises*, pp. 150–51. Cf. Charles Mathews, *op. cit.*, II, 102.

Chapter Two

1 "ADDRESS, *Spoken* by Mr. ELLISTON, and *Written* by J. C. CROSS," in J. C. Cross, *Recitatives, Songs, Duets, Chorusses*, &c. &c. &c. in the New Burletta, Melo Drama, in Three Parts, Founded on the Subject, Incidents and Diction, Carefully Compressed, of the Beggar's Opera (London, n.d.) n.p.

2 For a history of the Royal Circus see Edward W. Brayley, *Historical and Descriptive Accounts of the Theatres of London* (London, 1826), pp. 67–75; Jacob Decastro, *Memoirs*, (London, 1824), *passim*; Charles Dibdin, *The Professional Life of Mr. Dibdin* (2 vols., London, 1803), II, 104–64; *The Microcosm of London*, founded on the original edition published by Rudolph Ackermann (London, 1808–11), ill. by A. C. Pugin and Thomas Rowlandson (3 vols., London, 1904), III, 13–17; Thomas Read, *The History of the Royal Circus* (London, 1791), *passim*.

3 Leigh Hunt, *Critical Essays on the Performers of the London Theatres* (London, 1807), p. 190.

4 Two-paged handbill, dated June 13, 1809, Elliston Papers, Harvard Theatre Collection. Cf. *The Drama; or, Theatrical Pocket Magazine*, V (1823–4), 365–7.

5 J. C. Cross, *op. cit.*, act II.

6 Playbill, Royal Circus, undated [September 1809], Harvard Th. Coll.

7 *Morning Post*, September 6, 1809.

8 A. C. Sprague published the text of this promptbook, "A *Macbeth* of Few Words," in *All These to Teach: Essays in Honor of C. A. Robertson*, ed. Robert Bryan, and others (Gainesville, 1965,) pp. 80–101.

9 For example, see John Poole, *Hamlet Travestie, Lacy's Acting Plays*, X (London, n.d.), p. 21, where a revealing parody of such conventions is supplied. Cf. Andrew Halliday, *Comical Fellows; or, The History and Mystery of the Pantomime* (London, 1863), pp. 63–4.

10 Sprague, "A *Macbeth* of Few Words," p. 92.

11 See William Thomas Moncrieff, "Remarks" to *Tom and Jerry, Richardson's Minor Theatre*, vol. I (London, 1828).

12 Sprague, p. 101.

13 MS, "Theatrical Miscellany, c. 1826-1851," James Winston Collection, Folger Shakespeare Library.

14 *Morning Post*, September 30, 1809.

15 Advertisement, *Morning Chronicle*, November 1, 1809. A MS entry in *Hughes' Royal Circus*, vol. 2, Stead Collection, New York Public Library, gives the closing date of the Royal Circus as November 6.

16 *Morning Chronicle*, September 30, 1809.

17 Immortalized in *English Bards and Scotch Reviewers* (vv. 638ff.) as "the patron and the pile/Of vice and folly, Greville and Argyle!" Henry Fulke Greville organised the Pic Nic Club in 1802 and was first in the field in the drive to found an English opera house. See Watson Nicholson, *The Struggle for a Free Stage in London* (Boston and New York, 1906), pp. 161ff.

18 MS, Elliston Papers, Harvard Theatre Collection.

19 *Morning Chronicle*, September 22, 1809. Cf. Nicholson, pp. 215, 250–1. George Raymond points out, *Memoirs of Robert William Elliston Comedian*, I, 377ff., that because of a mixup between Lingham, the proprietor of the Lyceum, Arnold and Sheridan, to both of whom Lingham had leased the Lyceum, Arnold emerged as lessee by mistake, while the Drury Lane company became his tenants. Arnold's licence for English opera being only for the summer, there was need of another party with a licence for the winter: hence the introduction of Greville.

20 *Morning Chronicle*, October 25, 1809.

21 *Ibid.*, November 6, 1809. See Nicholson, *op. cit.*, pp. 140ff. for a full account of the "dormant" patent.

22 Raymond, I, 428.

23 Elliston to Lord Chamberlain, November 17, 1809, Elliston Papers.

24 Quoted Raymond, I, 430.

25 Allen to Elliston, February 14, 1810, Hoblitzelle Theatre Arts Library, University of Texas at Austin.

26 *Hughes' Royal Circus*, vol. 2, Stead Coll., New York Public Library.

27 "Petition of Magistrates & Inhabitants of the Boro' of Southwk & various other Places in the Coy of Surry," MS, Hoblitzelle Theatre Arts Library.

28 Elliston to Richard Brinsley Sheridan, March 2, 1810, Hoblitzelle.

29 Raymond, I, 432. What was in question, of course, was the second Licensing Act, 25 Geo. II, within which Elliston claimed to be staying.

30 "A Bill to exempt the Proprietor of the Theatre called the Royal Circus in the County of Surrey from certain penalties under the laws for restraining Dramatic Exhibitions," MS, Hoblitzelle.

31 Elliston to Perceval, March 21, 1810, Hoblitzelle.

32 Allen to Warner Phipps, March 12, 1810, Hoblitzelle.

33 *Account of the Proceedings before his Majesty's Most Honourable Privy Council upon a petition for a Third Theatre in the Metropolis* (London, 1810), Appendix I, pp. 23–5. Cf. Nicholson, pp. 192–220.

34 Letter, probably from Warner Phipps, to Elliston, quoted Raymond, *Life and Enterprises of Robert William Elliston, Comedian*, p. 170.

35 Clipping, dated March 31, 1810, Elliston Papers, Harvard Theatre Collection. Cf. *Monthly Mirror*, VII (April 1810), 311–12.

³⁶ Elliston to Richard Ryder, March 10, 1810, Uncatalogued Letters of R. W. Elliston, Harvard. Cf. *Account of the Proceedings*, Appx. I, p. 23. Letters from Phipps and Allen to Elliston, Hoblitzelle, discussed the plans for improvements during January 1810.

³⁷ *Morning Chronicle*, April 24, 1810.

³⁸ "Particulars of certain works to be executed by Contract for W. R. Elliston [*sic*] Esqʳ at the new Royal Circus under the direction of Mr. C A Busby Architect," MS, Hoblitzelle.

³⁹ Clipping, dated April 23, 1810, Elliston Papers.

⁴⁰ Pierce Egan(?), *Real Life in London* (2 vols., London, 1831), II, 44.

⁴¹ Thomas Dibdin, *Reminiscences* (2 vols., London, 1837), II, 113. See also *London Chronicle*, April 24, 1810.

⁴² *Ibid.*, pp. 110–11.

⁴³ John Ashton, *Social England under the Regency* (London, 1899), pp. 36–7.

⁴⁴ [R. W. Elliston], *Elliston's Whim*, being a Choice Collection of Popular New Songs, Now Singing with Unbounded Applause at Surry Theatre (London, 1810), pp. 28–9.

⁴⁵ Thomas Dibdin, *op. cit.*, I, 366.

⁴⁶ Playbill, Surrey Theatre, August 9, 1810, Folger Shakespeare Library.

⁴⁷ Advertisement, *Morning Chronicle*, August 17, 1810.

⁴⁸ *The Lady of the Lake: A Melo-Dramatic Romance, in Two Acts*, in *Cumberland's Minor Theatre*, vol. III (London, 1826). Cf. Raymond Mander and Joe Mitchenson, *The Artist and the Theatre* (London, 1955), pp. 207–9.

⁴⁹ Walter Scott, *The Lady of the Lake* (3rd ed., Edinburgh, 1810). Canto II, 6, vv. 7–20, becomes a song in the play, I, v.

⁵⁰ *The Times*, September 25, 1810.

⁵¹ James Robinson Planché, *Recollections and Reflections* (2 vols., London, 1872), I, 59–60.

⁵² Thomas Dibdin, *op. cit.*, I, 435.

⁵³ Raymond, *Memoirs*, II, 40.

⁵⁴ Handbill, dated November 23, 1810, Enthoven Collection.

⁵⁵ Clipping, dated December 10, 1810, Elliston Papers. As early as March 1810, Greville was trying to interest Elliston in a winter "proposal," Greville to Phipps, March 2, Hoblitzelle. In November 1810, Greville once again made suggestions for an opera scheme, Elliston to be manager: MS note, Elliston Papers.

⁵⁶ Thomas Dibdin, *The Harper's Son and the Duke's Daughter; a Grand Melo-Dramatic Romance, interspersed with Songs, Duets, and Chorusses, performing with the Greatest Applause, at the Surrey Theatre* (London, 1810).

⁵⁷ See William Oxberry, *Memoirs of Celebrated Performers* (New York, n.d.), pp. 3–10.

⁵⁸ *Morning Chronicle*, February 18, 1811.

⁵⁹ Quoted in Raymond, II, 16.

⁶⁰ "Mentor" to Elliston, March 6, 1811, Uncatalogued Letters of R. W. Elliston, Harvard Theatre Collection.

⁶¹ "Mentor" to Mrs. Elliston, May 6, 1811, *loc. cit.*

⁶² Raymond, II, 46ff. Colman's partner refused to pay this high salary, to Elliston and two others, and a walk-out and court case developed in July. See *London Chronicle*, July 22, 1811; Jeremy F. Bagster-Collins, *George Colman the Younger 1762–1836* (New York, 1946), pp. 220–5.

⁶³ See Watson Nicholson, *op. cit.*, p. 256.

64 *The Times,* May 16, 1811.

65 "Mentor" to Elliston, May 1811, *loc. cit.* At Bath, Elliston's Hamlet and three Singles, in particular, had won high praise in the *Bristol Gazette,* Jan. 3, Feb. 21. In London, the *Monthly Mirror* was severely critical of Elliston's performances at the Surrey.

66 In the occasional address recited at the Haymarket on May 15. (See n. 64 above.)

67 See Elliston to Mathews, April 6, 1811, Enthoven Collection. Mrs. Charles Mathews testifies that this letter refers to the Surrey Theatre, and she affirms that Mathews would not act in a minor theatre. See *Memoirs of Charles Mathews* (4 vols., London, 1838), II, 118–9.

68 Raymond, *Memoirs,* II, 39.

69 Clipping, dated June 11, 1811, *Hughes' Royal Circus, loc. cit.* For the horse craze in general, see Arthur H. Saxon, *Enter Foot and Horse* (New Haven, 1968), *passim.*

70 Playbill, Surrey Theatre, Dec. 30, 1811, Folger.

71 *Morning Chronicle,* October 25, 1811.

72 Copy of a letter from Walter Scott to Elliston, in the hand of James Winston, Elliston Papers. Winston's punctuation has been modified for intelligibility.

73 Playbill, Surrey Theatre, March 1812, Folger.

74 *Morning Chronicle,* May 21, 1812. The playbill provided a "Prospectus" of the action, in full detail.

75 "Memoir of S. T. Russell," in *Oxberry's Dramatic Biography,* N.S. (London, 1827), II, 48.

76 Dennis Lawler, *The Earls of Hammersmith; or, The Cellar Spectre!* Dunscombe's Edition of Plays (London, n.d.), scene 3.

77 Playbill, Surrey Theatre, April 30, 1812, Folger.

78 The lease expired on March 25, 1814, and Elliston gave notice he would not renew. MS note, *Hughes' Royal Circus,* vol. II, NYPL. Elliston's original lease for seven years was revised around January 1810, allowing him to give up the theatre after two years, "provided he gives written Notice to one of the Trustees . . . previously to the 29th September in this season." See "Alterations named by Mr Elliston in his first proposal, and acceded to by the Trustees of the Circus," MS, undated, Hoblitzelle Library.

Chapter Three

1 Errol Sherson, *London's Lost Theatres of the Nineteenth Century* (London, 1925), p. 77.

2 William Dunlap, *The Life of George Frederick Cooke* (2 vols., London, 1815), I, 312. For a full account of the early history of the Olympic, see Raymond Mander and Joe Mitchenson, *The Lost Theatres of London* (London, 1968), pp. 253–64.

3 See Walter Thornbury, "London Theatres and London Actors," *Belgravia,* VIII (1869), 401.

4 John Astley to Elliston, January 17, 1813, Collection of Professor William W. Appleton. On January 19, Elliston wrote to Thomas Cooke in Dublin that he had bought the Olympic outright, Uncatalogued Letters of R. W. Elliston, Folger Shakespeare Library. Cf. *Londina Illustrata,* II, 173.

⁵ "Extracts from the Lease and Assignments," MS, dated March 1813, B. Mus. Th. Cts. 47. This MS is a continuation of that recording Lord Craven's lease to Astley, dated August 21, 1805.

⁶ Walter Thornbury, *op. cit.*, p. 403. Cf. George Raymond, *Memoirs of Robert William Elliston Comedian*, II, 89.

⁷ Elliston to an unknown addressee, September 29, 1813, Uncatalogued Letters of R. W. Elliston, Folger. It may be noted that Elliston was still involved also in hiring actors for the Haymarket: Bellamy to Elliston, April 28, 1813, Collection of the Professor W. W. Appleton.

⁸ See H. N. Hillebrand, *Edmund Kean* (New York, 1933), pp. 98–103; pp. 362–3. Cf. George Raymond, *Life and Enterprises of Robert William Elliston, Comedian*, pp. 219–22.

⁹ Raymond, *Memoirs*, II, 123–4. According to a clipping, dated August 19, 1815, Elliston Papers, Harvard Theatre Collection, Elliston was asked to take a reduced salary.

¹⁰ *Theatrical Inquisitor*, VII (July 1815), 9–10.

¹¹ *Examiner*, May 17, 1818. Cf. John Genest, *Some Account of the English Stage*, VIII, 647–50.

¹² R. W. Elliston, *Copy of a Memorial Presented to the Lord Chamberlain by the Committee of Management of Theatre-Royal Drury-Lane and by the Proprietors of Theatre-Royal Covent-Garden*, against the Olympic and Sans Pareil Theatres; with Copies of Two Letters, in Reply to the Contents of such Memoirs, Addressed to the Lord Chamberlain by Robert William Elliston, Comedian (London, 1818), Advertisement, p. i.

¹³ Elliston to James Winston, September 26, 1815, Elliston Papers.

¹⁴ Playbill, Olympic Theatre, October 30, 1815, Enthoven Collection.

¹⁵ Winston to Elliston, postmarked January 30, 1816, Hoblitzelle Theatre Arts Library, University of Texas at Austin.

¹⁶ *Ibid.*, undated, ca. January, 1816.

¹⁷ Elliston to Winston, October 24, 1815, Elliston Papers.

¹⁸ Winston to Elliston, April 2, 1816, Hoblitzelle.

¹⁹ Winston to Mrs. Elliston, November 10, 1815, Elliston Papers.

²⁰ Winston to Elliston, April 2, 1816, Hoblitzelle.

²¹ MS, dated March 17, 1817, Elliston Papers.

²² *Theatrical Inquisitor*, IX (December 1817), 471.

²³ On its first production, Dec. 26, 1817, this "comic extravaganza entertainment" was called *Giovanni Let Loose;* the title was changed after four nights. For the text see *Cumberland's British Theatre*, vol. XVII (London, 1828). Cf. Oscar Mandel, *The Theatre of Don Juan* (Lincoln, Nebraska, 1963), pp. 403–46.

²⁴ William T. Moncrieff, "Sayings and Doings of the Celebrities of the London Theatres, for upwards of the Last Half Century," Clipping, undated, Harvard Theatre Collection. The subsequent anecdote is drawn from this source.

²⁵ John Larpent to Charlton, March 2, 1818, Collection of Professor Appleton. Cf. John Genest, VIII, 669–70.

²⁶ R. W. Elliston, *Copy of a Memorial*, p. 5.

²⁷ Elliston to Winston, October 23, 1815, Elliston Papers.

²⁸ See Allardyce Nicoll, *A History of English Drama*, IV, 92. Cf. Henry A. White, *Sir Walter Scott's Novels on the Stage* (New Haven, 1927), pp. 34–56;

White does not mention Moncrieff's version of *Rob Roy*, the MS text of which is in the Larpent Collection, Huntington Library.

²⁹ *Copy of a Memorial*, pp. 29–30.

³⁰ *Ibid.*, p. 68.

³¹ *Ibid.*, p. 140.

³² *Ibid.*, p. 78.

³³ See *British Stage and Literary Cabinet*, September 1818.

³⁴ Clipping, dated November 16, 1818, Elliston Papers. Cf. Raymond, *Memoirs*, II, 185–6.

³⁵ Clipping, dated August (?) 1818, Elliston Papers, Cf. Raymond, *Life and Enterprises*, p. 254, where the figure is given as £2500.

³⁶ [George Robins], "Particulars of the Olympic Theatre, in Drury Lane: which will be sold by Auction, by Messrs. ROBINS, . . . on TUESDAY, the 13th of June, 1820, at Twelve o'Clock," B. Mus., 11795.k.31. Elliston once got 675 people into the pit: Accounts form, B. Mus., Th. Cts. 47.

³⁷ *Morning Post*, November 16, 1818. Cf. Edward W. Brayley, *Historical and Descriptive Accounts of the Theatres of London* (London, 1826), p. 88.

³⁸ December 7, 1818.

³⁹ November 22, 1818.

⁴⁰ LXXIV (1818), 535. Cf. also *Theatrical Inquisitor*, XIII (1818), 392; *British Stage and Literary Cabinet*, III (1819), 50.

⁴¹ *Morning Post*, November 17, 1818.

⁴² *Theatrical Inquisitor*, XIII (1818), 468.

⁴³ MS, in Winston's hand, March 1817 (?), B. Mus., Th. Cts. 47. Raymond Mander and Joe Mitchenson, *op. cit.*, p. 260, give the dimensions of the stage for 1812 as 50′ wide and 60′ long, but only three-fifths of the stage was used for scenery.

⁴⁴ In "Remarks," prefacing *Rochester*, in *Richardson's Minor Theatre*, vol. I (London, 1828), and in *Cumberland's Minor Theatre*, vol. XI (London, n.d.). Cf. E. B. Watson, *Sheridan to Robertson* (Cambridge, Mass., 1926), p. 38.

⁴⁵ MS application in Elliston's hand, November 14, 1818, Huntington Library.

⁴⁶ William T. Moncrieff, *Rochester; or, King Charles the Second's Merry Days*: A Burletta, in Three Acts. As Performed at the Olympic New Theatre, Newcastle Street, Strand (London, 1819), p. 2.

⁴⁷ In "Remarks," *loc. cit.* Cf. *The Times*, January 18, 1819.

⁴⁸ Elliston had a contract with one Marquis de Chabannes, owner of a foundry at 121 Drury Lane, whereby the steam apparatus was to be installed for £100. MS agreement, dated January 16, 1819, Elliston Papers.

⁴⁹ See *Rodolph the Wolf; or, Columbine Red Riding Hood*. A comic Melodramatic Pantomime (London, 1819).

⁵⁰ MS note, undated, Elliston Papers.

⁵¹ *The Times*, April 5, 1819.

Chapter Four

¹ William Hutton, *The History of Birmingham* (London, 1819), pp. 61–4.

² Birmingham had a theatre in Moor Street in 1740 and one in King Street 1751–80, but only the New Street theatre survived the 18th century. See James Winston, *Theatric Tourist* (London, 1805), pp. 57–60; T. Edgar Pemberton,

The Theatre Royal, Birmingham 1774–1901 (Birmingham, 1901), pp. 5–7; John E. Cunningham, *Theatre Royal* (Birmingham, 1950), pp. 11–16; Allardyce Nicoll, *A History of English Drama 1660–1900*, IV (Cambridge, 1955), 234.

3 William Hutton, p. 207. Cf. Robert K. Dent, *Old and New Birmingham* (Birmingham, 1880), pp. 220–56.

4 George Raymond, *Memoirs of Robert William Elliston Comedian*, I, 413–14. Cf. James Winston, *Bibliotheca dramatica et histrionica* (London, n. d.), item 196; Winston also lists a manager's account book for Croydon 1813–14. Cf. also "A Supplement to the Memoir of Mr. Elliston," *Lady's Magazine*, N.S. 3 (1822), 46. Croydon was seized by Elliston's creditors in 1826.

5 MS note, dated November 1815, Elliston Papers, Harvard Theatre Collection.

6 Kathleen M. D. Barker, *The Theatre-Royal Bristol: The First Seventy Years* (Bristol, 1963), p. 13. See also "Proprietors' Minute & Account Book," II, 10, dated July 10, 1817.

7 T. L. G. Burley, *Playhouses and Players of East Anglia* (Norwich, 1928), p. 126. Cf. *Theatrical Inquisitor*, April 1818; *British Stage and Literary Cabinet*, April 1818.

8 Clipping, dated August 1818, Elliston Papers. Cf. George Raymond, *Life and Enterprises of Robert William Elliston, Comedian*, p. 250.

9 George Raymond, *Memoirs*, II, 183.

10 *Theatrical Inquisitor*, September 1819. Cf. MS agreement between Elliston and John Boles Watson, whereby E. leased the theatre for 18 years from Dec. 21, 1819, at £60 p.a., Elliston Papers. E. acquired considerable other property in Leamington, including the Library where Charles Lamb first made his acquaintance. His two eldest sons, William Gore and Henry Twistleton, were placed in charge of Leamington in 1819, but the theatre, in practice, remained under their father's control.

11 Raymond, *Life and Enterprises*, p. 308. Elliston may have possessed Coventry before 1821, however. E. to Davenport, June 18, 1821, grants him permission to open T. R. Coventry on certain terms: see Gabriel Harrison, *Life and Writings of John Howard Payne* (2 vols., Philadelphia, 1885), I, 104, extra-illustrated, Harvard Theatre Collection. Cf. MS clause written in on Articles of Agreement between E. as manager of Drury Lane and Sampson Penley, dated June 14, 1821, Enthoven Collection. E. was still renting Coventry in 1824, according to a MS note by Winston, dated Nov 25, 1824, Elliston Papers.

12 *Twenty-Six Years of the Life of an Actor and Manager* (New York, 1847), p. 60.

13 "Minute Book of the Proprietors of the Theatre Royal, 1773–1821," MS, Birmingham Public Libraries (Local Studies Library). Quotations by permission of the City Librarian.

14 *Ibid.*

15 MS Articles of Agreement between Elliston and the committee of proprietors of T. R. Birmingham, dated March 23, 1813, Pierpont Morgan Library.

16 The proprietors doubled this in 1807, according to Cunningham, *op. cit.*, p. 26. One assumes this included Tavern and Assembly Rooms. Cf. Winston, *Theatric Tourist*, p. 60, where Macready's rent is given as £700.

17 Figure cited by Elliston to Thomas Cooke, April 4, 1816, Uncatalogued Letters of R. W. Elliston, Folger Shakespeare Library.

18 Quoted in Dent, *op. cit.*, pp. 380–1.

19 Playbill, Theatre Royal, Birmingham, July 12, 1813, British Museum. See Plate 3.

20 From January 23, 1813, for 20 nights. *Remorse* was announced as in preparation at Birmingham T.R. on June 14, 1813. See John Alfred Langford, *A Century of Birmingham Life* (2 vols., Birmingham, 1871), II, 376. At Drury Lane Elliston, as Alvar, so outshone the lead, Ordonio, played by Rae, that Coleridge referred to him as "the blundering coxcomb" who "by mere dint of Voice & Self-conceit" stole the limelight. See Samuel T. Coleridge, *Collected Letters*, ed. Earl L. Griggs (4 vols., Oxford, 1959), III, 436–7.

21 Playbill, July 12, 1813, *loc. cit.*

22 Quoted in Langford, *loc. cit.*

23 *Aris's Birmingham Gazette*, September 6, 1813, quoted in Langford, p. 377.

24 "Minute Book," February 28, 1814. The architect's name is variously spelt 'Carbanell' and 'Cabonel.' It is assumed this was Cabanell Jr., who had designed the new Royal Circus in 1805–6. Cf. Jacob Decastro, *Memoirs* (London, 1824), p. 159; also *Microcosm of London* (3 vols., London, 1904), III, 16.

25 May 13, 1814; quoted in Langford, p. 380. For a description of the 1795 structure see Dent, *op. cit.*, 321–2, and Cunningham, *op. cit.*, pp. 23–4.

26 See Chapter Three above, p. 50.

27 Joseph Moore to Elliston, November 1814, Collection of Professor W. W. Appleton. The name of Miss Norton, an actress with whom Elliston was having a lover's quarrel, gave unsavoury publicity to the theatre.

28 After a farce in which a real reaping machine was used on stage, October 1814. See Langford, p. 381; Pemberton, *op. cit.*, p. 16.

29 Collection of letters from Brunton and Ashley to Elliston, May-July 1815, Hoblitzelle Theatre Arts Library, University of Texas at Austin.

30 Brunton to Elliston, May 18, 1815, *loc. cit.*

31 "Receipts and Disbursements. Birmingham Seasons 1815 and 1817," MS, Boston Public Library. It supplies details from October 23, 1815 to August 22, 1817.

32 Playbill, May 2, 1816, Harvard Theatre Collection.

33 Raymond, *Life and Enterprises*, pp. 239–41.

34 Quoted in Langford, p. 390.

35 Elliston to Lee, October 23, 1817, Henry E. Huntington Library.

36 See T. L. G. Burley, *op. cit.*, pp. 21, 126.

37 "Memoir of Robert W. Elliston," *Dramatic Biography* (5 vols., 1825–6), III, 82. Oxberry's portrait of Elliston, it should be noted, is, quite literally, squinted.

38 "Minute Book," January 12, 1818.

39 Raymond, *Life and Enterprises*, pp. 249–50.

40 Langford, *op. cit.*, p. 395. Receipts had averaged just over £24 nightly.

41 *Ibid.*, p. 394. Elliston supplied a list of 11 performers, the figure "secured" to each, and the actual sum each benefit night comprised. The discrepancies totalled some £123. *The Times*, September 4, 1818, reprinted this list and quipped: "It is worthy of the classical reputation of Birmingham, to have patronized Mr. Conway and Miss Somerville three times more than Miss Kelly."

42 Mr. Brendan O'Brien, "Amateur Drama," a Thomas Davis Lecture, unpub., RTE Radio, October 14, 1969. Transcript courtesy of Mr. O'Brien.

43 William Hazlitt indicates in *London Magazine*, VIII (August 1820) that

"the Green Man is adapted by Mr. Jones from a French *petite pièce*, which was itself taken from a German novel, we believe one of Kotzebue's."

44 Playbill, September 26, 1818, Harvard Theatre Collection.

45 Elliston to Spurrier and Ingleby, March 8, 1819, Elliston Papers.

46 In October 1819 Elliston paid £300 of his arrears, but in January 1821 there was still a balance due of £485, according to "Minute Book." The theatre was destroyed by fire on January 6, 1820. For his part, E. lost his scenery, on moving it unprotected in a storm. See Raymond, *Life and Enterprises*, pp. 255–6.

47 Clipping, dated Aug 10 [July?], 1931, Enthoven Collection.

Chapter Five

1 For a full account of the years 1812–19 see Samuel J. Arnold, *A Letter to All the Proprietors of Drury-Lane Theatre* (London, 1818); [Anon.], *An Authentic Statement of Facts Connected with the Interior Management of Drury-Lane Theatre* (London, 1818); H. N. Hillebrand, *Edmund Kean* (New York, 1933), pp. 174–85; W. J. Macqueen-Pope, *Theatre-Royal Drury Lane* (London, 1945), pp. 228–51; [Peter Moore], *Facts are Stubborn Things!* (London, 1818); F. H. W. Sheppard, ed., *Survey of London*, vol. XXXV, *The Theatre Royal Drury Lane and the Royal Opera House Covent Garden* (London, 1970), ch. 2.

2 *Theatrical Inquisitor*, XIV (1819), 428.

3 *Ibid.*

4 Elliston to Ward, June 7, 1819, Elliston Papers, Harvard Theatre Coll.

5 George Raymond, *Memoirs of Robert William Elliston Comedian*, II, 197.

6 G. Wathen to Elliston, postmarked July 5, 1819, Research Library of Performing Arts, New York Public Library.

7 A copy of the lease, dated September 8, 1819, is in James Winston's "A Collection of Memoranda," 1819, British Museum C. 120.h.1.

8 "Ellistoniana," in *The Dramatic Essays of Charles Lamb*, ed. J. Brander Matthews (New York, 1891), p. 110.

9 See Elliston to Hunt, August 24, 1819, B. Mus., Add. MSS. 38523, f. 51. Hunt's tragedy, on the Cid, was accepted, but Hunt then withdrew it. See *The Autobiography of Leigh Hunt*, ed. Roger Ingpen (2 vols., London, 1903), I, 167–8. Keats's tragedy, *Otho*, was similarly withdrawn after acceptance. See *The Letters of John Keats*, ed. M. B. Forman (2 vols., Oxford, 1931), II, 483, ff. Shelley's *The Cenci* was rejected as being too horrible. See *Letters*, ed. Roger Ingpen (2 vols., London, 1912), II, 768.

10 In scenery there were 178 pairs of flats, 462 wings, 461 setpieces, and 31 "Side Pieces," valued at almost £3500; drop scenery and machinery were valued at a further £2000. MS inventory in Winston's hand, Elliston Papers. In costume, men's dresses were valued at £3133, ladies' at £807; properties at £642; banners, tripods, etc., at £561: a grand total of some £5000. MS inventories in Winston's "A Collection," B. Mus.

11 Elliston to Winston, September 5, 1819, Elliston Papers.

12 MS letter of application to Winston, September 13, 1819, in "A Collection," B. Mus. The idea of a 'dress circle' was an innovation.

13 John Gardner to Winston, September 25, 1819, in "A Collection."

14 *The Times*, October 1, 1819. Many papers carried the same "release."

15 John O'Keeffe, *Wild Oats*, in *Cumberland's British Theatre*, vol. XXXIV (London, n.d.).

[16] *Theatrical Inquisitor,* XV (1819), 211.

[17] R. W. Elliston, "Advertisement," *Shakespeare's Tragedy of King Richard III. As Altered by Colley Cibber* (London, 1819). Copy in the Folger Shakespeare Library, PR 2821/1819a/Copy 1 Sh. Col. Cf. *Theatrical Inquisitor,* XV, 324–6.

[18] Clipping, in Portraits of R. W. Elliston, Harvard Theatre Collection.

[19] See George C. Odell, *Shakespeare from Betterton to Irving* (2 vols., New York, 1920), II, 56–8.

[20] *Shakspeare's Coriolanus; an Historical Play* (London, 1820). Copy in the British Museum, 11764, bbb. Cf. Odell, II, 149–51.

[21] I (January-June 1820), 168.

[22] *Shakspeare's King Lear.* Printed Chiefly from Nahum Tate's Edition, with some Restorations from the Original Text, by R. W. Elliston (London, 1820). Copy in the Folger, PR 2819/1820b. Sh. Col. Three years later, on February 10, 1823, Elliston did in fact stage *Lear* with act V fully restored. See Odell, II, 154–6.

[23] Kean to Elliston, March 31, 1820, Letters of Edmund Kean, Folger Shakespeare Library, Y.c. 400 (12–21). On the back Elliston wrote, "Mr Kean respecting the 3d Act of King Lear, & the General Costume," signed this, and dated it April 3, 1820.

[24] *London Chronicle,* April 25, 1820.

[25] Joe Cowell, *Thirty Years Passed among the Players* (New York, 1845), p. 47. Cf. *The Times,* April 25, 1820; *European Magazine,* LXXVII (Jan-June 1820), 428; George Raymond, *Life and Enterprises,* pp. 281–2.

[26] Elliston to Booth, August 14, 1820, containing terms of engagement, Walter Hampden Memorial Library, New York. Having failed to sell the Olympic at auction on June 13, 1820, Elliston leased it to Reeve and Barlow on October 24 for 14 years at £1077 annual rent; MS note, Elliston Papers. Cf. *Belgravia,* VIII (1869), 404.

[27] MS note, dated September 1820, Elliston Papers.

[28] Memorandum, dated September 4, 1820, signed by Harris and Elliston, in Winston's "A Collection," 1820–1, B. Mus.

[29] The portico, begun in September, was not finished until December 4, at a cost of £1050. It was immediately compared to a cowshed; it still stands today.

[30] Lines by Tom Duncombe, Clipping, Enthoven Collection.

[31] Macready said that the king's praise of Miss Wilson packed Drury Lane for 20 nights afterwards. See Henry Saxe Wyndham, *Annals of Covent Garden Theatre* (2 vols., London, 1906), II, 12.

[32] John Howard Payne, Preface, dated February 11, 1821, to *Thérèse* (New York, 1821). See also Gabriel Harrison, *Life and Writings of John Howard Payne* (2 vols., Philadelphia, 1885), I, 98–9.

[33] Thomas Moore was the go-between, if it is accepted that Elliston was the addressee of a letter, November 16, 1820, stating, "I forwarded your letter to Lord Byron, but I fear that your hopes about his tragedy will be disappointed, for it has been some time in Murray's hands, &, from what I can understand, is neither fit nor indeed intended for representation." See *Letters of Thomas Moore,* ed. Winifred S. Dowden, II (Oxford, 1964), 486. Cf. *Letters and Journals of Lord Byron,* ed. Thomas Moore (3 vols., London, 1833), III, 147.

[34] Elliston to Winston, April 11, 1821, Elliston Papers. The Hon. George Lamb had been on the Drury Lane sub-committee with Lord Byron during

1815–16, and was again on the sub-committee in 1822; his endorsement, therefore, would seem to indicate official approval of Elliston's action.

35 Elliston to Winston, April 13, 1821, Elliston Papers. Winston was to follow Byron's dating, and consult with Hamilton Smith for authorities.

36 Winston and Dunn (the Treasurer) were ordered to go to Murray's on the day of publication, buy two copies of *Marino,* and sign them as having been bought there on April 21; this was a "necessary precaution." One copy was to be cut according to Lamb's instructions, the omitted parts covered with slips of paper and whole leaves sewn up: this was the copy for the Lord Chamberlain. Elliston to Winston, April 12, 1821, Elliston Papers. Elliston himself wrote the letter of application to the Lord Chamberlain on April 22. See Dougald McMillan, *Catalogue of the Larpent Plays* (San Marino, 1939), pp. 365–6.

37 See Paul Sawyer, "Processions and Coronations on the London Stage, 1727–1761," *Theatre Notebook,* XIV (Autumn 1959), 7–12.

38 *European Magazine,* LXXX (July-Dec. 1821), 188–9. For a full account, see Christopher Murray, "Elliston's Coronation Spectacle, 1821," *Theatre Notebook,* XXV (1970-71), 57–64.

39 See *The Times,* December 24, 27, 28, 1821; *European Magazine,* LXXXI (Jan.–June 1822), 72–4. For the text, see W. T. Moncrieff, *Songs, Duets . . . in Giovanni in Ireland* (London, 1821). Copy in National Library of Ireland, 7821.

40 See Watson Nicholson, *The Struggle for a Free Stage in London* (Boston & New York, 1906), pp. 272–9. Cf. *London Chronicle,* April 3, 1822.

41 Clipping, October 1822, Elliston Papers.

42 Edward W. Brayley, *Historical and Descriptive Accounts of the Theatres of London* (London, 1826), p. 10.

43 See *The Times,* October 14, 1822; Edward W. Brayley, *op. cit.,* pp. 8–12; "Description of the Theatre," in *Illustrations of the Public Buildings of London,* ed. J. Britton & A. Pugin (2 vols., London, 1825–8), I, 247–61; *Survey of London, op. cit.,* ch. 4.

44 The otherwise excellent account of Elliston's reconstruction given by the editors of *Survey of London, op. cit.,* fails to mention this. The 1812 structure did not have stage doors, but at some time between 1812 and 1819 they were restored—Charles Dibdin says by Elliston, "An Account of the Theatre Royal Drury Lane," in *Illustrations,* ed. Britton & Pugin, I, 246–7; but cf. *The Times,* September 21, 1814. The address written for opening night, October 16, 1822, made clear reference to the removal of the stage doors: the new *Sunday Times* printed this address in full, October 20. See also Allardyce Nicoll, *A History of English Drama 1660–1900,* IV (Cambridge, 1955), 31.

45 Frederick Reynolds, *Life and Times* (2 vols., London, 1826), II, 416.

46 Enthoven Collection. Young, who had been paid £20 a week at Covent Garden, got £20 a night from Elliston; Miss Stephens got £10 a night; Liston got £50 a week.

47 See William Charles Macready, *Reminiscences,* ed. Sir Frederick Pollock (2 vols., London, 1875), I, 201 ff.

48 The *London Magazine,* VII (Jan.-June 1823), 196, singled out a Fairy Lake by Moonlight, "the painter of which, a Mr. Stanfield, must be an ingenious and powerful artist."

49 It is noteworthy that from October 1, 1823 Barrymore was described in the playbills as "Director of the Spectacle and Pantomime Department."

⁵⁰ *Drury Lane Journal*: *Selections from James Winston's Diaries* 1819–1827, ed. Alfred L. Nelson and Gilbert B. Cross (London, 1974), p. 97.

⁵¹ Reynolds to Elliston, September 16, 1823, Elliston Papers.

⁵² *British Monitor*, November 2, 1823.

⁵³ *London Magazine*, VIII (July–Dec. 1823), 638.

⁵⁴ See J. Britton, "An Account of the Diorama," in *Illustrations of the Public Buildings of London*, I, 66–71; also Helmut and Alison Gernsheim, *L. J. M. Daguerre, The History of the Diorama and the Daguerrotype* (London, 1956), pp. 14–23.

⁵⁵ *European Magazine*, LXXXIV (July–Dec. 1823), 557. This diorama cost £1380 to execute: see *The Drama*, V (1823–4), 289–90. See also David Mayer III, *Harlequin in His Element* (Cambridge, Mass., 1969), pp. 70–3.

⁵⁶ William Thomas Moncrieff, *Zoroaster; or, The Spirit of the Star* (London, 1824).

⁵⁷ See Christopher Murray, "Elliston's Productions of Shakespeare," *Theatre Survey*, XI, No. 2 (November 1970), 116–18.

⁵⁸ Clipping, November 7, 1824, Elliston Papers. Cf. *The Times*, October 29, 1824; *Examiner*, October 31; *European Magazine*, LXXXVI (July–Dec. 1824), 461.

⁵⁹ George Soane, *Der Freischütz: A Romantic Opera, in Three Acts* (3rd edition, London, 1825). Soane described his work as "partly original, and partly altered from the German opera of Friedrich Kind."

⁶⁰ *Extracts from Goethe's Tragedy of Faustus*, Explanatory of the Plates, by Retsch (London, 1820).

⁶¹ Soane translated a total of 546 lines. See Leonard L. Mackall, "Soane's Faust Translation Now First Published, from the Unique Advance Sheets Sent to Goethe in 1822," in *Archiv fur das studium der neueren sprachen und literaturen*, Band CXII, Heft 3/4 (1904), 277–97.

⁶² George Soane, *Faustus: A Romantic Drama, in Three Acts* (London, 1825), Speck Coll. zTa 3/S6/825 Copy 1, Copy 2. The latter is marked as belonging to John Pritt Harley, who played Wagner, and is copiously marked for cues, etc. Cf. *Cumberland's British Theatre*, vol. XXXIII (London, n.d.), where the ending is quite different. See Christopher Murray, "Robert William Elliston's Production of *Faust*, Drury Lane, 1825," *Theatre Research*, XI, Nos. 2 & 3 (1971), 102–13.

⁶³ Prologue, part of the MS version of *Faustus* sent to the Lord Chamberlain, April 21, 1825, and approved May 3. B. Mus., Add. MSS. 42,871, ff. 322–379b.

⁶⁴ The play's ten songs were published separately as *Faustus, A Musical Romance*, as Performed at the Theatre Royal Drury Lane, Composed by T. Cooke, Charles E. Horn, and Henry R. Bishop (London, n.d.).

⁶⁵ *London Magazine*, N.S., II (May–Aug. 1825), 300–301. Cf. *Times*, May 17, 1825.

⁶⁶ Henry Crabb Robinson, *The London Theatre 1811–1866*, ed. Eluned Brown (London, 1966), pp. 110–11.

⁶⁷ *Examiner*, July 10, 1825. Cf. *Times*, July 6; the *Age*, July 10; *New Monthly Magazine*, 2, XV (1825), 346. The authorship of *Five Minutes* is uncertain, but either Moncrieff or Colman seems likeliest.

⁶⁸ Quoted in George Raymond, *Memoirs*, II, 14–15.

⁶⁹ MS note in Winston's hand, dated October 20, 1824, Elliston Papers.

⁷⁰ *Ibid.*, dated July 8, 1825. Winston quotes Calcraft as saying that others would pay more to lease the theatre.

71 *The Times*, July 25, 1825.

72 MS note in Winston's hand, dated August 5, 1825, Elliston Papers. Cf. Raymond, *Life and Enterprises*, pp. 374–5; *Memoirs*, II, 452.

73 Certificate from Dr. George Pearson, MS, dated August 11, 1825, Elliston Papers. Cf. Raymond, *Life and Enterprises*, p. 375.

74 Elliston to George Robins, January 5, 1826, denied emphatically the charge of such neglect, citing the letters he dictated daily "when I could not move a finger," and explained how his instructions were "frustrated" by circumstances beyond anyone's control, a matter to which every theatre "will always be subject." Uncatalogued Letters of R. W. Elliston, Folger Shakespeare Library.

75 Winston, Diary entry, dated September 18, 1825, quoted by Alfred L. Nelson and Gilbert B. Cross, *op. cit.*, p. 115.

76 MS note in Winston's hand, dated November 16, 1825, Elliston Papers. It should be noted that the report of the meeting in *The Times*, December 5, is quite misleading.

77 Elliston to George Robins, January 5, 1826, *loc. cit.*

78 Elliston had refused £7000 for the Olympic, as being only half what he expected, Clipping, October 13, 1825, Enthoven Collection. The present purchaser was John Scott, proprietor of the Sans Pareil.

79 *Reminiscences*, I, 307–8.

80 An extra who carried Elliston off stage gives the dialogue used by Wallack; quoted by William Archer in "Robert William Elliston," *Actors and Actresses*, ed. J. Brander Matthews & L. Hutton, II, 185–6.

81 Among the conditions upon which Drury Lane was now leased was a significant new clause. The lessee, during his term, was not to be a "proprietor, manager, or partner, or to be concerned, directly or indirectly, in any theatre or place of public amusement, nor act or perform at any other place." See "Outline of the Conditions," etc., in Winston's "A Collection," vol. XXII, B. Mus.

82 To June 16, receipts totalled only £40,600, the lowest since Elliston took over management; expenses, at £44,600, were about average.

83 See Clipping, dated July 3, 1826, Enthoven Collection; also Raymond, *Memoirs*, II, 477–83.

84 *The Times*, March 3, 1827.

85 Entry dated May 23, 1826, quoted Nelson and Cross, *op. cit.*, p. 122.

Chapter Six

1 MS in Elliston's hand, dated October 22, 1827, Folger Shakespeare Library, Y.d.23 (190g). Cf. George Raymond, *Memoirs of Robert William Elliston Comedian*, II, 487–90.

2 "Case relative to shareholders in the Royal Brunswick Theatre placed before Mr. Christy for his opinion by F. G. & H. Baddeley," MS in Elliston's hand, undated, Boston Public Library. That the plans for the new theatre were far along is evidenced by a letter from Elliston to Charles Robert, his son, February 22, 1827, Collection of Mr. Roy Plomley.

3 MS in Elliston's hand, dated October 22, 1827, *loc. cit.*

4 MS note in Winston's hand, *Hughes' Royal Circus*, vol. 3, Stead Collection, New York Public Library. West, however, refused to transfer the lease from

Charles Robert to Elliston in 1828, and also insisted on £870 deposit in 1828, indicating a change in attitude.

[5] The scenery included 48½ pairs of flats, 102 wings, 187 set pieces, 27 borders, "Inventory/Surry Theatre No 1 1827," Winston Collection, Folger, W.a.215. Charles Robert and Elliston himself made these inventories: Winston, it may be pointed out, remained at Drury Lane.

[6] *The Morning Chronicle,* June 5, 1827. Cf. *The Examiner,* June 24.

[7] Quoted in W. Clark Russell, *Representative Actors* (London & New York, 1888), pp. 296–7.

[8] "Memoir of Henry Kemble," in *Oxberry's Dramatic Biography,* N.S. (1827), I, 151.

[9] *Biography of Master Burke, the Irish Roscius; the Wonder of the World; and the Paragon of Actors* (7th ed., Philadelphia, n.d.). Cf. "Memoir of Master Burke," in *The Dramatic Magazine,* II (1830), 129–30.

[10] This agreement was terminated after eighteen months, not because of, but for fear of, a diminution in Burke's appeal. Clipping, November 14, 1828, Harvard Theatre Collection. (After a year's absence, Burke returned to the Surrey in 1830.)

[11] *Biography of Master Burke,* p. 6.

[12] Hermann furst von Pückler-Muskau, *Tour in England, Ireland, and France, in the Years 1826, 1827, 1828, and 1829* (trans., Philadelphia, 1833), p. 227.

[13] Playbill, Surrey Theatre, December 26, 1827, Enthoven Collection.

[14] December 27, 1827.

[15] See George E. Wellwarth, "The Disappearance of the New Royal Brunswick Theatre: or The Mystery of the Iron Roof," *Theatre Notebook,* XXII (Winter 1967/8), 56–63.

[16] *Examiner,* September 14, 1828. Of importance this year also, in establishing the Surrey, were the redecoration of the theatre at Easter, and the placing of some performances under the patronage of the Lord Mayor, the Duke of York, the Marquis of Worcester, etc., two well-tried gambits in Elliston's *modus operandi.*

[17] Clipping, 1829, Enthoven Collection.

[18] Edward Fitzball, *Thirty-five Years of a Dramatic Author's Life* (2 vols., London, 1859), I, 119–21.

[19] *Ibid.,* p. 125.

[20] *The Inchcape Bell,* A Nautical Burletta, in Two Acts, II, v. In *Cumberland's Minor Theatre,* vol. I (London, n.d.).

[21] W. T. Moncrieff, *The Pestilence of Marseilles,* A Melodrama in Three Acts, in *Cumberland's Minor Theatre,* vol. XI (London, n.d.).

[22] See text, in *Cumberland's Minor Theatre,* vol. VII (London, n.d.).

[23] Quoted by Walter Jerrold, *Douglas Jerrold* (2 vols., London, 1914), I, 110.

[24] *Ibid.,* p. 120.

[25] R. Dodson, "Theatrical Scraps," Clipping, Enthoven Collection.

[26] Douglas Jerrold, *Black-Eyed Susan; or, All in the Downs,* A Nautical and Domestic Drama in Two Acts, in *Lacy's Acting Edition of Plays,* vol. XXIII (London, n.d.).

[27] *Ibid.,* "Scenery and Properties." Cf. the playbill, June 10, 1829, Harvard Theatre Collection.

[28] Playbill, June 15, 1829, Enthoven Collection. The "illustrious Charlatan"

in question was one George Davidge, manager of the Coburg. Earlier in the year, Davidge had been criticized for packing his theatre with shilling "orders," leading to unruly audiences; Elliston, in contrast, was awarded a piece of silver plate by his company because of his refusal to participate in this mode of audience attraction. See *The Atlas*, April 19, 1829. Thereafter, Elliston made a point of feigning ignorance of Davidge's existence.

29 See Walter Jerrold, *op. cit.*, p. 131. Raymond attributes this instant melodrama to Moncrieff, *Memoirs*, II, 512.

30 In *Richardson's Minor Theatre*, vol. III (London, n.d.).

31 See Walter Scott, *Poetical Works* (12 vols., Edinburgh, 1833), vol. XII. Elliston's version was probably in three acts.

32 Playbill for second performance, November 19, 1829, Harvard Theatre Collection.

33 Cf. the "Remarks" of George Daniel to the edition of *Thomas à Becket* published in *Cumberland's Minor Theatre*, vol. XI (London, n.d.).

34 *Othello, Macbeth, Richard III, Hamlet, Romeo and Juliet, Merchant of Venice, King Lear, 1 Henry IV, Henry VIII*, and *Coriolanus*.

35 *The Times*, December 10, 1829. On the basis of his new affluence, the irrepressible Elliston dreamed for a time of running for Parliament. See Raymond, *Life and Enterprises*, p. 404.

36 On his last night at the Surrey, Burke played the lead in *Richard III* (3 acts), Tristram Fickle in *The Weathercock*, Sholto in *Old Heads on Young Shoulders*, and Jerry in *A Day at the Fair* (farces). This represented a total of 18 different characters, 12 costume changes and 3000 lines. He also played an overture on the violin, an accompaniment on the 'cello, and a prelude on the piano. Finally, he spoke an address with the natural charm which was his greatest attraction, "in such language as a boy might use . . . taking leave of his home and friends." *The Atlas*, October 3, 1830. Burke left England on October 16, made his debut at the Park St. Theatre, New York, on Nov. 22, and went on to the Tremont in Boston on Jan. 31. He was a huge success in the U.S. until about 1839. In later years Burke was a concert violinist, and in 1850–1 toured as accompanist to Jenny Lind. He died in New York, January 19, 1902.

37 See W. T. Moncrieff, *Van Diemen's Land*, An Operatic Drama, in Three Acts, in *Cumberland's Minor Theatre*, vol. X (London, n.d.).

38 George Daniel, "Remarks," *Shakespeare's Festival, or A New Comedy of Errors*: A Drama, in Two Acts, in *Cumberland's Minor Theatre*, vol. X (London, n.d.).

39 *The Atlas*, April 27, 1828.

40 Clipping, April 24(?), 1831, Enthoven Collection.

41 Quoted by Raymond, *Life and Enterprises*, p. 407.

42 MS note in Winston's hand, *Hughes' Royal Circus*, vol. 3, *loc. cit.*

Chapter Seven

1 See Jeremy Bagster-Collins, *George Colman the Younger 1762–1836*, pp. 243–4.

2 Elliston to Winston, January 8, 1816, Elliston Papers, Harvard Theatre Collection. This meticulous approach was habitual with Elliston. The present writer knows of only one instance where E. was outsmarted over agreements.

On May 24, 1824 he signed articles with Andrew Ducrow, engaging, as he thought, the equestrian along with his horses for Drury Lane; it soon emerged that Ducrow considered the horses only to be engaged. Since horses without a trainer were useless to Elliston, he was forced to make out a second agreement, on July 5, whereby Ducrow was to perform "in such pieces as his Equestrian Troop may play in," at £4-10s. per week in addition to the £60 going to the horses. Memorandum of an agreement, Folger Shakespeare Library, Y.d.82(242). Cf. George Raymond, *Life and Enterprises of Robert William Elliston, Comedian*, pp. 340-1.

³ Elliston to Winston, January 28, 1816, Elliston Papers.

⁴ *The Atlas*, July 17, 1831.

⁵ Articles of Agreement between Elliston and Henry & Phoebe May, dated November 20, 1809, Enthoven Collection; also between Elliston and Thomas Ellar, dated November 1, 1809, Harvard Theatre Collection.

⁶ Articles of Agreement between Elliston and Sloman, dated October 21, 1815, B. Mus., Th. Cts. 47.

⁷ Elliston to Winston, January 25, 1825, Elliston Papers.

⁸ George Raymond, *Memoirs of Robert William Elliston Comedian*, II, 434. Cf. Alan S. Downer, *The Eminent Tragedian William Charles Macready*, pp. 101-2.

⁹ Clipping, January 6(?), 1821, in James Winston's "A Collection of Memoranda," 1820-1, B. Mus.

¹⁰ Quoted by H. N. Hillebrand, *Edmund Kean*, p. 255. Unfortunately, something Hillebrand does not report, this was not the parting note between Kean and Elliston. In mid-July 1825, Kean brought the law on Elliston for failure to pay £350, for 7 out of 15 nights for which Kean had contracted (MS agreement, March 17, 1825, Folger, Y.d.387-8). Winston appended a MS note, dated July 18, 1825, to this agreement, blaming Kean for his action in view of the fact that E. had paid him £150 in advance, and 2 private boxes nightly (one for his wife and one for his "whore"), while Kean, for his part, played every night "under expenses." The Kean v. Elliston case came before the courts on Nov. 7, 1825, by which time Kean had gone to the U.S. and Elliston was on the verge of bankruptcy: the outcome has not been determined.

¹¹ Elliston to Cooper, March 12, 1820, Uncatalogued Letters of R. W. Elliston, Folger.

¹² *Thirty Years Passed among the Players*, p. 44.

¹³ Elliston to Thomas [T. P.?] Cooke, January 19, 1813, Uncatalogued Letters of R. W. Elliston, Folger.

¹⁴ Elliston to T. P. Cooke, July 17, 1816, Collection of Professor W. W. Appleton.

¹⁵ See Hillebrand, *op. cit.*, pp. 234-7; Downer, *op. cit.*, pp. 94-7. Cf. William Charles Macready, *Reminiscences*, I, 294-7. A fragment of a letter from Kean to Elliston indicates his general attitude: "though they have *stole* from me half my reputation—[they] shall not strike at the other half—by forcing me into characters I *dislike*." Undated MS, University of Chicago Library.

¹⁶ Elliston to Cooke, September 3, 1816, Uncatalogued Letters of R. W. Elliston, Folger.

¹⁷ *Recollections and Reflections* (2 vols., London, 1872), I, 36.

¹⁸ William T. Moncrieff, *Rochester; or, King Charles the Second's Merry Days* (London, 1819), III, i.

¹⁹ Clipping, in Portraits of R. W. Elliston, Folger.

20 That is, £700. Clipping, 1829, Enthoven Collection. There is no evidence to indicate that Kean ever complied.

21 He was so credited by the critics, e.g., *The Examiner*, February 27, July 10, 1831; James Elmes, *Metropolitan Improvements* (London, 1829), p. 135.

22 See Watson Nicholson, *The Struggle for a Free Stage in London*, pp. 323–55; E. B. Watson, *Sheridan to Robertson*, pp. 41–57; Dewey Ganzel, "Patent Wrongs and Patent Theatres: Drama and the Law in the Early Nineteenth Century," *PMLA*, LXXVI (1961), 384–96. The committee's findings were published in *Reports from Committees*, vol. VII (London, 1832).

23 Preface to Douglas Jerrold's *Flying Dutchman*, in *Richardson's Minor Theatre*, vol. III (London, n.d.).

24 *The Stage: Both before and behind the Curtain* (3 vols., London, 1840), I, 19.

Index

Note: A question mark is used within parentheses to indicate doubt over a Christian name if it comes first and over a profession if it appears after a professional designation.